PHILIPPIANS
The Mind of Christ

PHILIPPIANS
THE MIND OF CHRIST

NORMAN MELLISH

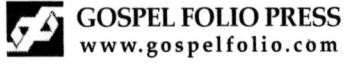
GOSPEL FOLIO PRESS
www.gospelfolio.com

PHILIPPIANS: THE MIND OF CHRIST
by Norman Mellish
Copyright © 2006
GOSPEL FOLIO PRESS
All Rights Reserved

Published by GOSPEL FOLIO PRESS
304 Killaly St. W.
Port Colborne, ON L3K 6A6

ISBN 1897117213

Cover design by Rachel Brooks

All Scripture quotations from the
King James Version, unless otherwise noted.

Printed in the United States of America

CONTENTS

INTRODUCTION TO THE EPISTLE — 1
   THE FORMING OF THE ASSEMBLY — 1
   THE FRAMING OF THE LETTER — 10

THE SINGLE MIND — 13
   1:1-11—THE FELLOWSHIP OF THE GOSPEL — 14
   1:12-18—THE FURTHERANCE OF THE GOSPEL — 39
   1:19-26—THE FOCUS OF THE GOSPEL — 49
   1:27-29—THE FAITH OF THE GOSPEL — 60

THE SUBMISSIVE MIND — 65
   2:1-4—THE PROBLEM: THE EXHORTATION TO THE SAINTS — 67
   2:5-11—THE PATTERN: THE EXAMPLE OF THE SAVIOUR — 76
   2:12-16—THE PRACTICE: THE EXERCISE OF THE SAINTS — 91
   2:17-30—THE PICTURES: EXPOUNDED IN THE SERVANTS — 101

THE SPIRITUAL MIND — 117
   3:1-8—PAUL'S PAST: LOSING — 118
   3:9-16—PAUL'S PRESENT: LONGING — 135
   3:17-19—PAUL'S PAIN: LAMENTING — 154
   3:20-21—PAUL'S PROSPECT: LOOKING — 159

THE SAME MIND — 169
   4:1-7—GOD'S PEACE — 169
   4:8-9—THE GOD OF PEACE — 184
   4:10-19—THE GIFT FROM THE SAINTS — 191
   4:20-23—GREETINGS TO THE SAINTS — 210

BIBLIOGRAPHY — 213
SCRIPTURE INDEX — 217

Preface

The present work is written in the same style as my book on Revelation. This is a system that I find helpful to me to set forth divine truth, and I trust it will enable others to appreciate further the truth that is set forth in this epistle.

Again, like the book of Revelation, it has been written in different parts of the world as it has been my privilege to serve the Lord in these parts. Often, one would desire to be in one's own study, but this is not possible, and I am very thankful to the Lord for His grace that has given the help that one needs when touching the holy things of God. I trust that the Lord will use this work to encourage His own to manifest the mind of Christ in every aspect of their daily lives. As I move among believers throughout the world I am becoming more conscious that the truth of Philippians does not seem to be seen as it ought to be among some Christians, though the Lord alone knows the heart. The desire to "seek our own things and not the things of Jesus Christ" seems to become more apparent in these last days of the Church's history on the earth. Philippians has a very practical lesson to all who love the Lord and we trust that He will use this present work to further our devotion to Him as we wait for His coming.

As with the book of Revelation, I am again thankful for the many aids that are at the disposal of the student of Scripture, and for the help that has been given to me by those who have written on this book for the good of the saints of God. The Greek words that are quoted are taken from *Wigram's Word*

Study Concordance or directly from the *Englishman's Interlinear Greek New Testament.*

I write this book with the prayer that the Lord will encourage some to seek further His mind and will in the precious things that have been revealed to us by the Holy Spirit of God.

Norman Mellish.
Chesterton.
Newcastle.
Staffs.

My Thanks

No book could ever be written without the help of others in their encouragement to put one's studies into a written form and I am indebted to the many that have encouraged me to do this. We trust that their support in the desire to spread the truth of God will prove to be a blessing to all who read this commentary.

The present volume could not have been completed without the labours of Bill McLeod of Mayfield, Scotland, who undertook to type my manuscript and who also gave invaluable help by giving very sound advice that he felt would help to make the book what it has become. I value highly all he has done over the past few months.

I am again thankful to Mike Baker of Burton-on-Trent for his diligence in proof reading the original manuscript and making the corrections where needed. I appreciate the effort that he put into this, especially as he is still recovering from illness.

Dedicated to my wife Ann and family:

Gillian, Helen, Andrew, Timothy, Peter, Stephen, Ann, Judith, and Alison.

The Lord has blessed us with them and we are thankful for the love they show.

Introduction to the Epistle

The Forming of the Assembly

Acts 15:36—The Conflict

> *And some days after Paul said unto Barnabas, Let us go again and visit our brethren in every city where we have preached the word of the Lord, and see how they do.*

The origins of the work at Philippi are recorded in the book of Acts in chapter 16. The ministry there forms part of Paul's second missionary journey, which commenced with a desire to visit those of the brethren who were *"in every city where we have preached the word of the Lord, and see how they do"* (Acts 15:36). The journey commenced with a conflict of interests between the servants of God. When Paul and Barnabas could not agree regarding the value of the service of John Mark at that time, *"Barnabas determined to take with them John, whose surname was Mark"* (Acts 15:37). The determination of Barnabas was no doubt formulated by natural ties, Mark being his sister's son (Col. 4:10). How often rifts have come into the work of God, not on doctrinal ground, but because of family relationships. The determination of Barnabas caused a division between the servants of God, with Barnabas taking Mark and sailing to Cyprus, and on that boat, he sailed right out of Scripture. Mark returns and it seems as if he did turn out to be valuable. The Spirit of God and the testimony remained with Paul.

Acts 15:40–16:3 — His Companions

> And Paul chose Silas, and departed, being recommended by the brethren unto the grace of God. And he went through Syria and Cilicia, confirming the churches.
>
> Then came he to Derbe and Lystra: and, behold, a certain disciple was there, named Timotheus, the son of a certain woman, which was a Jewess, and believed; but his father was a Greek: which was well reported of by the brethren that were at Lystra and Iconium. Him would Paul have to go forth with him; and took and circumcised him because of the Jews which were in those quarters: for they knew all that his father was a Greek.

Having separated from Barnabas, Paul departed in the company of Silas, being recommended by the brethren. The conflict of interests regarding those who would be an asset to the work did not curtail the exercise of Paul's heart; he went on with the work. On the way, Timothy is added to the company, and at Troas, Luke joined them. Up until this point in their service, Luke speaks of the work and journeys as being carried out by the three servants mentioned (see Acts 16:4, 6-8), but from Troas, as they begin to bring the gospel to Europe, Luke links himself with them (16:10-13), which is apparent from the introduction of the personal pronouns "we" and "us."

INTRODUCTION TO THE EPISTLE

Acts 16:6-10—The Call

> *Now when they had gone throughout Phrygia and the region of Galatia, and were forbidden of the Holy Ghost to preach the word in Asia, after they were come to Mysia, they assayed to go into Bithynia: but the Spirit suffered them not. And they passing by Mysia came down to Troas. And a vision appeared to Paul in the night; There stood a man of Macedonia, and prayed him, saying, Come over into Macedonia, and help us. And after he had seen the vision, immediately we endeavoured to go into Macedonia, assuredly gathering that the Lord had called us for to preach the gospel unto them.*

Having gone through the cities where they had formerly preached the word, helping to establish them as apostolic truth was taught, they now seek for a further field of service. At this point there is direct intervention by the Spirit of God. What began as a personal exercise to visit their brethren now becomes a movement orchestrated by divine persons, as the Spirit of God takes control of the servants of God. *"Having gone throughout Phrygia and the region of Galatia" (v. 6)*, they were forbidden by the Holy Spirit to continue their journey westward, even though as yet the gospel had not reached these parts. This would teach us that need does not constitute a call. If a door remains open, then the opportunity given by God should be taken, but we do not persist in a work merely for its own sake, but we look for divine guidance. The work in Asia is going to commence on their journey homeward, but for the present, they are **"forbidden"** (a word that means, to prevent by word or act) to preach in Asia. Still wishing to carry the gospel to the people, their thoughts turned northward towards Bithynia, but again divine intervention stopped any movement in that direction as the Spirit suffered them not, that is, did not permit them or leave them alone to fulfil their intentions. In verse 6, the Spirit withstood them, and in verse 7, He withheld them from their purpose of preaching the gospel in these unevangelized areas. It must be noticed that the gospel is to reach Bithynia, God will not leave them to perish, but it is others who will be used to take the gospel to these parts. It is evident that there are assemblies there, for Peter writes to them (1 Pet. 1:1). It would seem that some might have been among the three thousand that were saved on the day of Pentecost, for citizens of Pontus, Cappadocia and Asia are recorded as being among the multitude that was in Jerusalem at that time.

Paul and his company determined to pass by Mysia, that is, not to make it a sphere of gospel activity, and they came down to the seaport of Troas. During this time, Paul waited for the pillar cloud to move, not wanting to be outside the will of God. There is no evidence that there was a testimony for God in Troas at that time, though on his visit there, recorded in Acts 20:5-12, an assembly had been formed and New Testament principles were being carried out. It is at Troas that his future movements were revealed to him, as to God's plans for his service.

The mind of God is made known in the third of eight visions that Paul had, these visions being:

Acts		
	9:12	His Salvation
		His Sight
	16:9	His Service
	18:9	His Stay in Corinth
	22:17-18	His Safety (a past vision recorded here)
	23:11	His Support in Suffering
	27:23	The Shipwreck
2 Corinthians 12		His Scenes of Glory

As a result of this vision, generally known as "The Macedonian Call," Paul and his companions are convinced of their future service for God.

The call to *"come over and help us"* reveals that the greatest need of man is not physical or moral, but spiritual. The word "help" is used in connection with a need for deliverance from satanic power (Matt. 15:25; Mark 9:22-24). In this verse and also in 2 Cor. 6:2, the great need is that of salvation. The word "help" is used again in the book of Hebrews where it is used

INTRODUCTION TO THE EPISTLE

of the priestly ministry of our Lord Jesus for His own, where *"He is able to **succour** them that are tempted" (Heb. 2:18)* and to give *"help in time of need" (Heb. 4:16)*. Satan's power needs to be dealt with and salvation must be known, hence the vision to Paul that led the company to conviction, *"assuredly gathering that the Lord had called them for to preach the gospel unto them" (Acts 16:10)*.

ACTS 16:11-12—THE CROSSING

> *Therefore loosing from Troas, we came with a straight course to Samothracia, and the next day to Neapolis; And from thence to Philippi, which is the chief city of that part of Macedonia, and a colony: and we were in that city abiding certain days.*

Being in the will of God, Luke records *"We came with a straight course to Samothracia,"* which simply means "sailing before the wind." They had a comfortable and easy passage as they made their way. From Samothracia they sailed the next day to Neapolis. One wonders why they did not start the work of the gospel in Neapolis at that time. Perhaps the answer is in verse 12, for Philippi *"is the chief city of that part of Macedonia."* The Apostle Paul always carried out his work from a major centre, knowing that the commerce and traffic passing through would, from that core of gospel activity, carry the Word of God throughout the province. Philippi was situated on a major route for travellers in that part of Macedonia, the Ignation Way. This road stretched from Dyrrhachium on the western shores of Macedonia and it ran through to Byzantium on the eastern shores of Thrace, making an easy passage between Europe and Asia. Philippi was named after Philip of Macedonia, the father of Alexander the Great. It was made a Roman colony by Caesar Augustus, it used Roman Laws, "and its constitution was modelled on the municipal constitution of Rome" (F. F. Bruce, *The Acts*, page 330). They called themselves Romans and adhered to the Roman law that was given to them (Acts 16:21).

Acts 16:13-40—The Converts

And on the sabbath we went out of the city by a river side, where prayer was wont to be made; and we sat down, and spake unto the women which resorted [thither]. And a certain woman named Lydia, a seller of purple, of the city of Thyatira, which worshipped God, heard [us]: whose heart the Lord opened, that she attended unto the things which were spoken of Paul. And when she was baptized, and her household, she besought [us], saying, If ye have judged me to be faithful to the Lord, come into my house, and abide [there]. And she constrained us.

And it came to pass, as we went to prayer, a certain damsel possessed with a spirit of divination met us, which brought her masters much gain by soothsaying: The same followed Paul and us, and cried, saying, These men are the servants of the most high God, which shew unto us the way of salvation. And this did she many days.

But Paul, being grieved, turned and said to the spirit, I command thee in the name of Jesus Christ to come out of her. And he came out the same hour. And when her masters saw that the hope of their gains was gone, they caught Paul and Silas, and drew [them] into the marketplace unto the rulers,

And brought them to the magistrates, saying, These men, being Jews, do exceedingly trouble our city, And teach customs, which are not lawful for us to receive, neither to observe, being Romans. And the multitude rose up together against them: and the magistrates rent off their clothes, and commanded to beat [them]. And when they had laid many stripes upon them, they cast [them] into prison, charging the jailor to keep them safely: Who, having received such a charge, thrust them into the inner prison, and made their feet fast in the stocks.

And at midnight Paul and Silas prayed, and

INTRODUCTION TO THE EPISTLE

sang praises unto God: and the prisoners heard them. And suddenly there was a great earthquake, so that the foundations of the prison were shaken: and immediately all the doors were opened, and every one's bands were loosed. And the keeper of the prison awaking out of his sleep, and seeing the prison doors open, he drew out his sword, and would have killed himself, supposing that the prisoners had been fled. But Paul cried with a loud voice, saying, Do thyself no harm: for we are all here.

Then he called for a light, and sprang in, and came trembling, and fell down before Paul and Silas, And brought them out, and said, Sirs, what must I do to be saved?

And they said, Believe on the Lord Jesus Christ, and thou shalt be saved, and thy house. And they spake unto him the word of the Lord, and to all that were in his house. And he took them the same hour of the night, and washed [their] stripes; and was baptized, he and all his, straightway. And when he had brought them into his house, he set meat before them, and rejoiced, believing in God with all his house.

And when it was day, the magistrates sent the serjeants, saying, Let those men go.

And the keeper of the prison told this saying to Paul, The magistrates have sent to let you go: now therefore depart, and go in peace.

But Paul said unto them, They have beaten us openly uncondemned, being Romans, and have cast [us] into prison; and now do they thrust us out privily? nay verily; but let them come themselves and fetch us out.

And the serjeants told these words unto the magistrates: and they feared, when they heard that they were Romans. And they came and besought them, and brought [them] out, and desired [them] to depart out of the city. And they went out of the prison, and entered into [the house of] Lydia: and when they had seen the brethren, they comforted them, and departed.

Paul's usual policy when beginning a new work was to go *"to the Jew first" (Rom. 1:16)*. In all the places that he entered on his first missionary journey, he first found the synagogue and began to preach Christ unto them. The only exception seems to be at Lystra and Derbe, where after the healing of the lame man, they were taken for gods having come down to earth in the form of man.

In the time (recorded in verse 12) that Paul and his company were in Philippi, it is evident that they did not find a synagogue. J. Sidlow Baxter says, "Few Jews lived at Philippi, doubtless because it was a "military colony" rather than a "mercantile city." That is why there was no synagogue, but only the *proseuche*, or legally proper "place of prayer" " (*Explore the Book, Vol. 6*, page 181).

Having discovered such a place of meeting, the following Sabbath found them taking their place among the women who gathered there. They occupied the place of the teachers when they *"sat down,"* for this was the posture that the teacher took (Luke 4:16-21). It would seem that men did not gather at this prayer centre, and all that the women could do was pray. The truths of 1 Corinthians 14:34-40 and 1 Timothy 2:9-15 were as applicable to Jewish women as they were to Gentile women in the church era. For the silence of women in public meetings originated because of the fall, and Eve's part in it. Paul appeals to "the Law," that is to the first five books of Moses, when teaching the role of women in the church, and in particular the sentence that was passed upon Eve by God in Genesis 3:16. This is made plain in 1 Timothy 2:11-15.

The fact that men were now present gave opportunity for the Word of God to be taught. The effect of the teaching was immediate, leading Lydia to act in faith upon it, *"whose heart the Lord opened that she attended to the things that were spoken of Paul" (v. 14)*. Her heart was opened to the Word, and obedience to it brought her to faith in Christ. It would seem that

INTRODUCTION TO THE EPISTLE

from that prayer meeting she immediately stepped in the river Gangites to be baptized. This seller of purple, who did not let her business keep her from a prayer meeting, now becomes the source of support for the servants of God as she opened her home to them. It would become the centre from which the work of God was carried out in the city.

The rest of Acts 16 relates the further movements of God that led to the conversion of the jailor and his household. The incidents that led to a wealthy woman being saved turned to seeing a wretched girl delivered from the control of demons. There is no proof that this girl was converted, or that she promoted the gospel while under demonic power. It may be pleasant to think that she may have come into the blessing of eternal life as a result of Paul's intervention, but there is no definite record of it.

In the record of the jailor's conversion, it is interesting to see how God works to bring sinners to Himself. Some would virtually deny, at least in their teaching, that God has any direct dealing with a sinner apart from the provision being made, and the gospel being preached. From that point on, they imply that everything depends on man and human responsibility, without divine intervention, otherwise God is partial in His dealings, working in an arbitrary way. The fact that God does move in a very definite way in the conversion of a soul is evident throughout the whole of this book. The three conversions of chapters 8, 9 and 10 declare that, without divine intervention in a personal way, neither the Ethiopian, the Apostle Paul, nor Cornelius would have been saved. The same things can be said regarding those saved in this chapter. The Macedonian call to *"come over and help us,"* then, as far as Lydia is concerned, *"whose heart the Lord opened,"* the imprisonment of Paul, the earthquake as Paul and Silas sang to a captive audience, which brought the house down—these events were the direct movements of God to save the jailor and his family. In the face of this evidence of which I have touched but a little, let no man deny God's direct intervention in personal salvation. That man can receive the gospel when it is presented is also plainly taught in Scripture for, *"whosoever believeth on Him should not perish but have everlasting life" (John 3:16).*

In these converts the basis of the testimony for God in Philippi began. The final verse of chapter 16 would indicate that others had already trusted Christ. These were the firstfruits of the assembly that Paul now writes to.

It would seem that the epistle to the Philippians was written against the background of Paul's imminent trial before Caesar, for he is obviously expecting release (1:19; 1:25; 2:24). A note of joy and an air of anticipation mark the epistle. It differs in tone from Colossians, which seems to reflect a more settled state of imprisonment, though Paul does not dwell on it, nor does he make much of it. As the epistle ends, he draws attention to it— *"remember my bonds" (Col. 4:18)*. In 2 Timothy, the tone alters completely; his death is imminent and the appeals to his child Timothy are full of pathos and warning.

THE FRAMING OF THE LETTER

The Apostle wrote to the Philippians to express his thanks for a gift that had been sent to him to help sustain him in the ministry of God. In New Testament times, those who served God in a full-time way sought to adhere to the teaching of the Lord Jesus as recorded in Matthew 10. When the disciples were commissioned to take the message to the people, they were told to provide freely the things of God. They were instructed that God would provide freely for them, for they were to, *"Provide neither gold, nor silver, nor brass in your purses, nor scrip for your journey" (Matt. 10:9-11)*. When the seventy were sent forth at a later time (Luke 10:1), the same obligations were put upon them (v. 4). John also reminds Gaius of those men who moved for God carrying out the same principles in later New Testament times, when he speaks of those that *"went forth, taking nothing of the Gentiles" (3 Jn. 7)*. He reminds Gaius of the responsibility of the saints to help and support them (v. 8).

The Apostle Paul always moved on this principle, often resorting to his natural occupation as a tent maker for the support of himself and those that were with him (Acts 20:34).

INTRODUCTION TO THE EPISTLE

His dependence upon God alone is well expressed in 1 Thessalonians 2:9; 2 Thessalonians 3:8; and 2 Corinthians 11:9. He also taught throughout his epistles the responsibility of the saints to support by financial means those who were serving God. It is evident that the saints at Philippi looked to their responsibilities well. They ministered to him not only whilst he was with them, but also as he continued his work for God in other places (Phil. 4:15). Even now, when he was imprisoned in Rome, they were anxious to be a help to the Apostle and sent a gift by the hand of Epaphroditus (2:25) who took sick on the journey to Rome. That Paul was in need when this gift came is implied by his words to them in chapter 4:10-14, *"But I rejoiced in the Lord greatly, that now at the last your care for me hath flourished again; wherein ye were also careful, but ye lacked opportunity. Not that I speak in respect of want: for I have learned, in whatsoever state I am, therewith to be content. I know both how to be abased, and I know how to abound: everywhere and in all things I am instructed both to be full and to be hungry, both to abound and to suffer need. I can do all things through Christ that strengtheneth me. Notwithstanding ye have well done, that ye have communicated with my affliction."* It is little wonder that he wants to express his thanks for their care that had flourished again.

We are very thankful at this late stage in the church era, that God still has many who are wholly dependent upon Him. Having been taught the divine principle of looking to God alone to supply their needs, missionaries have taken the gospel to many lands. Many have carried the gospel to those in the land of their birth, serving God full-time without guaranteed salary, with no society to further them, and with no visible means of support. Hundreds have looked to God alone, and have found that *"he is faithful that promised" (Heb. 10:23)*. They are a shining testimony to the preserving hand of God as He has fed, clothed, and maintained both them and their families.

Whilst writing to express his thanks, Paul takes the opportunity to seek to correct a problem that has arisen among them. It is evident that a spirit of self-seeking and high-mindedness was marking the assembly. There is no doctrinal error exposed as in

Corinthians, Galatians, or Colossians. The trouble here is interpersonal issues, but like doctrinal error, interpersonal issues can have a devastating effect upon a company, as we witness too often in church life today.

The Apostle addresses "all" the believers on eleven occasions in the epistle. The book begins and ends with "all" (1:1; 4:23). In this, he is seeking to unite them whilst not supporting the factions that have become evident. Throughout the epistle he is setting forth Christ as the example to follow. The great thesis on the humility of Christ in chapter two is a practical truth for the believers to emulate, not a doctrinal passage that he formulates regarding the person of Christ.

That he is appealing for unity of mind throughout the epistle is apparent from chapter 1:27, where he desires that they *"stand fast in one spirit, with one mind striving together for the faith of the gospel"*; and chapter 2:3-4 *"let nothing be done through strife or vainglory; but in lowliness of mind let each esteem other better than themselves. Look not every man on his own things, but every man also on the things of others."* Then again, there is the appeal to Euodias and Syntyche, *"that they be of the same mind in the Lord"* (4:2). Much could be added to these examples, but this will become obvious during the course of the exposition.

1
THE SINGLE MIND

A. T. Robertson gives the title to his work on Philippians as *Paul's Joy in Christ*. In some ways this is merited, for Paul's joy regarding these believers is brimming over as he recalls both them and their service for God. Yet it would seem to me that though Paul gets great pleasure of mind from these his converts, (and what a source of encouragement it must have been during his captivity), running through the epistle as a constant thread is his longing to see the saints move in unity. Hence the title presently applied, *The Mind of Christ*, for the mind of Christ is a lowly mind, and this seems to be what is lacking among them.

The Lord Jesus is set before them in every chapter as the object on which to fix their gaze, for if we are occupied with Christ we will not be taken up with our brethren.

In chapter 1   We should be Living Christ—1:21
In chapter 2   We should be Learning Christ—2:5-11
In chapter 3   We should be Like Christ—3:10
                    We should be Looking for Christ—3:20-21
In chapter 4   We should be Leaning on Christ—4:13

In these Scriptures, the Lord Jesus is also set forth as:
Chapter 1   Christ my Purpose—1:21
Chapter 2   Christ my Pattern—2:5-11
Chapter 3   Christ my Prize—3:14
Chapter 3   Christ my Prospect—3:20-21

Chapter 4 Christ my Power—4:13

When we come to chapter 1, we find four simple divisions, which are:

1:1-11   The Fellowship of the gospel
1:12-18 The Furtherance of the gospel
1:19-26 The Focus of the gospel
1:27-30 The Faith of the gospel

The Fellowship of the Gospel
1:1-11

Paul and Timotheus, the servants of Jesus Christ, to all the saints in Christ Jesus which are at Philippi, with the bishops and deacons:

Grace be unto you, and peace, from God our Father, and from the Lord Jesus Christ.

I thank my God upon every remembrance of you, Always in every prayer of mine for you all making request with joy, For your **fellowship in the gospel** *from the first day until now; Being confident of this very thing, that he which hath begun a good work in you will perform it until the day of Jesus Christ: Even as it is meet for me to think this of you all, because I have you in my heart; inasmuch as both in my bonds, and in the defence and confirmation of the gospel, ye all are partakers of my grace. For God is my record, how greatly I long after you all in the bowels of Jesus Christ.*

And this I pray, that your love may abound yet more and more in knowledge and in all judgment; That ye may approve things that are excellent; that ye may be sincere and without offence till the day of Christ; Being filled with the fruits of righteousness, which are by Jesus Christ, unto the glory and praise of God.

1:1—THE PIONEERS

For the most part, the epistles carry the name of the penman as their opening words. The only diversion from this principle are the letters of the Apostle John, who neither appeals to his office, Apostle, nor to his fame as one of the twelve; he is content to give the Lord Jesus the first place, or to simply portray himself as the elder (2 Jn.; 3 Jn.). Even this would appear to be a reference to his age and not to an ecclesiastical position. The epistle to the Hebrews is the only other epistle that is unnamed, but it is consistent and fitting for a Jewish company when the true author of all divine revelation to that nation is given the foremost place, *"God, who at sundry times and in divers manners spake in time past unto the fathers"* (Heb. 1:1).

It is also noticeable that Silas is not mentioned among the authors of the epistle. Though he was instrumental with Paul and Timothy in seeing the assembly formed, nevertheless he does not seem to be with Paul in his later ministry, nor is he associated with Paul in his Roman imprisonment. His name does not appear in the epistles of the captivity. Others were linked to Paul in his imprisonment, or came to him, as Timothy and Luke, but Silas seems to be taken up with another sphere of ministry after the second missionary journey. In fact, his links with Paul may have ceased at Corinth, for there is no record of him after his arrival at Corinth with Timothy (Acts 18:5). That he preached the Word of God there faithfully is recorded in 2 Corinthians 1:19; after that no further light is shed on his whereabouts.

The two who wrote the epistle had a long and lasting partnership in the service of God. From the time that Timothy joined Paul, as he set out on his second sphere of service for God recorded in Acts 16, Timothy was never far from his side. Paul expected him to be present when his travels on earth were to be terminated by the executioner's sword in Rome, for he appeals to him to bring the cloak, the books and especially the parchments when he arrived (2 Tim. 4:13). The context of 2 Timothy 4 would cause many to think that

Paul's final trial had taken place, and that the sentence was his certain execution.

Paul does not appeal to his apostolic authority, but links Timothy with him as *douloi*, bond-slaves. When appealing for lowliness of mind in the Philippians, he is not exerting apostolic power, but he is showing the saints in a practical way that his desires are for their benefit. The term bond-slave is more in keeping with the character of the epistle. "At the very outset of his letter the Apostle wished to impress his converts with the fact that everything in the way of personal dignity became absorbed in the glory of the service of Jesus Christ" (Biggs).

1:1—THE PATTERN OF THE ASSEMBLY

> *Paul and Timotheus, the servants of Jesus Christ, to all the saints in Christ Jesus which are at Philippi, with the bishops and deacons:*

THE SAINTS

As we have seen, Paul appeals to "all." Unity is what is being called for throughout the epistle, and if Paul and Timothy demonstrate unity in serving together, Paul desires unity in fellowship among the Philippians.

The call is to all who form the assembly and also to those who have responsibility in it. The church of God can only be comprised of those who are saints, which is a word that means "holy." It is used of each of the persons of the Godhead. The Lord Jesus, in the prayer of John 17, speaks to the Father as *"**Holy** Father" (v. 11)*, and He Himself is spoken of as *"that **Holy** thing that shall be born of thee" (Luke 1:35)* or as *"the **Holy** One of God" (Luke 4:34)*. It is the same word that is constantly used of the "Holy" Spirit. Thus those who are brought to salvation and form part of the testimony that God raises to further His name in any locality must bear His character, "Holy." The practice of having a church roll which includes a membership of the lost sinner among them is not found in the early church. At a later date in church history, some linked this word, "saint," to a select company of deceased people, but in the New Testament, it is used of every child of God. It is the most frequent appellation in the New Testament of believers, indicating what the work of Christ has made us.

The believers of the church age are distinguished from believers of every other era by the phrase "in Christ Jesus." This is a dispensational expression that takes in only those who are converted between Pentecost and the coming of the Lord for the Church at the Rapture. Those of former ages are spoken of as *"they that are Christ's"* (1 Cor. 15:23). Every believer of every dispensation belongs to Him, but those of this church age alone are spoken of as being "in" Christ. It is a term used mainly by Paul in his epistles. Outside the Pauline epistles, it is only used by Peter on three occasions and by John once. It is not found in Hebrews, James, Jude, or Revelation. Paul, whose great ministry is that of the church, loves to dwell upon the unique relationship into which we have been brought. He speaks again and again of the eternal security into which we have been brought, as he states that we are "in Christ Jesus."

"Once in Christ, in Christ forever,
Thus the eternal covenant stands."

THE SHEPHERDS

There are various terms used for those men who have been given **responsibility** to care for an assembly by the Spirit of God (Acts 20:28). On five occasions, the word *Episcopos* is used. It is translated *Bishop* four times (Phil. 1:1; 1 Tim. 3:2; Tit. 1:7; 1 Pet. 2:25); it is translated as *Overseer* in Acts 20:28. It carries the thought of "to watch over" embodied in it. So the bishop has the responsibility of watching over things for God. We are enjoined in Hebrews 13:17 to *"obey them that have the rule* (guide, marginal reading) *over you, and submit yourselves: for they watch for your souls, as they that must give account, that they may do it with joy, and not with grief: for that is unprofitable for you."*

Along with the word bishop, these men are also called shepherds, recalling the **activity** that they are engaged in. They are also stated to be elders in their **maturity** (1 Pet. 5:1).

As elders, these are not young men. God desires those with experience of life to care for His own, and as Ecclesiastes 10:16 pronounced a woe upon Israel *"when thy king is a child,"* so the church would be in a perilous place with young men at the helm. It is said of Saul that he was a *"choice young man"* (1 Sam. 9:2), and we know the havoc that he caused. It is evident that Rehoboam was a young man when he came to the throne, and his appeal to *"the young men that were grown up with him"* (1 Kgs. 12:10) resulted in a divided kingdom. In the qualifications for elders in 1 Timothy 3, it is specifically stated that one in the place of responsibility in any church must not be a novice (v. 6). The margin says "one newly come to the faith," indicating one who is neither tender in years nor a recent believer. It should be noticed that the Bible knows nothing of one bishop over many churches, but always has many bishops in one church. The assembly is so precious to God that He desires many to watch over His own. It is also sad when a Diotrephes arises to lord it over his brethren, having his own interests at heart and not the Lord's (3 Jn. 9).

THE SERVANTS

It would seem that one of the most misunderstood words in relation to the service that is carried out by any local church, is the word *diakonos* that is translated deacon in this verse. The word is used in a twofold way in the New Testament. There are those who are seen as "deacons of the church," which is used simply of those who serve, and usually refers to a secular ministry. There are those who are said to be "deacons of Christ," which brings before us a very definite spiritual ministry. There is one who is named as *"a servant of the church which is at Cenchrea"* (Rom. 16:1). Phebe is not said to be a servant "in" the church but "of" it, and it would seem to be that as a *"succourer of many, and of myself also"* (v. 2), she was used by the church to give hospitality to those visiting the area. She is like the seven of Acts 6:5, who were chosen by the church to serve tables because of a dispute that arose between the Grecian and Hebrew believers, when certain women were neglected in the daily ministration. Many would take these seven as typical of deacon ministry, and state that their service is to be taken up with natural rather than spiritual things. It is interesting that the word deacon is not applied to these seven, nor is the word found in the book of the Acts. The word *"diakonia"* (the act of serving) is used both of the seven (6:2) and also of the Apostles in verse four when they give themselves unto the ministry of the Word of God.

The use of "deacon" in this verse has a vastly different idea from that which would come under the expression "deacon of the church," for these are not appointed by the church for a general work, but they are deacons of Christ (Col. 1:7). The word is translated minister in many passages, and speaks of those who are the teachers and preachers of the Word of God. There are four references to them in the book of Colossians where we can see the true meaning of the word expressed:

Col. 1:7 where Epaphras is seen to be *"a faithful minister (deacon) of Christ"*
Col. 1:23 where Paul states that he is *"a minister"* of the gospel
Col. 1:25 here Paul is *"a minister"* of the mystery
Col. 4:7 where Paul speaks of Tychicus as *"a faithful minister and fellowservant in the Lord"*

Paul would instruct us that these men were *"able ministers of the new testament"* (2 Cor. 3:6), and in chapter 6:4, *"the ministers of God."* There is a very definite distinction between deacons of the church and deacons of Christ. The latter should be a known body of men who are responsible for the public ministry in the assembly. That there was such a company of men in apostolic times is clear from Acts 13:1-3, 1 Timothy 3:8-13, and the present passage before us. Such must be proven men, who hold the mystery of the faith (1 Tim. 3:9-10). It is not for just any man to minister in God's assembly, but those who are called, fitted and put into the ministry by the Lord (1 Tim. 1:12). None of these are odd-job men doing a mundane work, but they are the teachers and preachers of the Word of God in the gatherings of God's children.

It is certain that in New Testament times there was nothing known of a one-man ministry in any church, be he priest or pastor. The gifts of the Spirit recorded in 1 Corinthians 12 completely contradict such a notion.

It should be noticed that the same distinction is made with the Apostles. There are those who are seen as the Apostles of Christ (1 Cor. 1:1), and those who are Apostles of the churches (2 Cor. 8:23), where the word "messenger" is the same word as Apostle), but these were chosen by the churches to fulfil a natural task of carrying the gift collected for the poor saints at Jerusalem to them. They do not fulfil a spiritual work, as do the Apostles of Christ.

1:2—THE PASTORAL BENEDICTION

Grace [be] unto you, and peace, from God our Father, and [from] the Lord Jesus Christ.

To every assembly Paul gives the apostolic benediction of grace and peace. A benediction is usually given at the end of a service; the Apostle always expresses this at the beginning of his letters. The fact that it is from God the Father and the Lord Jesus Christ is another proof of the deity of the Lord Jesus and of the equality that He has in the Godhead. We are thankful for the source of grace and peace, for only divine persons can truly dispense them. All God's dealings with His own are in grace from beginning to end. We are saved by grace (Eph. 2:8). It is a throne of grace that ministers to our needs along life's pathway (Heb. 4:16). Paul would desire that we are strong in the grace that is in Christ Jesus (2 Tim. 2:1), and Peter would have us know that it is grace that shall be brought to us at the revelation of Christ Jesus (1 Pet. 1:13). Paul desires that we will enjoy this grace as a constant feature of life. If we are living in the good of God's grace then we enjoy His peace. As a result of the grace of God, we have been brought into peace (Rom. 5:1). It is a peace that passeth all understanding (Phil. 4:7).

1:3-4—THE PRAYER OF THE APOSTLE

I thank my God upon every remembrance of you,
Always in every prayer of mine for you all making
request with joy,

The Apostle invariably gives thanks for the saints. He fulfils his own injunction recorded in 1 Thessalonians 5:18, *"in everything give thanks: for this is the will of God in Christ Jesus concerning you."* Some believers have a very censorious spirit, and criticise harshly, ever fault finding, being quick and eager to voice their disapproval. It is a lovely thing to emulate the Apostle and give thanks to God for that which is of value in the saints. In the Roman epistle, he gives thanks for the evidence of their salvation, *"that your faith is spoken of throughout the whole world" (Rom. 1:8).* Some Christians are very irate when they perceive other Christians moving away from the truth that is in Jesus, when they look at the testimony of such as those at Corinth, but Paul again gives thanks, *"for the grace of God that is given you by Jesus Christ. That in everything ye are enriched by Him, in all utterance, and in all knowledge" (1 Cor. 1:4-5).* The only believers he does not return thanks to God for are those of Galatia, for he fears they may not have genuinely come to the faith.

The thought behind Paul's giving of thanks is, "on my whole remembrance of you," (for such is the meaning of the Greek word used here) making his thanksgiving incessant, rather than intermittent, as in the phrase *"every remembrance."*

Paul draws attention to his consistency in prayer for the Philippians, *"always in every prayer of mine."* He is not merely uttering words in the presence of God but is making supplication for them. He also makes known his spirit as he is praying; he prays with joy. How blessed he is even in the prison cell at Rome, that there are things that bring him joy. As he reflects upon the converts that resulted from his former labours, he knows that his labour is not in vain in the Lord. The Philippians, like many others, must have been brought constantly before God for it was his habit to pray *"night and day" (1 Thess. 3:10; 2 Tim. 1:3).*

The repetition of the word "all" would run through these two verses, as he speaks of *"all my remembrance" (NASB v. 3)*, and *"always for you all."* There seems to be a delicate tact in which he uses the word, as he prepares the way for the ensuing exhortations to unity.

His prayer also brings forth his first reference to joy in the epistle. There are many things that bring him joy as he looks on the work of God at Philippi. His joy is seen as:

1:4	Joy in prayer
1:5	Joy in the progress of the saints
1:18	Joy in preaching
1:26	Joy in the presence of the preacher
2:2	Joy in unity
2:17-18	Joy in ministry
2:28	Joy in recovery

The highest form of joy is seen in chapter 3:1 where it is, **"rejoice in the Lord."** This is again desired in chapter 4:4 with the addition to it of, **"rejoice in the Lord alway."** It is evident that joy is not dependent on outward circumstances for Paul was in prison. It is rather in the appreciation that *"we know that all things work together for good" (Rom. 8:28)*, and that the Lord is in every circumstance that we pass through. It is this that gives us joy.

1:5—THE PROVISION OF THE PHILIPPIANS

For your fellowship in the gospel from the first day until now;

THE PROVISION

This verse expresses the reason for his thanksgiving in verse 3. This is a letter of thanks for a gift the assembly had sent him. Paul does not look on this as merely financial help, but as *"fellowship in the gospel."* It is rather fellowship "to" (*eis*) the gospel. The preposition used would lift the value of the gift that is given beyond that of the servant to whom it is given, for in giving we are not merely supporting a man, but Paul elevates all giving to the support of the gospel ministry. What a blessed thing to know that all who support a God-given ministry are helping to further that ministry. In chapter 4:18, Paul links giving to God, and again puts it beyond merely giving to the servant. Let all who support the work of God rejoice in the fact that the gift goes beyond those to whom they give, for it is to further the great work of God in the world.

THEIR PERSISTENCE

The arrival of the gift must have given great pleasure to Paul as he remembered the faithfulness of the Philippians toward him, for he speaks of their support as being *"from the first day until now."* The assembly was a liberal church, always looking to their responsibilities to further the work of God. In chapter 4:15-16, he recalls their faithfulness, *"Now ye Philippians know also, that in the beginning of the gospel, when I departed from Macedonia, no church communicated with me as concerning giving and receiving, but ye only. For even in Thessalonica ye sent once and again unto my necessity."* Here was a church that saw to Paul's needs not only when he was among them, but also as he moved further afield to serve the Lord. The Philippians were never far behind him, supporting the servant who was at the forefront of the battle. Often times with so many believers it is "out of sight, out of mind"; not so with this assembly. Even though Paul is in captivity in Rome, they will seek to support the work of God done through him. There are still many churches that resemble those that Paul speaks of here— churches that did not give to the work of God; churches that fail in their responsibilities to support the work. Many are like misers instead of ministers with the funds they have, which ought to be put into the work of God.

The Philippian believers would also recall that *"from the first day"* Lydia had set the example. The Lord not only opened her heart *"that she attended unto the things that were spoken of Paul,"* but when she was baptised, she opened her home to God's servants. Their giving to God began from the outset of the work.

1:6—Preservation of the Saints

> *Being confident of this very thing, that he which hath begun a good work in you will perform [it] until the day of Jesus Christ:*

It is to be noticed that in 1:5-6, two days are brought before us, *"the first day"* and *"the day of Jesus Christ."* Perhaps the two statements link the two verses together, giving two possible thoughts. First, the spirit of giving and consistent support to the gospel will be furthered by God until the day of approval, the Judgement Seat of Christ, which seems to be implied by the expression "the day of Christ." In this interpretation, Paul is confident that the ministrations of the saints will find their fulfilment in the day of approval when every man's work will be manifested.

There is of course, the thought that the eternal security of the believer is being emphasised. There are two thoughts regarding this wondrous truth, if we take this as the teaching of the passage.

The Confidence of Paul

Unlike the work that Paul had wrought in Galatia, where he started to have grave reservations about a true work of grace among them, as they turned from the work of Calvary as the basis of their salvation, and imbibed Jewish legalism as a necessity to find acceptance with God, Paul had no such concerns regarding these Philippian saints. Their evident interest in the gospel of our Lord Jesus as they supported the servant of God was enough for the Apostle to recognize that a true work of grace had taken place. Thus he can say, *"being confident."* The word simply means, "to be persuaded; to trust." There was sufficient evidence manifested in the lives of these believers to give Paul the assurance that genuine conversion had taken place. Other New Testament writers would lay stress regarding those who profess salvation, that there must be a true dependence on Christ, and that we have not merely accepted the statement of facts regarding Him. The Word of

God has a very prominent place in the salvation of a soul, for we are *"born again not of corruptible seed, but of incorruptible, by (dia-through) the Word of God, which liveth and abideth for ever"* (1 Pet. 1:23). Again, *"faith cometh by hearing, and hearing by the Word of God"* (Rom. 10:17). It is essential to note that the Word of God brings us to Christ, for as He said, *"Verily, verily, I say unto you, He that heareth my word, and believeth on him that sent me, hath everlasting life, and shall not come into condemnation; but is passed from death unto life"* (John 5:24). It is faith in a Person, not in a program about Him, that saves. I trust that all who read this will be able to say with the Apostle *"I know whom I have believed,"* not, "what I have believed" (2 Tim. 1:12).

Both Peter and John would encourage us to test the reality of our profession. See 2 Peter 1:10; 2:1. John is always testing profession. In his first epistle, he looks for the evidence of a soul walking in the light where God dwells. John hears many stating *"we say."* John says, "Let us see by your life, and then we can believe what you say." One brother has said, "We cannot hear what you say for the sound of your feet; their walk did not match their talk."

THE COMMENCEMENT

In this Paul looks back to the origins of the work in Philippi, and I suppose the believers as they read the letter would appreciate the startling way they were brought to faith—the Macedonian call, the Lord opening the heart of Lydia, the rabble mob that hounded Silas and Paul to prison, but then the earthquake that awoke the jailor from his spiritual as well as his natural sleep. Would not all look back and say *"he which hath begun a good work"* (Phil. 1:6)? The word "begun" occurs only here and in Galatians 3:3 *"having begun in the Spirit,"* where there is no doubt it refers to the commencement of their Christian life.

THE CONCLUSION

Such was the character of the work in the believers that Paul had no doubt of its ultimate success. It was a good (*agathon*) work. That is, "what is good in principle, in its character or constitution, and beneficial in its effect" (Vine). It is used of Mary's choice in Luke 10:42, *"Mary hath chosen that good part," and in* Nathaniel's astonishment at being told, *"We have found him of whom Moses in the Law, and the prophets, did write, Jesus of Nazareth, the son of Joseph" (John 1:45).* His reply was, *"Can there any good thing come out of Nazareth?"* All that Vine says of the word "good" was certainly seen in Christ. Paul sees the final end of the work of God in these believers, for he is assured that the work begun by God will be brought to its completion by God. How blessed to know that our salvation is in divine hands and does not depend on us. God began it and God will complete it. It is to be noted that being brought to the day of Jesus Christ, the time when rewards are given for faithfulness, in this present verse depends on God, but how we stand there, in verse 10, very much depends on us.

1:7-8—Partners in the Ministry

> *Even as it is meet for me to think this of you all, because I have you in my heart; inasmuch as both in my bonds, and in the defence and confirmation of the gospel, ye all are partakers of my grace. For God is my record, how greatly I long after you all in the bowels of Jesus Christ.*

There are divergent thoughts as to which is the correct reading of this verse; whether it is that recorded in the text *"I have you in my heart,"* or the reading inserted in the margin, *"ye have me in your heart."* It is not a point to be argued, for both are true. To Paul the important thing was that God *"is not unrighteous to forget your work and labour of love, which ye have shewed toward his name, in that ye have ministered to the saints and do minister" (Heb. 6:10).* For with the support of the assembly as it was, he says, *"it is meet for me to think this of you all,"* the word "meet" simply means righteous. It is a sad thing that those who are supported in the work of God cannot hold in affection those who show fellowship to the gospel. I have heard that there are those who, unlike Paul in this Epistle, cannot even acknowledge the kindness of believers towards them. The word occurs again in chapter 4:8, *"whatsoever things are just."* It is meet, righteous, just, to hold those in esteem who are faithful to God in their giving, and it must draw out your affection for them. I would judge this to be the correct reading, and verse 8 would confirm it, *"For God is my record, how greatly I long after you all in the bowels of Jesus Christ."*

I recall many years ago a Welsh schoolgirl sending us a small gift one Christmas time. She told us how she had set aside a portion from her weekly allowance from her parents, and she sought to help us in our work for God. The following year with a gift double the amount sent the previous year, she told us how she had led her school friend to Christ, and had taught her to set aside a portion of her allowance too. We still hold that lady in high esteem and are very thankful for her love toward us.

That there is truth in the marginal reading too is obvious; their love for Paul was evident by their continual support for God's work. Their affection leads to action and their giving linked them to him in a three-fold way, and Paul gives a three-fold response to it.

1:7—His Sufferings

If their giving in verse 5 was a fellowship to the gospel, it is now seen to directly associate them with Paul in his bonds. Such is giving; it links us with the servant of God no matter what his situation is.

1:7—His Service

Not only with *"his bonds,"* but also *"in the defence and confirmation of the gospel."* The word for defence is *apologia* and carries the thought of "pleading one's cause in court" (Lightfoot, *Philippians*, page 83). It is used in this way in 2 Timothy 4:16, *"at my first answer no man stood with me."* Yet how often do the brethren put the servant in the courtroom, as did the Corinthians with Paul in 1 Corinthians 9:3? These believers at Corinth, the fruit of his labours, rather than caring for him could only criticise him. He makes his defence in their courtroom of how he has a right as a servant of God to have his food supplied (v. 4), to support his family by the gospel (v. 5), and to leave the factory (v. 6), as it is the responsibility of the assembly to support him in his service. I notice that, like the Corinthians, there are many to whom you have been a great blessing in the hand of God, who later turn and oppose you for no apparent reason. Paul knew this from those in Asia also (2 Tim. 1:15), *"this thou knowest, that all they which are in Asia be turned away from me."* Could any give a legitimate reason as to why Paul and his ministry were rejected? The more abundantly he loved the less he was loved.

The Pulpit Commentary admirably sums up the two words used here, "There seems to be no reference in the words 'defence and confirmation' to his public defence before Caesar (which probably had not yet taken place), but generally to his work of preaching the gospel, which was both apologetic, meeting the objections of the adversaries, and aggressive, asserting the truth" (*Vol. 20, Philippians,* page 3).

1:7—HIS SPECIAL CALL

The giving of the Philippians linked them as one with him in his call and exercise of his gift for God. Paul speaks of them as being *"partakers of my grace."* The word partakers is *sugkoinonos.* As we noticed in verse 1, the prefix *"sun"* denotes as being one with, indicating that the support of the Philippian assembly by their giving associated them with Paul in the gift that he had received from the Lord Jesus. Whenever the Apostle speaks of his ministry, he refers to it as a "grace" (Rom. 12:3; 15:15; Gal. 2:9; Eph. 3:2; 3:8). It is the unmerited favour of God that gives gift to any, and to be able to teach divine truth is a great privilege given of God. The Philippian saints are seen to be a part of it by their supportive giving. May God unveil the blessed honour of giving financial support to those who serve Him.

One of the tragedies of our day is that some would forget the ability they have received is a grace and God-given. Sadly some would use this grace not for the purpose it was given, to edify saints, but to make much of self, and to use the platform to attack and destroy the teaching of their fellow-servants who move honestly before God to seek the blessing of the saints. The flesh has never been judged and worldliness marks them. As Kelly says they "seek to win persons as a party around themselves, by sparing the flesh and humouring the natural character, so as at least to have their own way without question" (2 Cor. 12:19-20) (*Philippians*, page 18). Some Christians also like to gather themselves around men rather than to using every gift that God has given for their spiritual benefit (see 1 Cor. 1:12-13; 3:21-23).

1:8—HIS SINCERITY

The response of the Apostle to the affections of the Philippian believers is now expressed. Love begets love in the hearts of those who are spiritual, and the fervent expressions of the assembly toward Paul bring forth a deep response from him. He expresses **his faithfulness.**

This is evident as he states *"God is my record"*; the word he uses is that for "witness." On five different occasions, the Apostle declares how that every aspect of his life and ministry is carried out under the eye of God, and that his motives for all his service are pure before God. He is like his blessed Lord, of whom it is said, *"who is the faithful witness" (Rev. 1:5)*. The Proverbs declare that *"a faithful witness will not lie" (Prov. 14:5)*, and Paul took on the character of his master who is *"the truth" (John 14:6).*

The Apostle calls upon God to be the witness of his **affections** for the believers at Philippi. His **supplications** for the saints in Rome are seen in Romans 1:9 as being the subject of God's witness, *"For God is my witness, whom I serve with my spirit in the gospel of his Son, that without ceasing I make mention of you always in my prayers."* His appeal in 2 Corinthians 1:23 is to his **reservations** against visiting the assembly there until his written ministry has been effective, *"Moreover I call God for a record upon my soul, that to spare you I came not as yet unto*

PHILIPPIANS: THE MIND OF CHRIST

Corinth." The **proclamation** of the gospel will bear the scrutiny of God, as he says to the Thessalonians, *"For neither at any time used we flattering words, as ye know, nor a cloak of covetousness; God is witness"* (1 Thess. 2:5). He will also put the manifestations of the **perfection** of his life in public service before the believers in verse 10 of the same chapter, *"Ye are witnesses, and God also, how holily and justly and unblameably we behaved ourselves among you that believe."* Would that all who serve God could order their lives and ministry in such a way before Him.

Paul adds to his faithfulness, **fidelity and fervour**.

All the ministry of Paul, carried out under the eye of God, came from his heart of love for the Christians. He adds another lovely word that he is fond of using when he says, "how greatly I long after you." On seven occasions, Paul uses this word for long (*epipotheo*). It carries the thought of, to dote upon, intensely crave, long after, or to desire earnestly. The assembly would understand the yearnings of his heart toward them as they read this statement. Paul uses it in other places where it reveals his true longings as he handles the precious things of God. Not for Paul what one brother advised a servant of God, when he said, "You take your ministry too seriously. You should just give your message then go home and forget about it." How sad to have such an attitude to the truth of God. No! Paul had a deep yearning heart over all that God had put into him. The word occurs again in the following passages, where the desire is:

Romans 1:11	to instruct the saints—"the School"
2 Corinthians 5:2	for a house from Heaven—"the Shelter"
2 Corinthians 9:14	Paul's Prayer for the Corinthians—"the Supplications"
1 Thessalonians 3:6	of the Thessalonians for Paul—"the Servant"
2 Timothy 1:4	of Paul for Timothy—"the Son"

It is also used in James 4:5 of the Spirit's longings that we should not sin, and by Peter, as he would seek to put a longing into us that we should desire the Scriptures (1 Pet. 2:2).

THE SUBMISSIVE MIND
1:9-11—Prayer of the Apostle

And this I pray, that your love may abound yet more and more in knowledge and [in] all judgment; That ye may approve things that are excellent; that ye may be sincere and without offence till the day of Christ; Being filled with the fruits of righteousness, which are by Jesus Christ, unto the glory and praise of God.

Paul's prayers in the epistles are a beautiful example to all of the character that prayer should take as we supplicate before the throne of God. It was not for Paul to simply commit the mundane things of life to the Father, *"he knoweth that ye have need of all these things" (Matt. 6:32).* The Lord Jesus Himself instructed us to take no anxious thought for food and drink, or for our clothing. The whole section of Matthew 6:28-34, though simple to read, should exercise our heart to be dependent on the Lord for our daily needs. To pray for them is one thing, to give thanks for the mercies of the day is another. We should, *"in everything give thanks: for this is the will of God in Christ Jesus concerning you" (1 Thess. 5:18).*

The prayers of the Apostle always tend towards the spiritual well-being of the believers. In his two prayers in the book of Ephesians, he stands like the high priest of old in garments of glory and beauty. For in the prayer of chapter 1 he has the saints on his *shoulders* as he desires that we know the *power* of God toward us. In the third chapter, all is on his *heart*, when the prime thought is that of the *love* that God has toward us to bring us to such great blessings. The priest of Israel bore the names of the children of Israel upon precious stones, both on his shoulders and on his breast. In the epistle to the Colossians, the prayer of the Apostle is once again for a spiritual appreciation of the full intention of God as He has purposed it in His will, and for us to place ourselves within the orbit of it (Col. 1:9-11). In the present verse, Paul, writing against the background of the self-centred lives of the Philippians, prays for spiritual discernment and fruitfulness.

1:8—Prayer for Affection to be Displayed

> *And this I pray, that your love may abound yet more and more in knowledge and [in] all judgment;*

Paul's prayer begins with a desire to see the love of the saints abounding toward one another. The word he uses in relation to prayer is one that is always directed to God, and has the thought of worship involved in it. How blessed must be the life that, when calling upon God, has a reverential spirit and thoughts of devotion to the Lord, while bringing petitions before the throne. The love that the saints should have one for another is *agape* love, the love of God that loves without a cause. It is a love that is divine in its origin. Paul is not content that we simply love one another, but he wants our love to abound. To abound would indicate that which is to be over and above, or to be extravagant, to exist in full quantity. He also desires their joy to abound (1:26) in the same way. Paul speaks from experience, for in the changing circumstances of life he also knows what it is to abound (4:12). The prodigal son could look toward his father's house from the swine troughs of the far country, and see how even the hired servants had *"enough and to spare."* Such is the word abound. God has *abounded* towards us (Eph. 1:8) and would desire that we abound in love one toward another (see 1 Thess. 3:12-13).

Love must ever be an intelligent love, for it must be in knowledge. Love must not be indiscriminate, but discerning with spiritual sense. We cannot love what God abhors, but the word used here for knowledge (*epignosis*) would indicate that love is to be carried out in a full knowledge whether acquired or experimental. Many would make love an excuse to overlook sin, and thus they fail to honour God when His word is set aside. But a true love will act in faithfulness to see God glorified in the lives of fellow believers. A true love will seek to correct what is contrary to His word; *"Faithful are the wounds of a friend"* (Prov. 27:6).

Again, this love is not only in knowledge but also in judgement. The word judgement is used only here but comes from a word meaning "to perceive." It has been translated "wise discretion." There should be moral sensitivity, not just an intellectual acuteness in all our relationships with fellow believers.

1:10—Prayer for Appreciation of our Destiny

> *That ye may approve things that are excellent; that ye may be sincere and without offence till the day of Christ;*

The Apostle always looks beyond our present pathway here in this world; our present life is determining our future destiny. How we live now will affect our place in the kingdom, which will be decided at the Judgement Seat of Christ. Present carelessness with the deposit of spiritual things that has been given to us could mean that we are casting away our crowns. The place of honour that the Lord desires to give can be lost if we do not take heed to the divine injunctions regarding our lives. We cannot live as we like and be careless with the truths of God, and then expect to be rewarded for it. We shall look at the crowns that the Lord sets before us when we come to chapter 4:1.

The present verse begins with "that" (*hina*, in order that). This would show that there is a very definite link with verse 9. The great truth revealed here is that we *"may approve things that are excellent."* Again, the expression needs to be carefully weighed, as much of our future enjoyment depends on our fulfilment of this truth. To approve simply means, to examine, to test, and to choose after the test is made. This will enable us to appreciate *"things that are excellent."* The marginal reading says, "things that differ." Vine's Dictionary states, "to carry through." It can be put as, "the more excellent way." I would appeal to every dear believer not to be content with just moving with the crowd, but to seek to discern the mind of God. There is a more excellent way that He desires us to tread, which will have eternal benefits for those who do so.

As we walk the more excellent way, it is again, *"that ye may be sincere and without offence."* The Greek word for sincere comes from two words, *heile* meaning, "warmth or light of the sun, and *krino*, to test; these words mean testing by sunlight" (Kittel, *one volume edition*, page 206). The word would be used of a jug purchased in the market place, having a fault line covered with wax and painted over, which when exposed to the sunlight caused the wax to melt and exposed the flaw. How often we seek to cover our failures, and to paint a pretty picture of our Christian lives, seeking to beguile other believers with a pretence of holiness. We are not sincere, and the light of the judgement seat will expose our hypocrisy. An unflawed life will mean that we are without offence. The word offence (*aproskopos*) occurs three times in the New Testament:

Acts 24:16 speaking of Paul's testimony before God and men
1 Corinthians 10:32 speaking of the Church's testimony before men
Philippians 1:10 speaking of Personal testimony before the Lord

A. T. Robertson states "the word is either intransitive, as in Acts 24:16 and means 'not stumbling', or transitive as in 1 Corinthians 10:32 and means 'not causing others to stumble'. Either will make good sense here" (*Paul's Joy in Christ*, page 38). Lightfoot would be a little more definite when admitting either interpretation can be taken, but favours the transitive, saying, "the former is to be preferred; for it is a question solely of the fitness of the Philippians to appear before the tribunal of Christ, and any reference to their influence on others would be out of place" (*Philippians*, page 85). This leads us to the expression *"till the day of Christ."* The preposition "till" would indicate that this is certainly going to be reached, and that all believers will stand there. It is just a little word *"eis"* but it is a guarantee of our eternal security, for the day of Christ brings us to the Judgement Seat of Christ, when our service and our faithfulness will be rewarded. It must be remembered that there is no future judgement for the believer regarding sin; that was fully dealt with by

Christ at the cross, and Romans 8:1 must always be kept in the heart, *"There is therefore now no condemnation to them which are in Christ Jesus."* Many believers get troubled in spirit regarding failure; sin does not affect our union with Christ, but it does affect our communion with the Father. It was for this reason that John wrote in his first epistle chapter 1:9, *"If we confess our sins, He is faithful and just to forgive us our sins and to cleanse us from all unrighteousness."* We must keep short accounts with God to see that nothing hinders the fellowship into which we have been brought. The first epistle of John gives a double assurance that our sins are eternally dealt with by both the work and person of Christ. Chapter 1:7 speaks of the constant value of the blood of Christ, which *"cleanseth us from all sin."* The present continuous tense confirms to us that the work of Calvary is still effectual as far as the sin question is concerned. We must also notice in chapter 2:1-2 that God gives further assurance to the heart, that sin, as far as the believer is concerned, cannot rise to His throne on account of the fact that the Lord Jesus is there, for, "if we sin" we have one who is both an advocate to present our cause, and who is Himself *"the propitiation for our sins."* The person of the Lord Jesus assures us that our sins are dealt with forever.

1:11—PRAYER FOR ABUNDANCE OF FRUIT DESIRED

Being filled with the fruits of righteousness, which are by Jesus Christ, unto the glory and praise of God.

The Apostle would keep before us, not only our own lives to be lived with the Judgement Seat of Christ in view, but also that we might glorify God both here and now. To this end, he prays that we might be filled with the fruit of righteousness. Its origin is seen to be by, or through, the Lord Jesus. There could be no thought of self-righteousness or righteousness by the Law. This fruit can only be imparted by divine persons and by having a divine link with the Lord Jesus. The Lord Jesus makes it clear that it is only as we abide in Him that we can bring forth fruit (John 15:1-17). Again, there are exhortations throughout the Scriptures to produce this fruit, which is the only evidence that divine life has been imparted for, *"by their fruits ye shall know them" (Matt. 7:20)*. This fruit of righteousness is also linked to the Holy Spirit in Ephesians 5:9, *"for the fruit of the Spirit is in all goodness and righteousness and truth."* If any fruit of the Spirit is to be seen then all must be seen, for the fruit is singular. Though there is a nine fold demonstration of it in Galatians 5:22-23, such fruit will be seen in all my life, for the first three are God-ward, the next trio is man-ward, and the final three are self-ward. O for a life full of the fruit of the Spirit where all that God desires for me will be displayed in all that I do. God Himself has a personal interest in us when He chastises His children, for it is to produce *"the peaceable fruit of righteousness" (Heb. 12:11)*. We also have a responsibility to further it in the lives of our fellow-believers, for James 3:18 indicates that *"the fruit of righteousness is sown in peace of them that make peace."* There are those that have bitter envying and strife in their hearts, who only produce confusion and every evil work, (see James 3:14-16). These will never contribute to producing the fruit of righteousness.

This fruit, which has its origin in Christ, has for its object *"the glory and praise of God."* Glory is a visible display of honour, and a life of righteousness, which is divine in origin, must be for God's glory and not for our honour. If the glory is displayed man-ward, the praise must be God-ward. That such conditions can be produced in the heart of sinful men must generate praise to Him who begat it. There are many features of the Christian life that bring glory to God as seen in:

FAITH—ROMANS 4:20

The faith of Abraham who, *"staggered not at the promise of God through unbelief; but was strong in faith, giving glory to God."*

FELLOWSHIP—ROMANS 15:7

The Roman believers are told not to make Jewish ordinances of days and diet a cause of division if some of the converts have scruples regarding these things, but rather, *"receive ye one another, as Christ also received us to the glory of God."*

THE SUBMISSIVE MIND

FOOD—1 CORINTHIANS 10:31

Some, again, would fear that food sold in the marketplace may have been first offered to idols, or even that eaten in the home of an unbeliever could come from the same source. Paul gives clear teaching on these subjects, then adds, *"Whether therefore ye eat, or drink, or whatsoever ye do, do all to the glory of God."*

FAITHFULNESS—2 CORINTHIANS 1:20

We have a God who will be faithful to all that He has said, and this will produce glory to Him, *"For all the promises of God in Him are yea, and in Him Amen, unto the glory of God."*

FURNISHED—2 CORINTHIANS 4:15

The ministry and the suffering of Paul, though severe for him (who knows what servants of God pass through for the good of the saints?), to Paul they were all, *"for your sakes, that the abundant grace might through the thanksgivings of many redound to the glory of God."*

FINANCES—2 CORINTHIANS 8:19

Even the way in which we handle the offerings that are given to support the work of God should be with such care as to bring glory to God, *"but who also chosen of the churches to travel with us with this grace, which is administered by us to the glory of the same Lord."*

FIRSTFRUITS—EPHESIANS 1:12

Paul realizes the honour that belonged to the first Jewish converts when he says, *"that we should be to the praise of his glory, who first trusted in Christ."* How thankful we are that he includes Gentile believers in verses 13 and 14.

FUTURE—EPHESIANS 3:21

It is fitting, if so many aspects of our lives should bring glory to God, that throughout the great eternity the saints of this dispensation will bring glory to Him. *"Unto Him be glory in the church by Christ Jesus throughout all ages, world without end. Amen."* I am sure that every true believer would add their "amen" to it, and may God be glorified in our lives as we live to glorify Him daily.

A further note may be added, having considered the appearance of believers at the Judgement Seat of Christ. There are three future judgements that must be distinguished if we are not to get into great confusion as we read the New Testament. They are:
1. The Judgement Seat of Christ: Romans 14:10
2. The judgement of living nations: Matthew 25:31-36
3. The judgement of the wicked unsaved dead: Revelation 20:11-15

There are major differences making each distinct:
1. Takes place in Heaven after the Rapture;
2. Takes place at Jerusalem after the Tribulation;
3. Takes place in space after the Millennium.

Again we see a difference in those who appear at the judgements:
1. All are believers;
2. Some are believers some are not. The Lord speaks of sheep and goats;
3. All are lost sinners.

Many have failed to recognise that God has various programs in His dealings with men, and all will not be settled at one last final great assize.

THE FURTHERANCE OF THE GOSPEL
1:12-18

> *But I would ye should understand, brethren, that the things which happened unto me have fallen out rather unto the furtherance of the gospel; So that my bonds in Christ are manifest in all the palace, and in all other places; And many of the brethren in the Lord, waxing confident by my bonds, are much more bold to speak the word without fear.*

> *Some indeed preach Christ even of envy and strife; and some also of good will: The one preach Christ of contention, not sincerely, supposing to add affliction to my bonds: But the other of love, knowing that I am set for the defence of the gospel. What then? notwithstanding, every way, whether in pretence, or in truth, Christ is preached; and I therein do rejoice, yea, and will rejoice.*

1:12-13—The Prison Experience

1:12—His captivity

> *But I would ye should understand, brethren, that the things [which happened] unto me have fallen out rather unto the furtherance of the gospel;*

The Apostle seeks to relieve the minds of the believers in relation to his imprisonment. The natural inclination is to think that the work of God was greatly hindered by this mighty servant of God being incarcerated and removed from the front line of gospel activity, where naturally he would seem to be required. The Apostle introduces a "rather" into his letter to them, making his movements a comparison between the actual and the expected results for the gospel. For rather than the gospel being hindered, it has fallen out to *"the furtherance of the gospel,"* reaching to places inside the prison and into other parts it would not have been able to go but for Paul's bonds. It not only reached places inside, but it also caused brethren outside (1:14-18) to take up the cause of the gospel of Christ.

Paul uses a word that would greatly encourage the Philippians when he speaks of the *"furtherance of the gospel."* It is a word that would speak of the pioneer who is going before to open up the path, removing that which obstructs the way for those who are following. It occurs again in verse 25, where Paul would not only open the way for the gospel, but also look to see growth in the lives of the saints. The fact that it is the furtherance of the gospel is seen geographically—reaching places; numerically—reaching people; spiritually—as in verse 25, producing *"your joy and faith."* Sadly, some who see the way open would use it antagonistically—verse 16, for they *"preach Christ of contention."*

The prison experience of the Apostle was beneficial in a threefold way as it furthered the work of God; the Lord makes no mistakes as He directs the movements of His servants. Here in Philippians, his preaching is prominent. The epistle to the Colossians would speak of *his prayers*. Far from hindering his ministry, he records how he is in *"great conflict,"* as the wrestler or the athlete struggles in the arena, to see the saints of God have their hearts, *"comforted, being knit together in love, and unto all riches of the full assurance of understanding, to the acknowledgement of the mystery of God" (Col. 2:2)*. We must all be thankful for the imprisonment of Paul, as we are indebted to his *pen* for the wondrous truths we have received from his many prison epistles. It can truly be said, *"The things which happened to me have fallen out rather unto the furtherance of the gospel."*

1:13—HIS CHAINS

> *So that my bonds in Christ are manifest in all the palace, and in all other [places];*

Within the prison wall it became self-evident the Apostle was not where he was because of desperate crimes, but for devotion to Christ. The words *"my bonds in Christ"* carry the thought of, *"as being in Christ."* This was manifest in the Praetorium, which is the word used for "palace." It is the place to which the soldiers took the Lord Jesus to prepare Him for crucifixion, where they mocked and arrayed Him in a scarlet robe 'ere they placed the crown of thorns upon His head, giving Him the reed as a sceptre and bowing the knee in scorn and derision. The religious leaders saw none of it, as they would not go in lest they be defiled (John 18:28). The Praetorium was evidently the quarter where the guards would meet. What incidents must have been related among them, as they spoke of the prisoner to whom they were chained? Would they themselves have been asked to bow the knee in the season of Paul's prayers? Would not the gospel have fallen from his lips as they were by his side? The implication is that they not only recognised the purpose of his imprisonment, but some believed on the Lord Jesus.

Historians tell us that this guard was the elite of the Roman army, numbering ten thousand hand-picked men, all of whom were Italians and formed part of the imperial guard. They were the most powerful body in the land and carried the rank of centurion. It is plain to see how such men, hearing and receiving the gospel, would have far-reaching effects as they carried the message even to those in high places. Little wonder the imprisonment of Paul had fallen out rather unto the furtherance of the gospel.

Coneybeare and Howson, in their book, *The Life and Epistles of Saint Paul*, state regarding the Praetorium "that it denotes here, not the palace itself, but the quarters of that part of the imperial guard which was in immediate attendance upon the Emperor. The Emperor was praetor or commander-in-chief of the troops, and it was natural that his immediate guard would be in the Praetorium near him" (*Vol. 2*, page 510).

1:14-18—THE PROCLAMATION OF THE GOSPEL

1:14—THE CHRISTIANS

And many of the brethren in the Lord, waxing confident by my bonds, are much more bold to speak the word without fear.

If the Apostle makes known the gospel inside the prison walls, his imprisonment caused the Christians outside *"to speak the word without fear."* The text makes a division in those who take up the gospel. Here he speaks of the majority, *"most"* of the brethren (translators say it is "most" here for "many"), whilst from verse 15 he would speak of a minority who were not honest in their preaching. For the most, the bonds of the Apostle stirred them to declare Christ, not fearing the face of man or the consequences that might follow.

The Pulpit Commentary indicates that, "the words, 'in the Lord' are perhaps better taken with being 'confident'." This is also set forth in the *Bishops Commentary*, "the words 'in the Lord' naturally though they attach themselves to 'the brethren', are better joined with the following. There is no true parallel in the N.T. for the expression 'brethren in the Lord', which would in fact be tautological; 'the brethren' (without 'in the Lord') sufficiently denoting Christians'" (page 598).

The word "confidence" occurs six times in the epistle:
- 1:6—Confidence in the finished work of God's salvation
- 1:14—Confidence of the saints in freely making proclamation
- 1:25—Confidence in the furtherance of the saints in their progression
- 2:24—Confidence in the faithfulness of Paul in his considerations
- 3:3—Confidence of Paul in the futility of the flesh for sanctification
- 3:4—Confidence of Jews in the flesh as they made their professions

These believers were not only faithful to preach the Word, but they were fearless as they made Christ known. The word that is used of them is *"aphobos"* and occurs four times in the New Testament:
- Luke 1:74—The prayer of Zacharias spoke of the time when Israel would serve God without fear in their worship;
- 1 Corinthians 16:10—Paul exhorts the assembly to receive Timothy so that he can move among them without fear in his walk;
- Philippians 1:14—The believers have no fear as they make their witness known;
- Jude 12—The evil teachers move among the saints at their love feast, feeding without fear in their wickedness. As all fours in Scripture divide into a three and

a one, so here we find that three are fearless in a good way, with the last being bad.

1:15—THE CRITICS

Some indeed preach Christ even of envy and strife; and some also of good will:

The Apostle turns his attention to the minority who were not sincere in their preaching. Some have looked for various reasons as to why these preach as they do, setting forth the Jewish element as the possible source of the opposition. They would tenaciously hold on to their former doctrines regarding days and diets, and they set themselves against Paul as seen in Galatians and Colossians. But is there any need to look beyond what is recorded by the Spirit here, as He relates the source of their enmity as being *"envy and strife"*? One has called them terrible twins, and such they are. Having being in fellowship with believers for over fifty years, it is sad to see this spirit still exists in many that profess Christ. Worse still, is to see it mark those who have been called to serve God and who breathe out bitter opposition to others, as they move in enmity and strife. Envy seeks to put itself up, while strife would put others down. Many believers have suffered because of this spirit in men, and many assemblies have been torn apart by it. We should look to ourselves that we do not fail in this matter, causing trouble among God's children. Such a spirit is seen in James 3:13-4:5, where we see it will deny the truth, it descends from the devil, and it destroys peace.

If Paul denounces the motive of their preaching, he is thankful for the matter that they preach, "Christ." The word for "preach" is that used to describe the herald as a public crier. It is used of John the Baptist, and of the Lord Jesus, also of His disciples as they make known Christ and the Kingdom. We find it occurs frequently in the Acts and the epistles as the gospel is told out. Those who carried the gospel in a former day did not mumble into their shirt collars as we find some do today, but they lifted their head and raised their voice to declare the glad tidings.

The verse also brings before us the manner that some preached, as he speaks of *"some also of good-will."* They acted as Paul did towards his nation as he records *"my heart's desire"* (Rom. 10:1) was to see Israel saved. The word is used of God's *"good pleasure"* towards us in Ephesians 1:5 and also in verse 9. Would that such a spirit would mark us as we would proclaim the gospel.

1:16—THE CALLOUSNESS

The one preach Christ of contention, not sincerely, supposing to add affliction to my bonds:

One wonders how such men as revealed in these verses could name themselves among believers, as we see the character they display. Whilst making a public declaration of Christ, it is in the spirit of strife and, sadly, they were not pure in their actions, *"not sincerely"* indicates impurity of motive. They were filled with the leaven of ill-feeling.

As the believers at Philippi were told that Paul's imprisonment was contrary to expectations in verse 12, so we find that these had not gained their objective when they thought to add the whip to afflict Paul along with his chain. When they desired to *"add affliction"* to his bonds, they looked for tribulation and anguish to be added to him. Such tribulation should only come from the world (John 16:33). The day will dawn when God will cause the world to pass through tribulation (Matt. 24:21). Paul knew much tribulation in his service for God. There are six references to it in 2 Corinthians. When he wrote that epistle, he must have been feeling the strain of the opposition he knew as he served God (see 2 Cor. 1:4; 1:8; 2:4; 4:17; 6:4; 7:4). Yet, in all his trials he could look to God *"who comforteth us in all our tribulation"* (2 Cor. 1:4). How sad when he cannot get comfort from the saints, but finds them acting like the world, seeking his hurt. We can hardly imagine such base carnality rising from the hearts of those who profess Christ. It would be well if such conditions were confined to Paul's day, but such is the bitter opposition against some servants, that some will do all that they can to oppose them.

1:17—THE CARING

> *But the other of love, knowing that I am set for the defence of the gospel.*

Paul is thankful that this was not the desire of all who preached as a result of his imprisonment. He discriminates between them as he recognises that others preach out of love that is divine in origin (*agape*), as they are intuitively (*eidotes*) taught by the Spirit that Paul is *"set for the defence of the gospel."* Rather than the gospel being hindered, they know that Paul is imprisoned by the will of God, being "set," that is "to lie outstretched" (Strong). The word is used of the Lord *"lying in a manger" (Luke 2:12)*, and by Simeon as he knows that the Lord Jesus is *"set for the fall and rise again of many in Israel" (Luke 2:34)*. In Revelation 4:2, it relates to *"a throne set in Heaven,"* and again in chapter 21:16 to the city that *"lieth foursquare."* Along with the others of its twenty-six occurrences, it seems he associated with the thoughts of purpose and definite action. Paul's imprisonment was not a plight but a purpose in the hand of God.

1:18—HIS CONFIDENCE

> *What then? notwithstanding, every way, whether in pretence, or in truth, Christ is preached; and I therein do rejoice, yea, and will rejoice.*

It is good to see the Apostle rise above the pretensions of men, and, though it is evident he does not condone the attitude of some, still he is not obsessed by it. It is apparent that Paul does not find a doctrinal difference in those that preach out of contention, for he will not endorse those that preach another gospel as the Judaisers in Galatia. Rather he reveals that they leave themselves open to a curse (Gal. 1:6-9). Nor will he sanction the Gnostic error of the Colossian epistle. Where error is mixed with truth, the honour of Christ is impugned, and this must be exposed as false. The preaching here is full of personal opposition not doctrinal error. The former means little to Paul; if Christ is preached, he will rejoice in it.

The use of the word "pretence" should cause us to be careful as we serve the Lord, for, as the Lord exposed in: Matthew 23:14; Mark 12:40; Luke 20:47—it can be seen in **prayer**. Here—it can be seen in our **preaching**. In 1 Thessalonians 2:5, it can make preachers greedy of **possessions**, for the word "cloak" is the word used here for pretence. Well might the Lord Jesus use the word again in John 15:22, as the revelation of Christ and the word He spake gives *"no cloak for their sin."*

Many years ago, it was my privilege to spend a Friday evening in the home of a venerable man of God, John Douglas of Lanarkshire. During the course of the evening as we spoke of the Scriptures together, he made two simple but sublime statements that opened my mind to consider some beautiful links between the book of Philippians and other Scriptures. He quoted chapter 1:12 and said *"the things that have happened unto me have fallen out rather unto the furtherance of the gospel"*; to which he added, "Joseph." Then quoting verse 17, *"I am set for the defence of the gospel,"* again in his own terse way he said, "Nehemiah." Knowing the history of both these men of God, it was easy to see how these statements beautifully summarised their life and ministry. We know that Joseph's rejection was according to the will of God for Israel's future preservation, both personal and national. This is seen in Genesis 45:4-8:

> *And Joseph said unto his brethren, Come near to me, I pray you. And they came near. And he said, I am Joseph your brother, whom ye sold into Egypt. Now therefore be not grieved, nor angry with yourselves that ye sold me hither: for God did send me before you to preserve life. For these two years hath the famine been in the land: and yet there are five years, in the which there shall neither be earing nor harvest. And God sent me before you to preserve you a posterity in the earth, and to save your lives by a great deliverance. So now it was not you that sent*

THE SUBMISSIVE MIND

me hither, but God: and he hath made me a father to Pharaoh, and lord of all his house, and a ruler throughout all the land of Egypt."

In Nehemiah's day, there were hindrances from without that sought to stop the rebuilding of Jerusalem for God. Chapter 4 records the defensive measures that were taken to build for God in spite of the opposition.

As we look further into Philippians we can see other examples of Old Testament saints that should be an encouragement to us. Would not verses 1:20-21 remind us of Queen Esther, who, like Paul, was in the place of danger but put the claims of God first, as she says in chapter 4:16, *"if I perish, I perish."* It answers to Paul's words, *"Christ shall be magnified in my body, whether it be by life or by death. For to me to live is Christ, and to die is gain."*

Again, when we come to 1:28 we see the three Hebrew sons, Shadrach, Meshach, and Abed-nego, who were not prepared to bow down at the sound of Babylon's music to the image of gold. With the fire before them it proved to be *"an evident token of perdition"* to those who took them to it, *"but to you of salvation, and that of God"* (see Dan. 3). The following verse 29 would keep us in Daniel as it describes Daniel's experience in chapter 6, who not only believed as he made his public petition to God, but was also to suffer for His sake. Like his three compatriots he was not *"terrified by your adversaries."*

The example of David can be seen in chapter 2:3-4. In verse 3, we see his reaction to the enmity and strife of Saul, when in 1 Samuel 24:4-12, having Saul at his mercy, he would not raise his hand against him for nothing should be done through *"strife or vainglory."* He left all the issues of the difference between them with God (v. 15), something we are taught to do in Romans 12:17-21. Again in verse 4, David is portrayed as not seeking his own things, as he cared for his father's sheep, dealt with his nation's foe, and sought his enemy, Saul's, good.

A cursory glance at chapter 2:15 is enough to see Gideon as he goes to war against the Midianites, *"a crooked and perverse nation,"* with *"lamps within the pitchers" (Judg. 7:16)*, and *"holding forth the word of life"* as they sound the trumpet (v. 18) that is to give them victory.

Does not 2:17 beautifully illustrate the offering up of Isaac in Genesis 22? He could say, *"if I should be offered upon the sacrifice and service of your faith."* The same could be said of Jephthah's daughter in Judges 11:36-40 as she bowed to her father's vow. It must be added that she was not offered in sacrifice but kept in perpetual virginity, not being given in marriage (v. 39).

We have very contrasting conditions in chapter 2:20-21. In the former, I think of the Shunamite in 2 Kings 4:9-10, who recognized Elisha's relationship with God and had a natural care for his state, when she provided a little chamber for his comfort with all that a servant would need, a bed for sleep, a table and a stool for study, and a candle to give light as he was there.

But the following verse, 21, seems to typify so many. It marked the first man, Adam, and has continued in his progeny, of whom Korah (Num. 16), Abimelech (Judges 9) and Saul (1 Samuel) are but a few examples. It definitely marked the whole assembly at Philippi for *"all seek their own."*

As we turn to chapter 3, features of other Old Testament characters are seen, such as Moses in verse 7. The epistle to the Hebrews 11:24-26 expounds its own commentary as an example of one who could say *"what things were gain to me, those I counted loss for Christ."*

The history of Ruth readily springs to mind in verse 10. Her beautiful statement of chapter 1:16-17 follows the spirit of Paul here, where both want to be completely identified with all that God would have for them.

Abraham's life can be seen in 3:13-14. Again, Hebrews 11:8-16 would tell of those who are *"forgetting those things which are behind, and reaching forth unto those things which are before."* The patriarchs are said to *"declare plainly that they seek a country. And truly, if they had been mindful of that country from whence they came out, they might have had opportunity to have returned."*

The sad affairs linked with Eli's sons, recorded in 1 Samuel 2:12-17, 22 reflect those who are spoken of in 3:17-19; those from within who are, *"enemies of the cross of Christ: Whose end* is destruction, whose God is their belly and whose glory is in their shame, who mind earthly things."

I am sure many more examples could be found, but it is sufficient to say that in chapter 4:1, Shammah's stand to guard a patch of lentils against the Philistines could be seen as, he stood fast (2 Sam. 23:11-12). I suppose a number of David's mighty men could be introduced into verse 1.

I often link the experience of Job, as Satan sought to find a weak point in his life, with verse 13, *"I can do all things through Christ which strengtheneth me."* I suppose, despite his moral weakness, Samson's name could be added to it. I am thankful for the comments of Mr. Douglas that opened up a mine of spiritual wealth to me.

THE FOCUS OF THE GOSPEL
1:19-26

For I know that this shall turn to my salvation through your prayer, and the supply of the Spirit of Jesus Christ, According to my earnest expectation and my hope, that in nothing I shall be ashamed, but that with all boldness, as always, so now also Christ shall be magnified in my body, whether it be by life, or by death. For to me to live is Christ, and to die is gain. But if I live in the flesh, this is the fruit of my labour: yet what I shall choose I wot not. For I am in a strait betwixt two, having a desire to depart, and to be with Christ; which is far better: Nevertheless to abide in the flesh is more needful for you. And having this confidence, I know that I shall abide and continue with you all for your furtherance and joy of faith; That your rejoicing may be more abundant in Jesus Christ for me by my coming to you again.

1:19-26—THE PROSPECT OF PAUL

It is difficult to discern if there is a break between verses 18 and 19, though the experiences of the former verse have caused him to review his life and to disclose its purpose and character.

There are three thoughts on which to meditate in verse 19: Paul's salvation, their supplication ("your prayer") and the supply of the Spirit.

1:19—THE LIBERATION OF THE SERVANT

For I know that this shall turn to my salvation through your prayer, and the supply of the Spirit of Jesus Christ,

Lightfoot, among others, would link Paul's salvation with his eternal salvation as he writes "'Salvation' is in the highest sense. These trials will develop the spiritual life of the Apostle, will be a pathway to the glories of heaven" (J. B. Lightfoot, *Philippians*, page 89). This would hardly seem to fit the context of these verses, as Paul is absolutely assured of his destiny (1:19-23), and the glory of heaven fills his spirit as he speaks of death as "gain" and "far better." Of the three appearances of salvation in the epistle, none would have a bearing on the salvation of the soul. In verse 28, the opposition of the world is a confirmation that we possess salvation, and in chapter 2:12, it is for the assembly to work out its problems, which will result in its salvation from the ills that characterise it. The three references to salvation are, 1:19 **the preservation of Paul,** verse 28, **the assembly's protection,** and in 2:12, **assembly problems.** Others, and I must confess that I once held with them, think that the salvation is his release from prison. A. T. Robertson would be among those who are the advocates of this; "To my salvation (*eis soterian*), for his release from prison as he strongly hopes to see them again (v. 26)." As one has continued to meditate on the verses, it would appear that the preaching of those who thought that they could add affliction to his chain

THE SUBMISSIVE MIND

would hardly move the Roman authorities to release him. It is evident that he was expecting with hope an early release for the benefit of the saints (v. 26), but I cannot see how this was behind the expression *"turn to my salvation."* Would not verse 20 express the salvation that Paul looked for, as he desired that he would not be marked by shame for Christ? I know that we would find it difficult to think that such a spirit could mark Paul, but such are the conditions and the reasonings of the injustice of his situation, that it could have led to a period of despondency. Paul did not want to be brought low by the events around him, and he was thankful for the provision God had made for his preservation. God's promise is twofold.

I. THE SUPPLICATION OF THE SAINTS

The Apostle realizes the value of prayer on behalf of others. We see how he prays for them, and is thankful for their prayers for him. How thankful we are for an omnipotent God who listens to the prayers of His own and is pleased to grant an answer. Well might Paul encourage us to be *"careful for nothing; but in everything by prayer and supplication with thanksgiving let your requests be made known unto God"* (4:6). There is not only the supplication of the saints to sustain us but there is:

II. THE SUPPLY OF THE SPIRIT

How thankful we are for that which the Spirit supplies. F. B. Meyer makes the following comment that draws out beautifully what Paul was to experience to keep him out of the slough of despond. "The word *'supply'* demands our attention. It occurs with its kindred verb several times in the New Testament. It contains the suggestion of a choir or singing entertainment, which was supplied on public occasion by some wealthy citizen to grace a triumphal entry, or celebrate some auspicious anniversary. It stands for the free and spontaneous furnishing of that which enriches and quickens the lives of others" (*Philippians*, page 49-50). What encouragement the Holy Spirit would be to the heart of Paul as He brought music to his heart. As the Spirit is seen to be *"the Spirit of Jesus Christ,"* we can see that the Lord Jesus is the rich man who will provide that which will lift His servant.

The fact that Paul looks to the prayers of saints and the supply of the Spirit to give him salvation would imply that it is not his eternal salvation, for that is dependent upon the work of Christ alone. It would also negate any thought of his release from prison, for though God could use the prayers of saints to that end, the desire for the supply of the Spirit would confirm that these things were to meet his present need in the circumstances in which he is found.

This is somewhat confirmed by Wuest in his commentary of *Word Studies in the Greek New Testament*. "The Greek word 'salvation' is used in the New Testament to refer not only to the spiritual salvation of the individual, but also to the healing of the body (Matt. 9:22), and of self-preservation in a physical sense, or of the well-being of the individual (Mark 15:30-31). Paul uses it here of his own well-being" (*Vol. 2, page 43*).

1:20—THE LOYALTY OF THE SERVANT

> *According to my earnest expectation and [my] hope, that in nothing I shall be ashamed, but [that] with all boldness, as always, [so] now also Christ shall be magnified in my body, whether [it be] by life, or by death.*

If, through his prison experience, Christ has been manifested in the preaching of the gospel, the desire of Paul's heart is to see Christ magnified in whatever circumstance he may be found. Such was his loyalty to Christ that it mattered not whether it be by life or by death.

This verse is typical of Paul as he heaps expressions one on top of another to make his desire known. The verse could have been condensed without the truth of it being lost, but he adds *"hope"* to his expectation, and links *"in nothing"* to being ashamed. If he speaks of boldness, he would add *"as always"* and *"so now."* Such words would unfold the deepest longings in the heart of Paul that nothing would stand in the way of Christ being magnified.

His *"earnest expectation"* is like that of the creation in Romans 8:19, where we have the only other occurrence of its use. It literally means, to watch with outstretched neck and keeping the object in view without turning aside or being distracted, as the creation waits for the future manifestation of the sons of God that it might be delivered from the bondage of corruption that bound it when God placed a curse upon it in Genesis 3:17. Paul's earnest expectation is that no shame would mark him, and that he will maintain his boldness, so that Christ will be magnified in his body.

The body is the place in which Christ will to be magnified. To "magnify" simply means, to enlarge or make great. I wonder if we as believers can take this verse and express these desires as if they were our own? It will begin with the body being presented a living sacrifice (Rom. 12:1). The epistle to the Romans reminds us of what our bodies were before conversion. In Romans 1:24, men *dishonour* their bodies, the body that *defiles* us, a body of sin that *"might be destroyed that henceforth we should not serve sin" (6:6)*. Romans 7:24 relates to us that it is *"a body of this **death**."* The body was subject to sin and death, but thanks be to God, it can now be a body in which Christ is magnified.

The Pulpit Commentary draws attention to, "after 'heaviness' (literally, boldness of speech) we can expect the active form, 'I shall be magnified'. Paul in his humility, prefers the passive 'Christ shall be magnified'. Boldness of speech was to be his part, the glory should be Christ's" (*Epistle to Philippians, Vol. 20*, page 5).

Paul is like the ox that is between the plough and the altar. Christ must be magnified either in the service of his life or on the altar of death. That Christ should be magnified, whether it be by life or death, leads naturally to the great truth expressed in verse 21.

1:21—THE LIFE FOR THE SERVANT

For to me to live [is] Christ, and to die [is] gain.

Many years ago, I was invited to lunch with a godly family in Mayfield, Scotland. Dear Mrs. Robertson, an elderly lady, followed me into the courtyard of their farmhouse, and, as I got into the car, said, "You know, all I want to do is to live for Christ." Then she paused and said, "No, no. All I want to do is live Christ." She had caught the truth of the verse and had the same spirit and desire as Paul. She too wanted Christ to be everything to her. The word "is" is not in the original text and has been placed in italics denoting this, and should be read just as Mrs. Robertson expressed it. I wonder what blessing every believer would know if this was the object of our lives, "to live Christ." It is evident that very few of us have this as our goal, as we set our sights on many things that rob us of a Christ-centred life.

The desire of Paul was **personal**, as he says *"for to me."* He is not speaking for others but expressing the whole object of his life here. We ought to ask the question, "What is my goal in life?" There are so many things that can come between Christ and the believer. Again, the Apostle is also *positive;* he leaves no room for doubt, *"to me to live, Christ."* Only Christ, always Christ, ever Christ. What pleasure this must give to the Lord. It is little wonder that with Christ the sole object of his life, he also has a glorious **prospect** *"to die is gain."* The word gain is that which we find in chapter 3:7, *"what things were gain to me, those I counted loss for Christ."* What a contrast there is between them. In chapter 1, we have a spiritual gain and he looks to be with Christ to enjoy it; in chapter 3, it is a temporal gain, which the world offers, and Paul counts this as dung. One is found in heaven, the other is from the world. Every believer should test his or her life by asking, "What is gain to me?"

1:22—THE LABOUR OF THE SERVANT

But if I live in the flesh, this [is] the fruit of my labour: yet what I shall choose I wot not.

Light is shed on this verse by Lightfoot when his opening thoughts on it state, "The grammar of the passage reflects the conflict of feeling in the Apostle's mind. He is tossed to and fro between the desire to labour for Christ in life, and the desire to be united to Christ in death. The abrupt and disjointed sentence expresses his hesitation" (*Philippians*, page 20).

With the gain before him of being with Christ on the one hand, and the need of the believers on the other, he knows not what to choose. If he remains, he knows that there will be fruit for his labour, and there are those who will benefit from his ministry, but the prospect of being *"absent from the body and ... present with the Lord," (2 Cor. 5:8)*, draws him toward the glory. Yet he is distracted from his personal desire and says, *"What I shall choose I wot not."* The word "choose" occurs three times and is linked with:

- Paul's choice of a Place—Philippians 1:22
- God's choice of a Purpose—2 Thessalonians 2:13
- Moses' choice of a People—Hebrews 11:25

For Paul, his choice was not yet fully formed. The will of God of course will determine the outcome. Would the saints benefit from his presence and labours here (which we have done as other epistles came from his pen), or would he receive his greatest joy, "to depart and be with Christ"?

How thankful every believer must be as we meditate on the choice of God who *"hath from the beginning chosen you to salvation through sanctification of the Spirit and belief of the truth,"* with the object of it being *"to the obtaining of the glory of our Lord Jesus Christ" (2 Thess. 2:13-14).* How blessed to know that we shall all share in the blessed hope that Paul had of being with Christ. The simplicity of the statement with its sublime truth can only cause us to wonder at the kindness of God toward us. It is precious to know that the thoughts expressed in 2 Thessalonians 2 are not isolated verses, for whenever the Lord reveals truth to the hearts of His children it is always at the mouth of two or three witnesses. Therefore we are thankful to see the same truth reiterated in Ephesians 1:4; 1 Peter 1:2; 2 Timothy 1:9; 2 Timothy 2:10; 1 Thessalonians 1:4; and Romans 8:28-30. All these verses express very clearly the great truth into which we have been brought, and cause us to value the personal dealings of God with us. How it rejoices the heart to know that we were ever in the thoughts and heart of God.

As far as Moses is concerned, his choice in Hebrews 11:25 was not based on natural or national ties, for he was *"choosing rather to suffer affliction with the people of God."* It was a spiritual interest that moved Moses for these were *"the people of God."* Some who profess Christ today are inclined to join themselves with the children of the wicked one as they indulge in *"the pleasures of sin."* Moses separated himself from the royal household, and he separated the people from Egypt. We are living in a day when separation is hardly known and the pleasures of sin are indulged in. Many years ago, a dear saintly lady in Scotland told me of a time when she and another Christian friend were suddenly caught in a severe rainstorm. Close by was the local cinema with a canopy over the doorway. The friend said "quick let us shelter under the cinema roof," to which the godly soul replied, "Na, ma godly feet will go naewhere near the place." How different things are today when many will warm the seats, having lost the truth of separation.

1:23—THE LONGINGS OF THE SERVANT

> *For I am in a strait betwixt two, having a desire to depart, and to be with Christ; which is far better:*

His **distraction** is evident as he proceeds to unfold the thoughts of his heart. He is in a strait, that is, he is held in, pressed, as if a crowd is restricting his movements; he knows not which way to turn. His foremost **desire** is evident; his love for Christ surpassed all, and he longs to depart that he might be with Him. He is like the pilgrim who has the object of his pilgrimage before him, and just wants to take up the tent pegs and reach his goal; or the shipmaster who has been hindered from entering the harbour, and longs to weigh anchor and finally reach his desired haven. His desire to be with Christ is one of great intensity. It is a word that is used of irregular and violent desire, lust, longings. *Strong's Concordance* says "especially for what is forbidden." The Apostle has alternative thoughts as he sets forth the object of his desire, and what kindles it—Christ.

His desire is aroused by the **destiny** that will be reached. You will notice that Paul does not dwell on the place to which he is going, but on the person he is going to meet. How often do we hear men preach of heaven as the goal of faith when the Bible speaks very little of it? For Paul the place mattered little, but Christ is everything. He has entered into the desires of the Lord Jesus Himself, who when speaking to the disciples in John 14:1-6, where most would dwell upon the place, the Lord said *"I will come again and receive you unto **myself** that where **I am** there ye may be also."* The blessed Saviour wanted His own to be in His presence, and Paul has entered into his Saviour's longings and made them his own. To be with Christ was to Paul *"far better."* The word "far" means, great, many, and much. It surpasses anything else that he has ever known, and is better, that is, nobler than the best. It is a word that is used often in the epistle to the Hebrews where everything that Christ is, surpasses all that has gone before. The verse not only brings before us the **distraction** of his mind, and the **desire** of his heart, but also the **destiny** he would reach, and the **delight** he would find when he was in the presence of the Lord Jesus.

1:24-26—LIBERATION OF THE SERVANT

The faithful servant is able to rise above personal desires, and knowing that he has a ministry to fulfil, his thoughts turn to the needs of others. He is not going to think *"on his own things"* (2:4).

1:24—HIS MINISTRY IS NEEDED

Nevertheless to abide in the flesh [is] more needful for you.

If there is anything that could hold the Apostle here, it is the need of the saints. His thoughts will rise above his own desires. 1 Corinthians 12:22 would express that the members of the body that seem to be more feeble are "necessary." This is the same word as needful, and as every believer is needful to the good of the whole, so Paul would see his ministry as being needful to the body.

1:25—HIS MIND IS SETTLED

> *And having this confidence, I know that I shall abide and continue with you all for your furtherance and joy of faith;*

The distractions that gripped him as he contemplated the grand possibility of being with Christ give way to the confidence that comes to him as he looks, not on his own things, but on the things of others. Their need is greater than his. It is this that gives him confidence that he will abide in the flesh. The Apostle is full of confidence in this epistle as he uses the expression six times throughout the book. The experience into which he has been brought cannot blight his faith in God. In the six references, we see his confidence in:

    1:6   His eternal security, "confident"
    1:14 In gospel activity, "confident"
    1:25 His personal liberty, "confidence"
    2:24 His visit personally "trust"
    3:3   A definite responsibility, "having no confidence"
    3:4   A glorious opportunity, "trust in the flesh"

In the latter, there could be no thought of being taken up with the character of his former life, which he renounced completely when he bowed to the claims of Christ. His desire *"to continue"* would have the thought of being one with them, and being continually around them. There was no desire in Paul's heart to have merely sporadic fellowship. Like the lame man who was healed at the gate Beautiful, who, on receiving strength to his ankle bones, also finds his jaw bone loosed as he *"entered with them into the temple, walking, and leaping, and praising God" (Acts 3:8)*. He is also *"standing with them"* at the inquisition by the priestly family (Acts 4:14). So we find Paul, from the moment of his conversion, immediately taken up with the things of Christ (Acts 9:20), and seeking the company of those who love the Lord as *"he assayed to join himself to the disciples" (Acts 9:26),* and *"was with them going in and coming out" (Acts 9:28).* There is something radically wrong with those who profess Christ yet who do not want to be in the company of the redeemed. For Paul, he wanted to "go in" in worship, and "go out" in witness, as in this verse he wanted to continue (*sunparameno*) with the saints who needed his support for their *"furtherance and joy of faith."* The Bible knows nothing of "independent" Christians, nor of spiritual gypsies who wander from one place of worship to another without taking a place of responsibility where they can serve the Lord with others of a like mind. At all times the Lord would look for the experience of those first converts, who upon receiving the Word *"were baptised: and the same day [they] were added,"* and of whom it is said *"they continued steadfastly in the Apostles' doctrine and fellowship, and in breaking of bread, and in prayers" (Acts 2:41-42).*

The thoughts that fill the mind of God's servant are for the spiritual progress and full enjoyment of the truth of God that he will be able to impart. He uses the word "furtherance" again as he does in 1:12. Whereas in verse 12 he is the pioneer opening the track for the gospel to reach sinners, here he is the teacher opening the truths of the Word of God for their joy of faith.

1:26—THE MOTIVE OF HIS HEART

That your rejoicing may be more abundant in Jesus Christ for me by my coming to you again.

The motive of Paul is emphasised in his use of "that" (*hina*) and of which it could be said "in order that." There was no thought of feathers in his cap being added as a result of his ministry; it was not gain for him but their interests that filled his mind. He wanted their boasting, their glory, to be paramount, for the word "rejoicing" has these thoughts in it. In fact, Paul wanted this boasting to overflow, to super-abound. It is expressed "excel" in the words of A. T. Robertson who writes "Paul therefore strikes again the triumphant, victorious note in his message to the Philippians. There is no 'hark from the tomb' religion for him. The Christian ought to be the happiest man alive, full of spiritual ecstasy and rapture. Joy is more than Epicurean sensualism. Baskerville quotes the Yorkshireman who found so great joy in his religion that he had 'a happy Monday, a blessed Tuesday, a joyful Wednesday, a delightful Thursday, a good Friday, a glorious Saturday, a heavenly Sunday'. Indeed Paul wished that their 'glorying' might literally overflow all bounds, providing it is in Christ (because of Christ primarily, and under the control of Christ, in the sphere of Christ). If people have enough occasion to shout aloud their joy, let them do it. Let the redeemed of the Lord say so. Sing aloud the praises of our God" (*Paul's Joy in Christ*, page 56).

THE FAITH OF THE GOSPEL
1:27-29

Only let your conversation be as it becometh the gospel of Christ: that whether I come and see you, or else be absent, I may hear of your affairs, that ye stand fast in one spirit, with one mind striving together for the faith of the gospel; and in nothing terrified by your adversaries: which is to them an evident token of perdition, but to you of salvation, and that of God. For unto you it is given in the behalf of Christ, not only to believe on him, but also to suffer for his sake.

In the following verses, we see rising to the fore, in verse 27 **The problems of the assembly**, whilst in verses 28-29 **The persecution of the saints** is addressed.

1:27—THE PROBLEMS OF THE ASSEMBLY

Only let your conversation be as it becometh the

THE SUBMISSIVE MIND

gospel of Christ: that whether I come and see you, or else be absent, I may hear of your affairs, that ye stand fast in one spirit, with one mind striving together for the faith of the gospel;

From this point on, the Apostle is going to remedy the problem that he has merely alluded to in the earlier part of the epistle. He makes it clear that the response to his admonition should not depend upon his presence with them; it is *"whether I come and see you or else be absent."* He wants their conversation to be *"as becometh the gospel."* The word "conversation" is not the usual word that is so translated in many other places, which means our manner of life, but it is the word that is akin to that used in chapter 3:20, and is the word from which our word "politics" comes. As we have seen, Philippi was a Roman colony and its politics were those of Rome as it modelled itself on the great metropolis. Now, says the Apostle, let your politics be of equal weight to the gospel by which you are called. Your lives must be commensurate with your call; they must be "becoming." The word is that of being placed in the scale and being of equal balance. What a sad thing if our life and testimony were like that of Belshazzar in Daniel 5, where he was weighed in the balances and found wanting. Paul longed that news would reach him concerning them, that they were standing fast. In 1 Corinthians 16:13, he wanted the saints to stand fast in the faith; again in Galatians 5:1 to stand fast in the liberty wherewith Christ has made us free. He does not want Jewish legalism to entangle us again. He would also encourage the Thessalonian believers not to be discouraged by persecution and to *"stand fast in the Lord,"* whilst in 2 Thessalonians 2:15 he again would exhort them to *"stand fast and hold the traditions."* How blessed when believers continue in truth. He writes to these Philippians that they *"stand fast in one spirit with one mind."* It is a call to unity, and to so move together that they are "one souled," for the word mind is the word for soul. This would indicate that they should move in absolute unity, with one purpose and with one common desire to be in harmony in the things of God.

The call is for the saints to "strive together." We should not be striving against each other; this is both detrimental and destructive to the work of God in any gathering of His children (see Gal. 5:13-16; Jas. 4:1-3). As Christians we are athletes in the arena; we have here the relay race when all worked together for the good of the others as they bore the torch. And as the torch of testimony is ours for the faith of the gospel, let us not be like the two women of chapter 4:2-3, who had laboured (strive together—same word as here) with Paul, but now were at loggerheads with each other.

The verse begins with a reference to our character as citizens of heaven, that it must be as becometh the gospel; it ends by manifesting that our conduct should be that of unity for the faith of the gospel.

1:28-30—THE PERSECUTION OF THE SAINTS

These three verses are seeking to encourage the saints as they face opposition and persecution. Verse 28 would seek to calm them in the face of persecution, while verse 29 reveals that persecution will certainly come upon them. The last verse of the chapter unfolds that the path of persecution is familiar to them having both seen and heard of Paul's experiences in his sufferings for the gospel's sake.

1:28—CALMNESS IN THE FACE OF PERSECUTION

> *And in nothing terrified by your adversaries: which is to them an evident token of perdition, but to you of salvation, and that of God.*

The desire of the Lord is that when persecution arises there should be **confidence in the saints.** Virtually all expositors tell us that the thought of not being terrified, is that of a startled horse that will suddenly bolt with none able to stop it. The word only occurs here, but we could think of many that displayed terror in the face of opposition. The Lord would also encourage us when He says to the twelve on the occasion of

His sending them into public ministry, *"Fear not them which kill the body, but are not able to kill the soul: but rather fear him which is able to destroy both soul and body in hell"* (Matt. 10:28). The adversaries are those who oppose. Before us in this verse, we have those who oppose physically; in 1 Timothy 1:10, there is revealed those who will oppose us doctrinally; speaking of law teachers, he says they are *"contrary to sound doctrine."* The word contrary is that for adversary in this passage. Men little realize the object of false doctrine is to set itself against what is of God. Chapter 4:1 of 1 Timothy reveals the source of all false doctrine when men are *"giving heed to seducing spirits, and doctrines of devils."* Again the word is used concerning the man of sin *"who opposeth"* (2 Thess. 2:4). Here it is not *physical* or *doctrinal*, but *spiritual* opposition to every claim of God and of Christ.

The opposition is in itself a **condemnation of sinners.** The faithful giving of the saints to help the poor in Jerusalem is a proof ("evident token") of the love of the saints one for another (2 Cor. 8:24), but the bitter persecution of the world is a proof that these are heading for destruction.

Whereas the manner of life of the persecutors would reveal their ultimate destiny, so with those who are persecuted; it manifests a **confirmation of salvation.** If we were of the world, we would be free from opposition for *"the world would love his own: but because ye are not of the world, but I have chosen you out of the world, therefore the world hateth you"* (John 15:19).

1:29—Certainty of Feeling Persecution

For unto you it is given in the behalf of Christ, not only to believe on him, but also to suffer for his sake;

We are now informed that it is an honour to bear reproach for our blessed Lord. To us it has been granted, as a favour bestowed, *"not only to believe in him, but also to suffer for his sake."* Like the apostles in Acts 5:41 who *"[rejoiced] that they were counted worthy to suffer shame for his name,"* the same honour was given to those in Philippi. The Lord has said that *"we must through much tribulation enter into the Kingdom of God"* (Acts 14:22), and *"if we suffer, we shall also reign with him" (2 Tim. 2:12).* The present sufferings to Paul were but a *"light affliction, which is but for a moment"* and *"worketh for us a far more exceeding and eternal weight of glory" (2 Cor. 4:17).* As we link Romans 8:18 to these promises where Paul says, *"I reckon that the sufferings of this present time are not worthy to be compared with the glory which shall be revealed in (eis—to) us,"* we can see why the sufferings are seen as an honour conferred on those who are called to pass through them. May we, like Daniel, give a good testimony in the face of the world's enmity.

1:30—Constant Familiarity with Paul's Persecution

Having the same conflict which ye saw in me, and now hear [to be] in me.

There is a reminder in this closing verse that the same conflict they are passing through was witnessed by them when they saw Paul's agony when he was among them. The jailor would remember the many stripes of his prisoners when they were in Philippi, and would not forget the maltreatment to which they were subjected. The word had reached them of all that he was passing through in Rome, and the fact that they sought to relieve him in his afflictions in Rome with the gift that was sent to him was evidence that they were acquainted with his sufferings there also.

2

THE SUBMISSIVE MIND

In this second chapter, the Apostle Paul is now going to appeal to the Philippians to adjust their lives and to correct the problems that had been reported to him by Epaphroditus when he arrived with the gift from the believers to Paul. The gift obviously gave him great pleasure as it relieved him in his affliction (4:10-19), but how sore his heart must have been as he heard of the behaviour of the saints one toward another. We must be thankful to God that the problem was addressed by Paul. How easy it is to bury our head in the sand and hope those things that cause trouble among us will go away. I remember a servant of God, Peter Brandon, relating how, on visiting a certain country, he found some of the basic features that should mark any company of God's children, whenever they gather, being disregarded. He told me he had to call the elders together and warn them that if they wanted to please the Lord and to receive His blessing, then they would have to put right the errors that were evident among them. Often we hear those who have been called to serve God criticise conditions among God's children, but do nothing to seek their restoration to God and to His Word. I heard of one notable man who, when seeing the Word of God being set aside in one gathering, to relieve himself of the responsibility that was his to give a word of correction, simply made the excuse of that being the elders' responsibility and not his. But if the elders have failed to hold the things of God aright, unless someone brings a word of correction they will never recover. I might remind all who serve God in a public way, that in our ministry, we are honour bound to the Lord to seek to recover the saints to the desires of God for them. It should be done in love and in meekness, seeking to win saints and not to wound them. Another valued servant, now with the Lord, often said, "Our ministry might hurt you, but it will never harm you." We are thankful that every error or problem that would afflict the church arose in the apostolic era, and was answered by them, so that now, we have the authority of the Word of God to set the truth before the saints.

The chapter before us has four basic divisions:
2:1-4   The Problem, "The Exhortation to the Saints"
2:5-11 The Pattern, "The Example of the Saviour"
2:12-16 The Practice, "The Exercise of the Saints"
2:17-30 The Pictures, "Expounded in the Servants"

The book of Nehemiah records the rebuilding of the walls of Jerusalem on the return of some of the Jews from the captivity in Babylon. The gates of the city are given prominence in the record of the rebuilding in chapter 2. Among these gates was the Sheep Gate in chapter 3 verse 1. I suppose we could write over Philippians 1 **"the Sheep Gate,"** as the Apostle is concerned with the sheep of His flock, and of their welfare. In this chapter, we can see **the Valley Gate** (Neh. 2:13); here the desire is for a valley experience of humility among the believers. When we come to chapter 3, **the Dung Gate** of Nehemiah 3:14 is prominent, when the Apostle would gather up all his natural achievements that would have given him honour in this world, and in 3:8 he counts them but dung. What a blessed thing if we could count all that would keep us from getting to know Christ as dung and waste, if we had a Dung Gate in our own experience. Perhaps chapter four alludes to the **Gate of the Fountain or the Water Gate** (Neh. 3:15, 26). What refreshment the Apostle found from God in this chapter as the gift arrived through the hands of Epaphroditus. I notice that the gates begin with the Sheep Gate (3:1), and they also end with the Sheep Gate (3:32). Perhaps we can see Philippians end the same way, as we think of that gift that was *"an odour of a sweet smell, a sacrifice acceptable, well pleasing to God"* (4:18). Here we see the lamb in sacrifice.

The Problem:
The Exhortation to the Saints
2:1-4

> *If there be therefore any consolation in Christ, if any comfort of love, if any fellowship of the Spirit, if any bowels and mercies, Fulfil ye my joy, that ye be like-minded, having the same love, being of one accord, of one mind. Let nothing be done through strife or vainglory; but in lowliness of mind let each esteem other better than themselves. Look not every man on his own things, but every man also on the things of others.*

2:1—An Appeal to the saints

> *If [there be] therefore any consolation in Christ, if any comfort of love, if any fellowship of the Spirit, if any bowels and mercies,*

There is a fourfold appeal to the saints, as Paul would seek to rectify the conditions that had arisen among the believers. Strife and disharmony are dangerous enemies to the fellowship of believers and a strong appeal is made to them.

He first makes an entreaty

"If there be any consolation in Christ." The "if" is significant, and is linked to each of the appeals. The word seems to bring out the heartfelt feelings of the Apostle. It is as if he is saying "if this be so, then." Such experiences that believers are called to enjoy and manifest are dependent on moving in the divine will and not fulfilling our own selfish desires.

The word "consolation" (*paraklesis*) comes from the Greek

word *parakaleo*, and is used in the sense of encouraging action, to put heart into; hence its translation as *"comfort" (Rom. 15:4),* and in *"the God of all comfort" (2 Cor. 1:3-4).* It is also translated *"exhortation" (Acts 13:15),* when Paul is asked in the synagogue in Pisidia *"if ye have any word of exhortation for the people."* In this opening phrase, the Philippians are being encouraged to action, to correct the disunity that presently marked them.

SECONDLY, HE SPEAKS OF SYMPATHY.
"If there be any comfort of love." The word "comfort" is a unique word only found here in the N.T., but its root is found in John 11 where on two occasions it speaks of those who come to comfort Mary and Martha on the death of their brother. Paul does not doubt the love of the Philippians toward him, but the conditions that he had heard about were causing him much grief, like bereavement. He looks for the sympathy of the love of the saints toward him to be shown by responding to his exhortation.

THIRDLY, HE LOOKS FOR UNITY.
"If there be any fellowship of the Spirit." This is the second of three references to this word "fellowship" in the epistle. He recalls their **ministry** to him in 1:5, and is thankful that their support financially as he served the Lord, was *"fellowship in [to] the gospel."* In chapter 3:10, the desires to be all for Christ rise again when he would long for **conformity** to Christ in His sufferings, and says he wants *"fellowship in his death."* The longing of his heart before us is *"fellowship of Spirit"* where he would look for **unity** in the believers.

We must distinguish between things that differ. 1 Corinthians 12:4-11 speaks of the gifts of the Spirit. This has to do with exercise of gift in the assembly for no one can serve the Lord without receiving a gift to enable him to do it, and the gifts are given by the Holy Spirit. Galatians 5:22 would speak of the fruit of the Spirit; this would give us exercise in our own lives to produce the features here seen. Again there should be a manifestation of all the fruit displayed in us, for the Spirit of God would produce a truly fruitful life in all who are desiring to walk in His ways. In our present chapter, it is rather that which would speak of our relationships one with another. The Word of God is constantly calling us to unity. This unity is Spirit-made, for we are exhorted in Eph. 4:3 *"Endeavouring to keep the unity of the Spirit."* We cannot make it but we can keep it. It will take the *"lowliness and meekness with longsuffering"* of verse 2, and as God has brought opposing parties together at salvation into one body, we must not let these opposing factions rise again to mar this divine unity. Was not the prayer of the Lord Jesus to the Father in John 17:21, *"that they also may be one in us: that the world may believe that thou hast sent me"*? Well might the Psalmist declare *"Behold how good and how pleasant it is for brethren to dwell together in unity!" (Ps. 133:1)*. It is first for the divine pleasure, for *"It is like the precious ointment upon the head, that ran down upon the beard, even Aaron's beard: that went down to the skirts of his garments" (v. 2)*. The ointment was to raise a sweet perfume as he went about his daily service in the tabernacle. How precious must appear the unity of saints before God as we move in priestly exercise before Him (1 Pet. 2:5). The perfume would not only rise to God but those within close proximity would also be partakers of that odour.

It is also like *"the dew of Hermon, and as the dew that descended upon the mountains of Zion" (Ps. 133:3)*. If there is a fragrance in the precious ointment, there is freshness in the dew. The ointment would only be known to those in close proximity to it, whereas the dew would be seen from afar. Is the unity that Paul is calling for not like that? It makes for a sweet odour in worship and gives freshness to our witness.

FOURTHLY, HE LOOKS FOR PITY

"If there be any bowels and mercies." The burdens of the prison are enough without the added strain of knowing that there is disharmony among his converts. For this reason he appeals to them, that the tender compassions that should always mark believers be extended to him. He has longings for them *"in the bowels of Jesus Christ" (1:8)*; now he would desire loyalty from them, in bowels and mercies. The word for "bowel" is the word for spleen, and brings before us the inner feelings of our

being. The word "mercies" has the thought of having compassion. These are features that should mark every child of God, as we see exhorted in Col. 3:12, to *"Put on therefore, as the elect of God, holy and beloved, bowels of mercies, kindness, humbleness of mind, meekness, longsuffering."* These expressions are another commentary on the verses before us.

2:2—THE APPLICATION OF THE SCRIPTURES

Fulfil ye my joy, that ye be likeminded, having the same love, [being] of one accord, of one mind.

The opening expression of verse 2 *"Fulfil ye my joy"* is literally "to make full" his joy. We have seen how that joy marks this epistle, and how Paul has joy for them even as he makes request for them (1:4). Now he wants his joy to be filled to the brim, even for his cup to run over, as his ministry is put into practice to bring a true unity among the saints.

The desire of Paul is that there will be a fourfold response to the fourfold reflections of verse 1. He is looking for:

A. EXERCISE OF MIND

"That ye be likeminded." It is a sad thing when any company is drawn in different directions because we do not think the same things. Often times, as it was here in Philippi, the trouble is not doctrinal, but personal. It is evident that these were in unity regarding the faith (Eph. 4:13), for Paul makes no doctrinal corrections in this epistle, but personal differences can cause as much damage as any dispute regarding doctrine. Over the centuries, the devil has been busy as "doctrines of demons" (1 Tim. 4:1) have divided the church. We must remember also that God hates *"he that soweth discord among brethren" (Prov. 6:19)*. Did the Apostle remember the discord that came between him and Barnabas which caused them to take diverse routes before Paul was led to Philippi? He would know the sorrow such events cause. He also looked for them to:

B. EXHIBIT THE SAME LOVE

"*Having the same love."* Has he not written a treatise on love to the Corinthians? The purpose of bringing this to the attention of the saints is that, if love pervades the gatherings of God's children, then every problem that arises will be rectified. There were many problems in the Corinthian church, which calls for Paul to set before them in chapter 13:
- The Pre-eminence of love (1-3)
- The Perfections of love (4-7)
- The Permanence of love (8-13)

If only the believers were to take these exhortations to heart as to their personal lives. How could the **personal pride** of 1 Corinthians chapters 1-4 exist if the love that *"vaunteth not itself and is not puffed up"* was known and practiced? How could the man of chapter 5 have such **practice of life** if he had love, for love *"doth not behave itself unseemly"* (1 Cor. 13:5)? How would brethren **prosecute believers** by taking them to court as they were doing in chapter 6, for love *"seeketh not her own, is not easily provoked"*? Nor would they **pursue evil** as they associate with idol temples, for love *"rejoiceth not in iniquity"* (v. 6). How would they have desires to leave the gatherings, for love *"rejoiceth in the truth"*? In these things, they would please God. Love would also have an effect upon their **present expectations**, as it *"Beareth all things, believeth all things, hopeth all things, endureth all things"* (v. 7). Is it any wonder that here in Philippians 2 he calls the saints to have the same love, for love would rectify the seriousness of the spirit of self-seeking that was among them? It is to this end that he desires that they will:

C. EXPRESS THE ONENESS

"Being of one accord." This is expressed as Paul uses a word that only occurs here in the N.T. (*sumpsuchos*). This compound word is from the preposition "*sun*," meaning to be "one with," and "*psuchos*" which occurs 105 times in the N.T. and is invariably translated "soul" or "life." It is evident that Paul is seeking for them to move in the closest harmony that it is possible

to do; to be "one-souled." None would be seeking their own then; all would be moving for the good of the others. Finally, he would call them to:

D. EXPERIENCE THE UNITY

"*Of one mind.*" Once again the Apostle reverts to that which is a great burden to his heart for these saints, and that is, that they should think the one thing. A. T. Robertson expresses it as "clocks that strike at the same moment. Perfect intellectual telepathy. Identity of ideas and harmony of feelings" (*Word Pictures in the New Testament, Vol. 4*, page 445).

The word for "mind" (*phroneo*) occurs 11 times in the epistle, and each would have its own bearing on the lives of the saints. It is found in:
  1:7   where Paul has them in his memory, "think"
  2:2   where he is looking for unity, "likeminded"
  2:2   where he longs for harmony, "mind"
  2:5   where he desires humility, "this mind"
  3:15 where he wants all to be like in destiny, "thus minded" (2 refs)
  3:16 where he wants all to seek it objectively, "mind"
  3:19 where he exposes sensuality as earthly, "mind"
  4:2   where he encourages recovery, "same mind"
  4:10 where he is thankful for liberality, "care, careful" (2 refs)
In the last verse, as in 3:15, the word is used twice.

2:3—THE APPALLING SCHISM

> [Let] nothing [be done] through strife or vainglory; but in lowliness of mind let each esteem other better than themselves.

The Apostle is now seeking to dig out the root of the problem that has affected the assembly in Philippi. Sadly, too often the failings exposed here are seen among us in our day, as we either fail to understand the mind of God as revealed, or, such is our conceit and pride, we do not realize that this is what is being practised to the detriment of the believers.

Words are used in this verse that run throughout the epistle; it is as if they must have the mind of God, expressed by the Spirit, always set before them to keep them on the right track as they move in fellowship together. Fellowship will be greatly marred if we fail to practice these truths. We are exhorted to *"let nothing be done through strife or vain glory."* The word "nothing" occurs in 1:28, *"in nothing terrified by your adversaries,"* and is set against the background of *persecution*. Again, it is to produce **peace** in 4:6, *"Be careful for nothing."* Depend on the Lord and let nothing draw you in different ways. In this verse, it is that which could **pain** the saints that causes Paul to write as he does.

Nothing should be done through *"strife or vain glory."* The former will put others down; the latter will lift me up. There are seven references to the word "strife" in the N.T. The first to this word *eritheia* is in Romans 2:8, where it speaks of those who are "contentious" and reject *"the goodness of God that leadeth thee to repentance" (Rom. 2:4)*. This will cause men to experience the **wrath of God.** Sadly, as in this verse, it occurs in 2 Corinthians 12:20, in what seems to be the common **way of saints.** Paul hopes that these traits will not be among the Corinthians when he comes to visit them. Again we see the origins of strife when we read Galatians 5:20, where it is manifestly one of the **works of the flesh.** We now find the word occurring twice in the Philippians, first in 1:16 where "the one preach Christ of contention" (strife); here the **word of the gospel** is not rightly preached. In our present verse, there is a call to **watchfulness in the saints,** as Paul does not want this to characterise his children in the faith. The last occurrences of the word are in James 3:14, 16, where men who have been entrusted with divine truth as teachers of the word have **wickedness in the heart,** as they have *"strife in your hearts,"* and as their ministry produces *"strife, ... confusion and every evil work."* Sadly, in our movements among the saints as we travel to serve the Lord, we come across this too often. The exhortation of James 3 should be constantly read and applied by those who teach the word. We must also be careful that we do not seek "vainglory." Strong says "empty glorying," *i.e.* self conceit. With this spirit being possible in the lives of the Lord's children, it is little wonder that the truths of 2:5-11 are set before us. For the word used here (*kenodoxia*) is from the same family as that which speaks of the Lord making Himself "of no reputation." Why should we seek what He refused?

The call is that another spirit should mark us at all times, and rather than being high-minded we should be lowly-minded, and he wants all the saints to be like-minded in it. The word that is here translated "lowliness of mind" is a compound word, the prefix being the word that Mary used in her Magnificat when she said that the Lord had *"exalted them of low degree" (Luke 1:52)*, and also that used by the Lord Jesus when He would call us to *"learn of me, for I am meek and lowly in heart" (Matt. 11:29)*. Could we not seek to follow the example that has been set before us both by the Lord Jesus and by Mary? The desire of the Lord is that ye *"Humble yourselves therefore under the mighty hand of God, that He may exalt you in due time" (1 Pet. 5:6)*. The further we can get down, the higher God will exalt us. If, like the Pharisees, we seek the praise of men here, we shall have our reward. None has gone as low as our blessed Lord, and He has been exalted far above all. I notice the Lord Jesus did not say who could fill the chief seats that the mother of Zebedee's children wanted for her sons; *"it shall be given to them for whom it is prepared of My Father" (Matt. 20:23)*. Some would speculate that these are reserved for Peter and Paul, who were the Apostles to the Jew and the Gentile, but I like to think that, like the Lord Jesus, the two who among all the saints get the lowest will have the honour of occupying them.

The principle seen in lowliness of mind should make it easy to *"esteem other better than themselves."* Again, we see a repetition of the word "esteem" throughout the epistle. It is not only something that Paul asks the saints to do, but was also seen in Christ when He *"thought it not robbery to be equal with God" (2:6)*. Paul uses it four times of himself and his actions when he *"supposed* (esteemed) *it necessary to send to you Epaphroditus" (2:25)* and when looking over the credits of his former life that would have given him the vainglory of men, he three times over "counts" (which is the word here (esteem). He had no esteem for those former things as he counts them but loss and dung (3:7-8).

The note made by K. Wuest is worthy of quoting regarding the word: "Esteem is from a word referring to a belief that rests, not on one's inner feelings or sentiment, but on the due consideration of external grounds, on the weighing and comparing of facts" (*Word studies in the Greek New Testament, Vol. 2*, page 60). As we compare the facts, knowing what we are in ourselves, it should not be difficult to esteem other better than ourselves.

The use of the word "better" is in itself beautiful, for it carries the idea of one's person and not one's position. He does not say that we *"esteem other **greater** than ourselves,"* for some men hold positions of greatness. It is said of Naaman that he *"was great ... with his master" (2 Kgs. 5:1)*. Again the woman of 2 Kings 4:8, who constrained Elisha to eat bread, and made him a little chamber and put into it all the requirements for the needs of the prophet as he passed through, is said to be *"a great woman,"* speaking not of her size but her status in the locality.

It is also said of Daniel, *"Then the king made Daniel a great man" (Dan. 2:48)*. So-called Jehovah's Witnesses have gone drastically wrong when they infer that the Lord Jesus is inferior to the Father, when He said *"My Father is greater than I" (John 14:28)*. The Lord was not speaking of His Father being greater in His person, but in His position, for the Father did not humble Himself as we find the Lord Jesus doing in that chapter. The position of the Father never changed; that of the Son did.

The word "better" also occurs in 3:8 where Paul speaks of *"the **excellency** of the knowledge of Christ,"* and in 4:7 where *"the peace of God **that passeth** all understanding"* has the same word (*huperecho*). They would remind us of how much better we should esteem the saints, "excellently" and "that passeth" any thought regarding self.

2:4—Apparent Selfishness

Look not every man on his own things, but every man also on the things of others.

The discord that had manifested itself at Philippi is summed up in this verse where everyone was looking on his own things and not on the things of others. The word "look" is to aim, or fix our attention on. In this verse, we can see the foot washing of John 13 and its application being brought before us. According to Luke's account of the upper room, *"there was also a strife among them, which of them should be accounted the greatest"* (Luke 22:24). The Lord Jesus adjusted their thinking by ministry in verses 25-27, whereas in John's gospel, He taught them by example when He *"laid aside his garments; and took a towel and girded himself."* The actions continue as He looks on the things of others, *"he poureth water into a bason, and began to wash the disciples' feet, and to wipe them with the towel wherewith he was girded"* (John 13:4-5). The disciples had walked past the water, the basin and the towel, as they looked every man on his own things, who would be the greatest. For all who desire it, position is power, and how often we run after it. Oh may our God teach all His own the truth of these verses, and give us a longing, like our Lord to "look on the things of others."

There is a true comment by Wiersbe on these verses in his book when he says "In chapter 1 it is 'Christ first' and in chapter 2 it is 'others next'" (*Be Joyful*, page 50). We could add that in chapter 3 it is "self last." If this order were followed there would be no strife in the gospel as there is in chapter 1, nor in the fellowship as in chapter 2, nor would it raise its head in ministry as it does in 3:17-19, but the Peace of God would be with us as in chapter 4.

The Pattern:
The Example of the Saviour
2:5-11

THE SUBMISSIVE MIND

Let this mind be in you, which was also in Christ Jesus: Who, being in the form of God, thought it not robbery to be equal with God: But made Himself of no reputation, and took upon Him the form of a servant, and was made in the likeness of men: and being found in fashion as a man, He humbled Himself, and became obedient unto death, even the death of the cross. Wherefore God also hath highly exalted Him, and given Him a name which is above every name: that at the name of Jesus every knee should bow, of things in heaven, and things in earth, and things under the earth; and that every tongue should confess that Jesus Christ is Lord, to the glory of God the Father.

EQUALITY WITH DEITY. FROM GLORY TO GLORY

We now approach a most sublime portion of the Word of God that will see the Lord Jesus being exalted from glory to glory. It begins with His equality with Deity, and ends with His superiority as the Sovereign. It begins with Deity taking up humanity, and ends with humanity in absolute Sovereignty. As we approach this sacred chamber of Holy Scripture, we need to take the shoes from off our feet as we contemplate the Person of the Lord Jesus Christ, as He is portrayed here.

When we read these verses, we must remember that they were not written as a doctrinal thesis to extol the supremacy of the Lord Jesus over all created things, as when Paul deals in the book of Colossians with Gnostic heresy, nor to set Him forth as better than Jewish idealism, as He is in the Epistle to the Hebrews. The truth before us is introduced that the saints might adjust their lives from a spirit of self-seeking to a personal interest in one another. Though the verses hold great doctrinal truth, they are set before us as a practical example that every believer must emulate.

In verses 5-8 we could say *"a greater than Jonas is here"* (Matt. 12:41), for the Lord Jesus went far lower than Jonah; whereas in verses 9-11 we echo the words of Matthew 12:42 when they say *"a greater than Solomon is here."* For if the Lord Jesus is greater than Jonah in His depth, He far exceeds Solomon in the heights to which He has been exalted. We, like the queen of Sheba when she had seen something of the glory of that which she had heard, can say *"thy wisdom and prosperity exceedeth the fame which I heard"* (1 Kgs. 10:7).

2:5—A Plea for Conformity

Let this mind be in you, which was also in Christ Jesus:

The Apostle is now calling the believers not to look every man on his own things, but for the whole tenor of our lives to reflect that which was seen in the Lord Jesus. If in verse 2 he wants us like-minded, and in verse 3 lowly-minded, he now desires that we should be Christ-minded. That is, the mind that He displayed should now be reproduced in our minds, *"Let this mind be in you."* The words carry the thought that there should be an active, continual exercise of the will, that it might be accomplished.

One writer strangely translates the phrase "let this mind be 'among' you, as also in Christ Jesus," saying "which is the literal translation" (Ralph P. Martin, Tyndale, *Philippians*, page 95). Alford justly says "Not 'among' on account of the 'en'" (*The Greek New Testament, Vol. 3*, page 166). Though Martin would use the word "among" and see it as the desire of the church fellowship to look for and to practice the mind of Christ, it is quite evident that it is an individual and personal exercise that is in view. If each member of the gathering practiced it then the whole company would become the beneficiary. We will see that the mind of Christ is not that of self-seeking but rather of self-sacrifice.

2:6—A Place of Equality

Who, being in the form of God, thought it not robbery to be equal with God:

THE SUBMISSIVE MIND

When setting forth the mind of Christ, the Apostle must begin with all that Christ is in Himself. In these verses, all that is revealed in the four gospels concerning the Lord Jesus is brought before us. In verse 6 we have the gospel of John, where the deity of the Lord Jesus is described; in verses 7 and 8 we see Mark's gospel, where the perfect servant is depicted, and Luke where the perfections of His humanity are declared; and in verses 9-11 the monarchy of Christ is demonstrated, as in Matthew.

We could write over verse 6, "*Behold your God!*" (Isa. 40:9); in verse 7 it is rather, "*Behold my servant*" (Isa. 42:1), whilst in verse 8 we echo the words of Zechariah 6:12, "*Behold the man.*" The verses that follow (vv. 8-11) establish another quote from Zechariah 9:9, "*Behold thy king.*" The passage is full of the glory of the Lord, His deity, His humility, His humanity and His monarchy. His essential, personal and official glories are brought before us in this lovely section of the Word of God.

As we approach verse 6, we are immediately confronted with His "being" (*huparcho*). This would tell us all that He is; in verse 8, the statement "*and being found*" would express not all that He is, but how He was seen. The word in verse 6 must carry the thought of the pre-existent deity of the Lord Jesus, His essential being, what He is in Himself. Vine's *Dictionary of New Testament Words* states "implies his pre-existent deity, previous to his birth, and his continued deity afterwards" (p. 116). The Incarnation could not take away from the Lord Jesus what He is, His deity. He ever was, is, and shall be God. The Received Text uses the word "subsisting" for "being." Whilst the word is variously translated throughout the New Testament, it always carries the thought of that which is the permanent possession of the one with whom it is linked. It is a word much used by Luke, both in his gospel and in the Acts; of the 48 uses of the word, 33 of them are by Luke. He would speak of:
- the Pharisees also, "*who **were** covetous*" —Luke 16:14
- the rich man, "***being** in torments*" — 16:23
- Stephen, "***being** full of the Holy Ghost*" —Acts 7:55
- a man, "***being** a cripple from his mother's womb*" —14:8
- God, "***seeing that he is** Lord of heaven and earth*" —17:24

79

PHILIPPIANS: THE MIND OF CHRIST

Other verses where the word is used could be quoted, but these are sufficient to ascertain that *"huparcho"* always carries the thought of that which is unchanging.

The verse not only records the "being" of the Lord Jesus, but also speaks of His being *"in the form of God."* The word "form" (*morphe*) occurs but three times in the New Testament, and on each occasion it is linked with the Lord Jesus. In verse 7, He *"took upon him the form of a servant,"* and in the servant book of Mark, when that service had been completed, we are told in 16:12 of the Lord Jesus on resurrection ground, as one who *"appeared in another form."* The fact that we only have these three references compels us to look no further when seeking to fathom the unfathomable. One thing is certain, we cannot link the word "form" with shape, as when Luke speaks of *"the Holy Ghost descending in a bodily shape like a dove"* upon the Lord Jesus at His baptism (Luke 3:22). The word would relate to what the Lord is in Himself. As a dear brother in Christ, who was always a great help and encouragement to me in my ministry, particularly in Canada, Sydney Maxwell, has written, "The expression therefore insists on the pre-existent and unoriginated deity of Christ previous to his birth and its continuance. This surely is the meaning of 'the form of God'" (*What the Bible Teaches, Philippians*, page 204). W. E. Vine also states, "For the interpretation of 'the form of God' it is sufficient to say that (1) it includes the whole nature and essence of deity" (*New Testament Dictionary* under *form*). Vincent is very simple yet sublime, saying "that Christ was in the form of God is to say that He existed as essentially one with God" (*Philippians, Vol. 3*, page 431). Could we not draw on many other verses of Scripture that establish with certainty the eternal being of our Lord Jesus Christ, as John 1:1, Romans 9:5 (where I must retain the A. V. reading, *"who is over all, God blessed for ever"*), Hebrews 1:3, *"who being the brightness of his glory, and the express image of his person,"* or the same chapter and verse 8, *"But unto the Son he saith, Thy throne, O God, is for ever and ever."* Let all who would have the audacity to deny the fact of the Lord Jesus being God, repent and bow to the revealed word concerning Him.

Again, another word that would express the whole thought of the second clause of the verse stands at its head. As "being" opens the first clause, so "thought" begins the second. The word simply means a judgement based on facts. The facts are very clear in the first statement of the verse; the Lord Jesus is God. If this is so, then the Lord Jesus could not think it robbery to be equal with God. Others like Satan (Ezek. 28:11-17), being lifted up with pride, fell; or Adam, when offered the prospect of being like God, took of the fruit of the tree of the knowledge of good and evil. Were not these Philippians seeking to move into realms that manifest pride as they sought vainglory? The Lord Jesus did not look upon His co-equality with the Father as a prize to be snatched at, something to be carried away by force (the word "robbery" only occurs here, but comes from a word that has the idea of "to carry away by force"), or a treasure to be retained at all cost. As the Lord Jesus is God, this was not something He had to seek after, nor was it something He must retain at all cost. If the Lord Jesus is going to do anything at all, He can only move in one direction, and that is downward. This He is going to do.

2:7-8—The Humility of the Servant

2:7—The Pattern of Humility

> *But made himself of no reputation, and took upon him the form of a servant, and was made in the likeness of men:*

The verse before us expresses those things that were evident in the incarnation of the Lord Jesus.

First, He *"made himself of no reputation."* Is not this what men seek for, to have a reputation? Was not the spirit that marked these Philippians that which would seek to enhance their reputation in the eyes of men? The word that is translated "reputation" (*kenoo*) is found five times in the New Testament, where it is written as *"made void"* (*Rom. 4:14)*, or *"made of none effect"* (*1 Cor. 1:17)*, and in 1 Corinthians 9:15 it is set forth as *"void."*

The scholars tell us that it has the thought of "to empty." When using the word in this way, we must be careful to see what is involved in the voluntary stoop of the Lord Jesus. Vincent writes "The general sense is that he divested himself of that peculiar mode of existence which was proper and peculiar to him as one with God; he laid aside the form of God. In so doing he did not divest himself of his divine nature" (*Philippians*, page 433. Another has said "The pre-existent Lord is the subject. He remains himself, but changes his mode of being" (Kittel, *Theological Dictionary of the New Testament* (abridged), page 427). Many teachers as they speak on this expression use the terminology "veiled" as they would seek to express the fact that the Lord Jesus maintained His deity as He came into humanity, for at no time could the Lord Jesus be other than He is, God. It is evident that the Lord Jesus retained every attribute that was His, as He moved among men. Is He not *"God ... manifest in flesh" (1 Tim. 3:16)*? John would write of Him in His eternal existence and states *"In the beginning was the Word"*; as to His distinct personality, *"and the Word was with God"*; and speaking of His divine equality *"and the Word was God" (John 1:1)*. When speaking of His manifestation to men, it is *"And the Word was made flesh, and dwelt among us" (John 1:14)*. The one who is eternal is the same one who was manifest in flesh; there is a change of **position** but not of His **person**. There is a lovely contrast between John 1:1 and verse 14,

v. 1—In the beginning was the word	v. 14—The word was made flesh
v. 1—The word was with God	v. 14—And dwelt among us
v. 1—The word was God	v. 14—We beheld His glory

The Lord Jesus remained **omnipresent**, that is, He is in all places at all times. John 1:18 would set forth the eternal dwelling place of love that the Lord Jesus knew, *"which is in the bosom of the Father."* He is there as Son of God, whilst as Son of Man He is *"in heaven"* when speaking to Nicodemus in John 3:13. His **omnipotence** is evident in the fact that disease, death, demons, and the elements were subject to His almighty power. The fact of His **omniscience**, that He is all-knowing was constantly demonstrated as He moved among men. Does not Nathaniel say, *"whence knowest Thou me?"* (John 1:48). We could draw a multitude of verses to prove His Omniscience, but it is enough to remember that He could tell the disciples to cast the net on the right side of the ship, or for Peter to be told to go to the bank, the bank of the river, and there take a fish that would produce the *stater* to pay the tax for both him and Christ. Perhaps a statement by Motyer will help to express the beauty of the Lord's incarnation, "It is not 'of what did he empty himself?' but 'into what did he empty himself?' Christ Jesus brought the whole of his divine nature, undiminished, into a new and—had it not been revealed to us in Scripture—unimaginable state" (A. Motyer, *Philippians*, IVP, page 113). To which we say Amen!

> *"Christ, by highest heaven adored,*
> *Christ, the everlasting Lord,*
> *Late in time behold Him come,*
> *Offspring of a virgin's womb;*
> *Veiled in flesh the Godhead see;*
> *Hail th' Incarnate Deity,*
> *Pleased as Man with men to dwell,*
> *Jesus our Immanuel."*
>
> [S S&S, no 30]

The second thing evident in the Incarnation is that *"he took upon him the form of a servant."* The word "form" is the same as "being in the form of God" (*morphe*). If this would express His prior existence as God, we now would see His present existence as servant. It would unfold the true place the Lord Jesus took, and what He ever remained in His movements here. Did He not say *"I am among you as he that serveth"* (Luke 22:27); or again *"Even as the Son of Man came not to be ministered unto, but to minister, and to give his life a ransom for many"* (Matt. 20:28)? The last clause would express why He took up the form of a servant, for we must remember that He is the servant of Isaiah

42:1, where God says *"Behold My servant."* The Lord Jesus is never the servant of men, though His service reached men. He was always Jehovah's perfect servant, who was obedient unto death. He took upon Him the bondman's form to do the will of His Father and at no time did He deviate from it.

The third expression speaks of Him who *"was made in the likeness of men,"* and yet He was so unlike men. One has said, "likeness resembles and image represents." The Spirit of God is always careful when speaking of the humanity of the Lord Jesus, and it becomes us to take great care when looking at His humanity. As to His birth, Luke is very careful to protect the conception when he would write concerning the *Production*, *"The Holy Ghost shall come upon thee"*; also the *Protection* that would be known when *"the power of the Highest shall overshadow thee,"* and the *Perfection* that would mark the Lord Jesus *"therefore also that holy thing which shall be born of thee shall be called the Son of God" (Luke 1:35)*. Adam, created in innocence, could and did sin, but holiness cannot sin, and thankfully, all of Scripture attests to this. Paul the man of intellect wrote *"who knew no sin,"* intrinsically (2 Cor. 5:21); Peter, the man of industry says *"who did no sin,"* externally (1 Pet. 2:22); whilst John, the man of intimacy records *"in him is no sin,"* internally (1 Jn. 3:5). In Romans 8:3, the Spirit again records, *"God sending his own Son in the likeness of sinful flesh"*; He came not in the likeness of flesh, for He had flesh, *"handle me, and see; for a spirit hath not flesh and bones, as ye see me have" (Luke 24:39)*, but He did not have sinful flesh. Finally in this connection, the epistle to the Hebrews 2:14, as with other parts of Scripture, watches over the humanity of the Lord Jesus when it states, *"As the children are partakers of flesh and blood, he also himself likewise took part of the same."* There are differences in the words used; "partakers" (*koinōneo*) means to have in common, whilst "took part of" (*metecho*) has the thought of, to hold along with. The Lord Jesus never had what was common to us, fallen, sinful humanity. Let every believer submit to the Word of God and recognise the distinct sinless humanity of the Lord Jesus.

2:8—Perfect Humanity

And being found in fashion as a man, he humbled himself, and became obedient unto death, even the death of the cross.

If verse 7 manifests what the Lord Jesus became when, acting as God, He took upon Him the form of a servant, we now discover what the Lord Jesus did as He was found in fashion as a man, when He further humbled Himself and became obedient to His Father to such an extent as "unto death."

If we noticed in verse 6 His "being," we are now confronted with the expression *"and being found."* The word (*heurisko*) has the thought of, to make a concrete discovery. It is used of Mary when she was *"found with child of the Holy Ghost"* (Matt. 1:18), and of the Lord Jesus, *"Ye shall find the babe wrapped in swaddling clothes"* (Luke 2:12).

How was He found? *"In fashion as a man."* The word "fashion" (*schema*) is found only here and in 1 Cor. 7:31, where Paul states that *"the fashion of this world passeth away."* It has the thought of bearing, appearance, and look. It would portray the Lord Jesus as He appeared, not what He is essentially in Himself, for the Godhead was not changed into manhood, though as He moved among men they assumed He was like unto themselves, *"Is not this the carpenter, the son of Mary?"* (Mark 6:3); and they refer to His family circle. The woman of Samaria could say *"How is it that thou, being a Jew, askest drink of me, which am a woman of Samaria?"* (John 4:9); or the blind man of John 9:11, who said, *"A man that is called Jesus made clay, and anointed mine eyes."* He was found in fashion as a man.

The predominant theme of the verse is what He did as man, *"he humbled himself,"* that is, he made Himself low. He who took servant form now moves even further down; His obedience to the Father is going to involve His going into death. In this verse we see the true character of the humility of Christ, first to be marked by obedience, then that obedience taking Him to death, then thirdly, even the death of the cross.

There are various aspects of the death of the Lord Jesus,

and each would bring a different truth to us. When speaking of His:

DEATH, it is generally put for	the sinner's condemnation:	Christ bore that (Rom. 3:23; 5:10)
CROSS, this is seen as	the sentence of a criminal;	Christ took that (Matt. 23:15-22; 27:38)
TREE, for disobedient sons, the place of disobedient sons.	the shame of a curse; (Deut. 21:18-23; Gal. 3:13)	Christ stood in
CRUCIFIXION, the ordeal and pain,	the suffering and cruelty;	Christ knew the bitterness of human enmity (Acts 2:23)

When looking at the death of the Lord Jesus, we must remember that He had no liability to death, *"Who only hath immortality"* (1 Tim. 6:16), but He had the ability to die. If for men it is *"the wages of sin"* (Rom. 6:23), for Him it was, *"that he by the grace of God should taste death for every man"* (Heb. 2:9). Again, it was not by the act of man, for *"I lay down my life, that I might take it again. No man taketh it from me, but I lay it down of myself"* (John 10:17-18). In this, we see the voluntary act of the Lord Jesus as He attentively listened to His Father's voice and was obedient to His will. Ralf Martin, quoting Lohmeyer, says "only a divine being can accept death as obedience; for ordinary men it is a necessity" (*Philippians, Tyndale New Testament Commentaries*, page 102). The death of the Lord Jesus was not natural, accidental, suicidal or judicial, but devotional and sacrificial.

Many have drawn attention to the seven-fold stoop of the Lord Jesus in verses 7 and 8, when He made Himself:

    i. of no reputation   "His Standing in life"
    ii. form of a servant   "the Servant of the Lord"
    iii. likeness of men   "His Similarity to men"

iv.	fashion as a man	"but Separate from men"
v.	humbled Himself	"His Submission to the Father"
vi.	obedient unto death	"His Suffering at Calvary"
vii.	cross death	"the Shame that was lamentable"

2:9-11—SUPREMACY OF THE SOVEREIGN

How thankful we are that the history of the Lord Jesus does not end with His sufferings on the cross, for His voluntary humility is now followed by His exaltation to absolute supremacy, and that not of Himself, but set on the splendour of the throne by God the Father. His exaltation is not now voluntary but validated by the Father, who fully compensated the Lord Jesus for the stoop that He took. In verses 9-11, we will see these things unfolded before us in the exaltation, expectation and adoration of the Lord Jesus.

2:9—HIS EXALTATION

Wherefore God also hath highly exalted him, and given him a name which is above every name:

It is fitting that the verse begins *"Wherefore God also..."*; often we find a "wherefore" or a "therefore." We were taught in our younger days that if you saw a "therefore," take a look at what it is there for! A "therefore" is for contemplation. When we come to a "wherefore," that has the thought of continuation. The "also" should cause us not to forget the reason for the present exaltation and future glorification of Christ. Lightfoot says "It implies reciprocation" (*Philippians*, page 111). If the Son will take up servant form for the Father, then God must be true to Himself and glorify His Son.

The Lord Jesus is said to be "highly exalted" (*huperupsoo*), a word that only occurs here, and would express the unique place given to the Lord Jesus, over and above anything ever seen before. A. T. Robertson has two very sad reasonings as he seeks to expound these sections relating to the humility and exaltation of Christ. Of the former he writes, "He took upon himself limitations of place (space) and of knowledge and power, though still on earth retaining more of these than any mere man" (*Word Pictures in the New Testament, Vol. 4,* page 444). We have already set forth that this is a gross misconception of the incarnation of the Lord Jesus. In relation to this present section, he writes "Because of Christ's voluntary humiliation, God lifted him above or beyond (huper) the state of glory which he enjoyed before the incarnation" (page 445). Here again ignorance of divine truth manifests itself. How could the Lord Jesus be exalted above the state that is set forth in verse 6? Did He not Himself pray, *"Father, glorify thou me with thine own self with the glory which I had with thee before the world was" (John 17:5)*? There is no thought of the Lord Jesus taking a place that could be above that which He knew as He co-existed with the Father. The truth before us is the same as that expressed in Ephesians 1:20-23. In both passages, we have the Lord Jesus taking humanity to the highest place of honour. The Ephesian letter records the place He has been given, whilst in Philippians it is the prospect of universal acknowledgement that is prominent.

There has also been "given" to Him the name which is above every name. It has been granted to Him as a favour, or grace, for the word "given" derives from the word *charis* (*Word Study concordance*). Most translators state it should be "the name," and would link it to Lord or Jehovah (as Caffin in the *Pulpit Commentary on Philippians*, page 61). Or as Vincent takes it in his exposition of Philippians, "The Name is a very common Hebrew title, denoting office, rank, dignity." He goes on to link the name as that of a glorified man "raised now to a place of equal dignity with Deity" (*Word Studies in the Greek New Testament, Vol. 2,* page 71). He leaves the name unrevealed, but makes it very clear, "But it is not at the name 'Jesus' that every knee shall bow. 'Jesus' was the name given our Lord at his humiliation. It is at The Name that belongs to Jesus that every knee shall bow" (p. 72). But why all this? For verse 9 seems to make it very clear that it is the very name that He bore in His humiliation, "Jesus," that God is going to cause all to acknowledge with the honour that is rightfully His, as God has exalted the name borne by Him in rejection.

2:10—His Expectation—Submission

That at the name of Jesus every knee should bow, of [things] in heaven, and [things] in earth, and [things] under the earth;

The Person

The purpose of being given *"the name which is above every name"* is "that" (*hina*), in order that, God fully intends that the name the Lord Jesus bore, and that is treated with such scorn and contempt, will be honoured by all.

He took the name in His *Incarnation*, when it was divinely conferred upon Him; it was Heaven's choice, *"thou shalt call his name Jesus"* (*Matt. 1:21*). It was the name they wrote and placed above His head at His *Crucifixion*, *"and set up over his head his accusation written, **This is Jesus the King of the Jews**"* (*Matt. 27:37*). It is the name given Him in His *Exaltation*, as in the present verse. Again, in the day of His *Manifestation* the name will be borne, *"this same Jesus, which is taken up from you into heaven, shall so come in like manner as ye have seen him go into heaven"* (*Acts 1:11*). So that in His nativity, ministry, mockery and majesty, the Lord bore the name Jesus; that name is going to be acknowledged by all in a coming day.

The People

There will be universal submission to Him who bore the shame, whether it is by those of the heavenly realm, or by men who are linked with earth, or those also who are described as being "under the earth"—and will acknowledge the honour that the Father has conferred upon His Son. Where it is a question of reconciliation, the Lord only reconciles what He creates, which are things in heaven and things on earth (Col. 1:16), for Colossians 1:20-22 limits the reconciliation to these spheres. We are now looking at the submission of all realms, and from the present verse we could infer that the order of demonic beings moved to what is designated "under the earth," moved there of their own accord; they were not created for such a sphere. Revelation 5:7-14 unveils universal submission to the Lamb as He takes the book out of the right hand of Him who sits upon the throne. We are now brought face to face with that universal submission.

THE POSTURE
"Every knee should bow." The word "bow" (*kampto*) simply means to bend the knee in submission or worship. It occurs but four times in the New Testament where we are told of:

- The Steadfast—Rom. 11:4, God had reserved 7000 who did not bow to Baal
- The Searched—Rom. 14:11, at the Judgement Seat of Christ
- The Supplicator—Eph. 3:14, Paul in prayer to the Father of the Lord Jesus
- The Submission—Phil. 2:10, universal bowing to Christ

The statement *"that ... every knee should bow"* is a quotation from Isaiah 45:23 where Jehovah is speaking. That verse also adds *"every tongue shall swear,"* which is the theme of verse 11. In this we have another proof of the deity of the Lord Jesus, for it is only to Him who is God that this shall be done. It is a worthwhile study to see verses that are spoken of Jehovah in the Old Testament applied to Christ in the New Testament, thus revealing His eternal deity.

2:11—THE ADORATION—CONFESSION

And [that] every tongue should confess that Jesus Christ [is] Lord, to the glory of God the Father.

THE PROGRAM
The decree of God is that there will not only be universal submission, but also universal confession of the honour belonging to the Lord Jesus. The word "tongue" would represent all who have been named in verse 10, and would mean every language. As in Acts 2, where 16 nations hearing *"every man in our own tongue, wherein we were born" (v. 8)*, would speak of the various languages spoken divinely on the day of Pentecost, so

the word reveals this in our passage.

To "confess" is literally, to say the same thing, or to agree to something. What a day of honour it will be when all are going to take sides with God concerning His Son, and will verify and ratify God's assessment of the Lord Jesus Christ. They will acknowledge that He is Lord; for those who are saved, this was done at conversion, Romans 10:9, when the Lordship of Christ was owned to bring us to salvation. Here it does not have salvation in view, but the veneration of His person.

Some writers would make the expression "Lord" equivalent to "the name" of verse 9, and state that it is this to which they bow. They say the name "Jesus" was too common a name for this to be extolled by men, but I find this type of teaching difficult to subscribe to.

The Purpose

The whole purpose of the exaltation of the Lord Jesus is *"to the glory of God the Father."* He who glorified Him on the earth, John 17:4, will cause that glory to be brought to His Father eternally.

The Practice:
the Exercise of Saints
2:12-16

Wherefore, my beloved, as ye have always obeyed, not as in my presence only, but now much more in my absence, work out your own salvation with fear and trembling. For it is God which worketh in you both to will and to do of his good pleasure.

Do all things without murmurings and disputings: That ye may be blameless and harmless, the sons of God, without rebuke, in the midst of a crooked and perverse nation, among whom ye shine as lights in the world; Holding forth the word of life; that I may rejoice in the day of Christ, that I have not run in vain, neither laboured in vain.

2:12—Assembly Preservation

Wherefore, my beloved, as ye have always obeyed, not as in my presence only, but now much more in my absence, work out your own salvation with fear and trembling.

The Apostle is about to apply the sublime teaching of verses 5-11 to the hearts of the saints at Philippi. He is first looking for **realization** from them, that is, to understand the reason why the Lord Jesus has been so set forth. The "wherefore" should immediately cause them to have an inward look at the condition of their own heart.

Again, it is good to see that the condition that marked the assembly did not mar the **relationship** that Paul had with them, as he still calls them "beloved." The truth is that the relationship would be a means of inspiring the saints to have a desire to respond to his promptings.

The **response** is seen in that the assembly had always sought to apply the ministry that was brought to them. As Paul reflects on the past teaching and instruction he had brought to them, he recalls a spirit of obedience to the truth of God; they *"always obeyed."* To obey is, to listen attentively to, and to heed or conform to a command or authority (*Strong's Concordance*). How heart-warming to the servant of God when he could see that he had not laboured in vain among them. He recalls that there was "always" a desire to move according to the mind of God. The word is used four times in the epistle, as Paul thinks of his **prayer** (1:4), *"always in every prayer of mine"*; also of the **promotion** of Christ (1:20), *"in nothing I shall be ashamed, but that with all boldness, as always, so now also Christ shall be magnified in my body."* In our present verse it is used for the **preservation** of the assembly, whilst in 4:4 we should always find our **pleasure** in the Lord, *"Rejoice in the Lord always."*

The Apostle is seeking the same response to his written ministry from them as they gave to his oral ministry. The Word of God should not need the urgent promptings of verbal teaching to apply it to our lives. The written Word should also find the same ready reaction from the believer. It is to this end that he writes *"not as in my presence only, but now much more in my absence."* It is as if his absence demanded a greater response from them.

The saints are called not only to give a response to the ministry, but they also have a **responsibility** to see that the exhortation is put into practice, hence the expression *"work out your own salvation with fear and trembling."*

It must be noticed that we can only "work out" our salvation; we cannot "work for" our salvation. This is not the salvation of the soul but the salvation of the assembly. By working out the principles laid down in verses 5-11, the life and testimony of the believers would be preserved and harmony and unity would be maintained. W. Lincoln pithily says "It must be 'our own' before we can work it out" (*Assembly Writers Library, Philippians*, page 123).

The unity of the assembly is no trivial matter and should be looked to "with fear and trembling." There should be a fear of displeasing God, and I should tremble lest I fail to correct the problem that has arisen.

The local church is seen as a cultivated field in 1 Cor. 3:6-9, and the expression "work out" can carry the thought of, to cultivate an allotment. It would teach us to use the hoe to root out the weeds, but we must take care not to destroy the good plants whilst doing it.

In the following verses 13-16, we have the results of the truth being put into practice by the believers. The first benefit will be:

2:13—For God's Pleasure

> *For it is God which worketh in you both to will and to do of [his] good pleasure.*

The divine agent in the movements to rectify the failure among them is God Himself. That this spirit of self-seeking is not of God is evident because of the exercise of Paul by the Spirit of God to write regarding these matters. It is contrary to that displayed by the Lord Jesus, so we find God Himself willing and working to produce conformity to Christ in the lives of His own.

The divine activity is evident as God *"worketh"*; the word used (*energeo*) is that from which we get our word "energy." The word occurs twice in the verse, and it manifests that God Himself is putting energy into us, with a view to our putting energy into acting as God desires, as He would want us *"to do"* (*energeo*) of His good pleasure.

This can only be effected if we have a *"will"* to perform His desires. What a blessed thing when all is done by a submission of our own will to the will of God. That this is not a natural process is evidenced by the fact that God must first work in us to desire to do His will, before we can work to perform it.

All is for God's enjoyment; it is for His *"good pleasure."* Again we are drawn to a word that occurs, in the form that is used here, nine times. The Lord Jesus revealed that the manifestation of truth to babes must not be despised, as it brought pleasure to the Father so to do (Matt. 11:25-26; Luke 10:21). A servant of God told me recently that when, as a young man, he twice ministered divine truth to the assembly, an older man who for many years had ministered to the saints, rose immediately after him and publicly rebuked him, saying he was out of place as a young man to teach the Word of God. I wonder where Israel would have been without a Samuel (1 Sam. 2:18), or a Jeremiah, whom God raised up as he states, *"I am a child"* (Jer. 1:6). We also see the wondrous ministry of Zechariah, of whom it is said that he was a *"young man"* (Zech. 2:4). And what age was Daniel when God first used him?

The word is also used in Luke 2:14 to reveal that the purpose of the incarnation was to bring "good will" to men. It was for the pleasure of humanity that the Lord Jesus came from the Father, as He was also to bring "Glory to God."

If there is pleasure in divine revelation, and also by the incarnation, Paul reveals that his intercession for Israel's salvation sprang out of the pleasure in his heart to do so; his *"heart's desire"* was that they might be saved (Rom. 10:1).

The word is used to reveal the pleasure God has to bring

us to "adoption," the placing of sons in Ephesians 1:5, and again in verse 9 where the pleasure of God is seen in the fact that He desires us to come to an appreciation of that which He has decreed, both for Christ and for His own, in the day of His manifestation and return to earth to establish the kingdom.

Eudokia is also used in Philippians 1:15 to reveal the true character of the heart of those who, in the proclamation of the gospel, preached it with "good will." This brings us to our present verse, where conformation to the will of God is that which will bring pleasure to the Lord. The final use of the word, according to the Word Study Concordance, is in 2 Thessalonians 1, where the manifestation of the saints with Christ as He comes *"to be admired in all them that believe" (v. 10)*, will have a present effect upon the saints, causing us to live and *"fulfil all the good pleasure of his goodness, and the work of faith with power" (v. 11)*.

The working out of the will of God is not only for the divine pleasure, but also for:

2:14—THE BELIEVER'S PEACE

Do all things without murmurings and disputings:

The Apostle calls them to *"do all things without murmurings and disputings."* The fact that the believers were not likeminded, and all were seeking their own things, would cause murmurings and disputings to rise up among them. The Apostle leaves no room for this spirit to remain, *"Do all things"* without it. Paul could *suffer loss* of all things (3:8); God has power to subdue all things (3:21). Again, Paul could do all things as he was strengthened by God (4:13). Now he appeals to the Philippians to see that nothing is spoken or done to produce this among them; they are still working out their salvation. I recall hearing someone say, "If we can get murmurings out of the people, we will get disputings out of the church." Israel's sad experiences as they passed through the wilderness invariably began with a murmuring people. God's record is, *"[Ye] have tempted me now these ten times, and have not hearkened to my voice"* (Num. 14:22), and again, *"How long shall I bear with this evil congregation, which murmur against me?"* (14:27). We see how it cost that generation the Land of Promise, as their carcases fell in the wilderness (Heb. 3:17).

The book of Numbers, chapters 11-17 bring before us a record of Israel's murmurings, which led to disputings. They had only begun to take the journey from Sinai to the Land when they complained about the **pathway** where the pillar cloud led them, causing God to kindle a fire to burn among them. This is followed by murmuring against God's **provision** for them, when they spoke against the manna. Chapter 12 sees Miriam and Aaron speaking against God's **prophet**. It is a serious thing to speak evil of our brethren, and especially of those who would seek to be a help to God's children. Did this family dispute begin with Miriam? She is placed before Aaron, and it is she who is smitten with leprosy, as if God made a public exposure of the inward corruption. Such murmurings held the camp back and no progress was made as a result. How often since then have the children of God been kept back from progress because of the personal disputes that have arisen among us?

In chapters 13 and 14, they speak against the **promises** of God. The murmurings continue as they are brought to the edge of the Land. It was caused by the **princes** among them who had gone to spy out the Land and brought back their evil report saying *"We be not able"* (Num. 13:31). It caused both murmurings and disputings among the people, recorded for us in chapter 14. Often times since, those in places of authority among the saints have held back believers from entering into the good of all that God would have for us to enjoy, simply because they see difficulties in obeying the Word of God. Beloved saints, remember the words of Mary, *"Whatsoever he saith unto you, do it"* (John 2:5). Do not miss out on the blessing of God because of supposed difficulties. The Lord never asks us to do anything that is beyond our capabilities.

Again, in Numbers chapters 16 and 17, Korah with Dathan and Abiram raise their voice against the **priesthood** that had divine origin. Like the Philippians, *"all seek their own"* (2:21).

They are not content to abide in the calling wherewith they were called. Again the consequences of their murmurings are seen when *"the ground clave asunder that was under them: and the earth opened her mouth, and swallowed them up" (16:31-32)*. Well might 1 Corinthians 10:11 record, *"Now all these things happened unto them for ensamples: and they are written for our admonition, upon whom the ends of the world are come."* Let us see to it that we do all things without murmurings and disputings.

2:15—THE WORLD'S PROSPERITY

> *That ye may be blameless and harmless, the sons of God, without rebuke, in the midst of a crooked and perverse nation, among whom ye shine as lights in the world;*

Not only will the application of the ministry be for the believer's peace, but it will also cause our testimony to the world to be more effective. The character of our life affects the confession of our lips.

The opening expression of the verse, *"that ye may be,"* carries the thought *"that ye may become."* They had not reached this goal yet, and until the teaching of verses 13 and 14 was put into practice, it would still not be reached. It is evident that Paul expected an early application of the truth that would produce this in their lives.

He was looking for them to be *"blameless and harmless."* The former has to do with the **priests** and sacrifices, and would denote physical perfections. It is used of Zacharias and Elisabeth, who *"were both righteous before God, walking in all the commandments and ordinances of the Lord **blameless**" (Luke 1:6)*. Paul could also state of himself, *"touching the righteousness which is in the Law, **blameless**" (3:6)*. Concerning the Law of Moses it is said, *"If that first covenant had been **faultless**, then should no place been sought for the second" (Heb. 8:7)*. In each of these, we see what was, and what was not, acceptable to God. As far as the priestly activities of Zacharias or Paul were concerned, there was nothing to hinder their ministry, but the failure of the Law to be able to perfect the sinner made it unacceptable to God. It did the work for which it was given as it exposed sin, but it could not rectify the problem that it exposed. It carries the thought of our conduct being without fault in the sight of another.

The latter word "harmless" would emphasise the thought of our character, what we are inwardly and morally. There are but three references to it in the New Testament. The Lord would call the disciples to be *"harmless as doves" (Matt. 10:16)*, and Paul exhorts believers to be *"simple concerning evil" (Rom. 16:19)*. These are features that should mark those who are *"sons of God."* The word "sons" is strictly children; sons carries the thought of dignity, whilst children, that of relationship. Here we are seen as those born of God, and as having the seed of God, being partakers of the divine nature. As such, we must bear God's character to the world, blameless and harmless. This would leave me without rebuke as far as the world is concerned. The word *"rebuke"* is akin to the word "blameless," which is what I am, while rebuke is what others would do to me.

How different is the world in which we move, as its children are seen to be *"crooked and perverse."* Both words express the bent that marks it; it is untoward and froward, and, as in the word perverse, it is distorted and twisted. The Lord Jesus spoke of Israel as being a *"faithless and perverse generation" (Matt. 17:17; Luke 9:41)*, whilst Israel accused Him of *"perverting the nation" (Luke 23:2)*. This proves just how distorted and twisted they were as they spoke of the Saviour in such a derogatory way.

We must manifest that we are light bearers to the world. The word "shine" is the word "to appear." To the darkened hearts of men in their sin, believers appear so different as they give light to the world. The Greek word for lights is *phosteres*, and means luminaries, stars. It only occurs again in Revelation 21:11, where speaking of the future government of the saints of this present age, who are seen as a city administering the

Kingdom, it recalls *"her light was like unto a stone most precious."* Thus the saints are seen as both the present and the future light of the world. We are seen as lights in (*en*) the world. It is where we are, more than what we do, that is emphasised. We are to shine, not shout. Many years ago as a godless young man, I was placed alongside a Christian in the workplace; he was my manager. He did not preach to me or give me a gospel leaflet, but whenever you looked at him, you thought of God; he shone. One day, just walking into the department, I suddenly thought, "What if there is a God?" The end result was to go to a hall where the gospel was preached and, by the grace of God, I trusted Christ. This was because one man appeared *"as a light in the world."*

2:16—THE SERVANT'S PROFIT

Holding forth the word of life; that I may rejoice in the day of Christ, that I have not run in vain, neither laboured in vain.

The application of the ministry will be beneficial to Paul's future honour at the Judgement Seat of Christ. The present service of the saints will be for the completion of God's work in them, and for the final approval of his own labour bestowed upon them.

The expression *"the word of life"* stands at the forefront of the Greek text, revealing that it is the prime thing in Paul's appeal to them. If they are to be *"holding forth,"* that is, as if one were extending to another food or drink or such like, the believer's prime thought in offering with outstretched hand to a needy world should be *"the word of life."* The Word is set forth in many ways in the New Testament, and each designation carries its own particular theme, as:

The Word of Life	"its Entity"	Philippians 2:16
The Word of the Lord	"its Authority"	Acts 15:35
The Word of the Gospel	"the Opportunity"	Acts 15:7
The Word of Promise	"the Security"	Romans 9:9
The Word of the Cross	"the Enmity"	1 Corinthians 1:18

The Word of Truth	"its Veracity"	Ephesians 1:13
The Word of Christ	"its Supremacy"	Colossians 3:16
The Word of Faith	"its Objectivity"	1 Timothy 4:6
The Word of Righteousness	"its Purity"	Hebrews 5:13
The Engrafted Word	"its Activity"	James 1:21
The more Sure Word	"its Certainty"	2 Peter 1:19
The Word of God	"its Originality"	Acts 8:14

It is this Word of God, with all its diversity and ability to transform lives that we must set before the world for their blessing and salvation.

This would cause the Apostle to rejoice, the word is really to boast, not in himself but in the labours of the Philippians. It would be an evident token that, in his ministry among them, he had not *"run in vain"* — the figure of an athlete, as he knows the end of the race will bring its reward. He adds *"neither laboured in vain"*; again, the thought behind the word "labour" (*kopiao*) is to tire or wear oneself out with physical toil. Kittel's abridged version says of the word, "it became less prominent in later Christian authors, who perhaps think that *kopos*, with its nuance of manual work, is not a fitting term for ministry" (page 453). The word occurs 23 times in the New Testament, and covers both the labours of Paul, and of many of the saints. A true servant will know what it is to be like this, though many of the saints will not appreciate all that goes into the service of God. Someone once said to me, "Oh you only work for an hour a night." They know nothing of the hours spent over the Word and in prayer, as well as visitations to encourage both saint and sinner in the things of God. The late David Craig said, "You must spend at least 7 hours in the presence of God for one hour in public." Perhaps the reason for such deterioration in the present testimony for God is because we do not have men like Paul who "ran" and "laboured."

The Pictures: Expounded in the Servants
2:17-30

> *Yea, and if I be offered upon the sacrifice and service of your faith, I joy, and rejoice with you all. For the same cause also do ye joy, and rejoice with me.*
>
> *But I trust in the Lord Jesus to send Timotheus shortly unto you, that I also may be of good comfort, when I know your state. For I have no man likeminded, who will naturally care for your state. For all seek their own, not the things which are Jesus Christ's. But ye know the proof of him, that, as a son with the father, he hath served with me in the gospel. Him therefore I hope to send presently, so soon as I shall see how it will go with me. But I trust in the Lord that I also myself shall come shortly.*
>
> *Yet I supposed it necessary to send to you Epaphroditus, my brother, and companion in labour, and fellow soldier, but your messenger, and he that ministered to my wants. For he longed after you all, and was full of heaviness, because that ye had heard that he had been sick. For indeed he was sick nigh unto death: but God had mercy upon him; and not on him only, but on me also, lest I should have sorrow upon sorrow. I sent him therefore the more carefully, that, when ye see him again, ye may rejoice, and that I may be the less sorrowful. Receive him therefore in the Lord with all gladness; and hold such in reputation: Because for the work of Christ he was nigh unto death, not regarding his life, to supply your lack of service toward me.*

The last section of the chapter brings before us three of God's servants who are set forth as examples to the saints. That the spirit that marked the Philippians can be controlled and that the mind of Christ can be worked out in God's children is evident from these examples brought before us by the Apostle.

In this portion of the Word of God we will see:
a) The Sacrifice of Paul
b) The Service of Timothy
c) The Suffering of Epaphroditus

2:17-18—THE SACRIFICE OF PAUL

Yea, and if I be offered upon the sacrifice and service of your faith, I joy, and rejoice with you all. For the same cause also do ye joy, and rejoice with me.

We are brought face to face with the true character of the service of the saints before God in this verse. Let all that serve the Lord rise to the dignity and honour that God has put upon us in our service. This is no mundane routine of mere habit; we are called to act as priests in all that we do before God. A great honour was put upon Aaron and his sons to minister in the sanctuary for God; no less privilege is given to believers today. Nay, the sphere of our ministry is far higher than theirs, for they ministered in an earthly sanctuary, which was but a shadow of the true, but we in that which is an heavenly. Peter would speak of the gatherings of God's children as being a *"spiritual house,"* and the gathered saints as functioning in a *"Holy Priesthood" (1 Pet. 2:5)*. Paul, when reflecting on his activities in the gospel, speaks of it as a priestly work, and those who are saved through his ministry as an offering to God (see Rom. 15:16). The word "minister" in Romans 15:16 is the same as that here when he recalls the "service" of the Philippian believers. It is a word for priestly activity.

As Paul thinks of the *"sacrifice and service"* of their faith, he is referring to them *"holding forth the word of life."* He sees their labours as a great sacrifice to God. He knows that this could lead to him being *"offered upon"* their sacrifice and priestly service. The offering in Paul's mind is that of the drink offering; upon every sacrifice, a drink offering was poured out (see Num. 28-29). The drink offering would speak of joy associated with worship, and it is for this reason that the Apostle says, *"I joy and rejoice with you all."*

The drink offering, or pouring out, can refer either to wine or to the blood of the sacrifice, which was poured out at the foot of the altar. This second aspect of the pouring out is seen in 2 Timothy 4:6, where the same word is used, again in reference to Paul's death. In this latter verse, joy is not brought in, and we have the blood of the sacrifice poured out at the base of the altar. These are the only two instances of the word in the New Testament.

Again we notice that joy is pervading all. This joy is first, personal, *"I joy."* It is also corporate, for it would cause the Philippians to rejoice also. The Apostle adds the preposition, *sun* (together with), to his word for rejoice (*kairo*), thus *sunkairo*. In verse 18 it is also reciprocal, *"For the same cause also do ye joy, and rejoice with me."* The same words are used by Paul to express the feelings of their hearts, as well as his own.

2:19-24—THE SERVICE OF TIMOTHY

> *But I trust in the Lord Jesus to send Timotheus shortly unto you, that I also may be of good comfort, when I know your state. For I have no man likeminded, who will naturally care for your state. For all seek their own, not the things which are Jesus Christ's. But ye know the proof of him, that, as a son with the father, he hath served with me in the gospel. Him therefore I hope to send presently, so soon as I shall see how it will go with me. But I trust in the Lord that I also myself shall come shortly.*

The sacrifice of Paul even as a drink offering was because of his devotion to God. We shall see that the service of Timothy was because of his devotion to Paul. It is evident that the sufferings of Epaphroditus revealed the devotion in his heart for the Philippians. Where the mind of Christ is seen in the child of God, it will draw out devotion towards God and each other.

Timothy is now set forth as one who has the mind of

Christ. The Apostle is not setting the standard too high for the saints; it is being displayed in the lives of these servants of Christ, and it is attainable.

There is a beautiful simplicity in Paul's appraisal of Timothy. This young man, who accompanied Paul and his fellow-helpers in the truth when he commenced his second missionary journey, was not only well known to the Philippians, but also respected by them. Paul has linked himself to Timothy in writing this letter, and from the display of his character in these verses, he is evidently the right man to help the saints apply the ministry that is given to them.

2:19—THE SENDING OF TIMOTHY

> *But I trust in the Lord Jesus to send Timotheus shortly unto you, that I also may be of good comfort, when I know your state.*

The Apostle uses a word that manifests his dependence on God, not the definiteness of personal assertion. Paul is not seeking to control events, but he looks to God for his directions; he is not "seeking his own things." He states, *"I trust."* The same word is used again in verse 24 and carries the thought of "hope," and in all 31 occurrences of the word, it is always translated "trust" or "hope." His trust is also *"in the Lord Jesus,"* (see also verse 24.) This would indicate that all is in the Lord's will, and under His control. The truth of James 4:13-17 is very much before Paul's mind as he moves in dependence upon the Lord.

His desire for Timothy to visit the church at Philippi has a note of urgency about it as he adds "shortly." Again, it is the expectancy of Paul himself in verse 24. The word has speed as its essence, meaning quickly, hastily, suddenly. It is as if the need is so immediate that there is no time for delay in bringing the ministry of Timothy to them.

The object of Timothy's visit is not only for the good of the believers, but also for a source of comfort to Paul, who was evidently greatly concerned for their well-being. It is little wonder that he will write to the Corinthians that among the great trials of his life, there are not only perils to face, and pains to endure, but also the problems of the saints affect him, *"Beside those things that are without, that which cometh upon me daily, the care of all the churches" (2 Cor. 11:28).* He wants to feel encouraged when he knows their state. He actually uses a word that means "cheered in soul" (*eupsucheo*). The inner feelings of this mighty servant of God are revealed; the effect of his ministry upon the lives of his converts will bring cheer to his heart.

2:20—THE SERVICE OF TIMOTHY

> *For I have no man likeminded, who will naturally care for your state.*

Such is the character of Timothy that Paul knows he is just the man for this ministry. He is of exactly the same mind as Paul, in fact Paul uses a similar word to that which he has expressed in his desire to be cheered, when he speaks of Timothy as being "likeminded," that is "equal souled" (*isopsuchos*). There was no one so in tune with Paul's desires as Timothy; perfect harmony existed between them. The word that Paul uses to express his relationship with Timothy is only used here, and perhaps that may indicate that such relationships are very few, and hard to find. There was a unique bond between these two servants of God.

Another feature that marks Timothy is that he will have a *"natural care for your state."* There would be no worked-up emotion, no self-seeking ambition to make a name for himself, but a genuine, sincere and true desire to see the Philippians prosper. Does this not speak to us all? There should be a "natural" care in every believer towards all. This is evidently Spirit wrought, and will be one of the marks of new birth. The problem that is raised in verse 21 is contrary to every movement of God in the lives of the redeemed. The world and the flesh obviously dominate such, not the mind of Christ.

2:21—Self-seeking Saints

For all seek their own, not the things which are Jesus Christ's.

That the spirit of *"all seek their own"* is not of God is plain for all who know the Word of God to see. Every affliction that has brought distress to this world, and ultimately necessitated the death of the Lord Jesus to recover us to God's will, stems from this. Did not Satan "seek his own" when, as the anointed cherub, he sought to dethrone God? In this, the course was set that was to have dreadful repercussions upon the whole of creation. His temptation of Eve was similarly to affect the world, as the desire to seek their own, not the things of Jesus Christ brought the judgement of God upon them and upon their posterity.

Does the Apostle Paul have discernment here as to the damage the Philippian believers could cause, and the grave danger they were exposing themselves to? This is no minor sin; the whole truth of God displayed in Christ is being attacked. The fellowship will be destroyed, the testimony at Philippi finished. Would that I could appeal to all believers to look to themselves and examine their ways, as over the years one has seen this destructive spirit at work among believers. The end result has been the break-up of many places where once there was very sweet and precious fellowship. As I write, my own heart is grieved as I reflect on the sad character that marks many, to the detriment of God's work among us. This epistle needs to be read and understood by all saints of God. Much damage has been done by self-seeking believers.

2:22—The Support of Timothy

But ye know the proof of him, that, as a son with the father, he hath served with me in the gospel.

Timothy was altogether different from those who seek their own. His life and testimony are summed up in a fourfold way in this verse.

THE SUBMISSIVE MIND

THEIR APPRECIATION
The high regard in which Timothy was held by Paul was fully owned by the believers at Philippi, for among the things he writes concerning him, Paul can speak of the appreciation that the Philippians had come to themselves, regarding Timothy. He says *"ye know,"* that is, they had come to know. Timothy's presence among them on a former day had left its mark upon them, and left very firm impressions as to his character.

HIS APPROVAL
"Ye know the proof of him." As with all who believe, for one cannot help but make judgements and assess those who profess to walk with God, so Timothy's life had been tested and he had found approval. We recall another who was tested in the divine scales, Belshazzar, who was *"weighed in the balances and found wanting" (Dan. 5:27).* The Apostle has been reviewing the lives of the Philippians, and in many respects it made sorry reading. They were not like-minded, lowly-minded, nor did they bear the mind of Christ, as *"all seek their own."* They needed someone among them who could help them to heed the ministry this letter brought, and who better than one whom they themselves had witnessed to be true in his life and service.

HIS AFFECTION
Once again the value of Timothy is extolled before them. They were aware of Paul's interest in them, and of his love for them. They would also know that Timothy came out of the same stock, and would act in the same way. Is he not in his service for Christ, *"as a son with the father"*? Wuest expresses this as "Timothy was Paul's assistant. He was also Paul's spiritual child. He could have said "as a son to a father, he served me in the gospel'. The Greek makes it plain that Paul said 'as a son to a father', not 'as a son with a father'" (*Word Studies, Vol. 2*, page 80). This expresses the fact that the relationship was one of affection, but also of mutual concern to serve God together. This brings us to

His Activity

The service of Timothy, though carried out in affection to Paul, was done as a bondservant to God. Both recognised that it was God's work and both subjected themselves to their Master in the work of the gospel. If Timothy was a son to Paul, he was a slave to God.

2:23—The Selection of Timothy

> *Him therefore I hope to send presently, so soon as I shall see how it will go with me.*

It seems that it was a deliberate choice by Paul to have the hope of sending Timothy to them. This is drawn out by the word "him." This is a strong emphatic word, and carries the thought of "such a one as this." Who better to seek to help believers such as these than one who would act as Paul would have done among them?

It is again touching to see the spirit of dependence that marks Paul. There is no dogmatic assertion, but a trust that all is in the will of God, *"I hope."* The events in Rome will determine his mind on these matters. The expression, *"so soon as I shall see how it will go with me"* would seem to imply that he knew that his trial was drawing near. This may be the cause of his expectancy, that he anticipates release. His confidence in the legal system of Rome, especially to one born a Roman, causes him to hope for an early deliverance. How could such charges as were laid against him keep him in confinement? He had done nothing contrary to Roman law. Justice would be done and he looked to be set at liberty. Perhaps this is the trial he refers to in 2 Timothy 4:16, *"At my first answer no man stood with me, but all men forsook me."* It is evident that events took a different course to what he expected, ultimately to end, not with release, but with execution. I say nothing about a supposed release and visit to Spain. It seems to me that this is a theory based on speculation with no concrete evidence, and certainly not taken from scriptural evidence. This argument is set forth by Coneybeare and Howson, *Life and Epistles of Saint*

Paul, Vol. 2, chapter 27. The basis for the argument seems to be quotations from the Early Fathers, so called.

2:24—THE SENTIMENTS OF PAUL

> *But I trust in the Lord that I also myself shall come shortly.*

It is evident that he is expecting that all will turn out for his freedom as he says *"I trust in the Lord."* The word "trust" occurs six times throughout the epistle and carries the thought of confidence, trust, thinking. The Apostle uses it in the following places:

1:6	The Performance of God	"confident"
1:14	The Preaching of brethren	"confident"
1:25	The Presentation of Paul	"confidence"
2:24	The Presence of Timothy	"trust"
3:3	The Powerlessness of the flesh	"confidence"
3:4	The Persistence of Judaisers	"thinketh"

Paul's trust is *"in the Lord."* He wisely submits his hopes and desires, even where the spiritual welfare of his converts is concerned, to the higher will of God. Every desire of the child of God should be *"in the Lord."* The will of God must be supreme, and we must subject ourselves to it. Hope, whilst passing through the trials of life, must always remain in us, though there is no room for self-assertiveness. James 4:15 must always be before us, *"For that ye ought to say, If the Lord will, we shall live, and do this, or that."* Paul recognises this principle in his own life, and remains dependent upon the will of God.

2:25-30—THE SUFFERING OF EPAPHRODITUS

> *Yet I supposed it necessary to send to you Epaphroditus, my brother, and companion in labour, and fellowsoldier, but your messenger, and he that ministered to my wants. For he longed after you all, and was full of heaviness, because that ye had heard*

> *that he had been sick. For indeed he was sick nigh unto death: but God had mercy on him; and not on him only, but on me also, lest I should have sorrow upon sorrow. I sent him therefore the more carefully, that, when ye see him again, ye may rejoice, and that I may be the less sorrowful. Receive him therefore in the Lord with all gladness; and hold such in reputation: Because for the work of Christ he was nigh unto death, not regarding his life, to supply your lack of service toward me.*

The Apostle brings before us the last of this triad of examples of those who bore the mind of Christ. Without this epistle, nothing would be known of this delightful believer who exhibited those spiritual features that God loves to see in His children. Yet here he is seen and placed alongside those familiar names of Paul and Timothy, as one who lived Christ. It would seem that Epaphroditus carried his name well, for it means "agreeable, lovely." How blessed it is when one lives up to the name he bears and is characterised by it. Let us remember that we that call upon the name of the Lord bear the name "Christian." A great weight of responsibility rests upon us, that the name of Christ is not blasphemed because of careless living.

A number of lovely things are said of Epaphroditus, who was evidently held in respect and esteem in the assembly at Philippi, and also by Paul. I notice that one esteemed writer speaks in a somewhat derogatory way of him when he says, "For the Apostle to recognise an ordinary layman in such high commendation was generous of Paul and also expresses his appreciation for all Epaphroditus had done" (I omit the writer's name). How can any speak of the saints, who are God's elect, as "ordinary laymen"? It may suit Christendom to divide believers into various categories, but it is not of God. The word "layman" means "of the common people," and there is nothing common about any child of God. The ministry of Epaphroditus raises him to the highest rank among believers. Paul was not "generous" in his appraisal of this man, but truthful. We must discover what Paul really thought of the man in the portion of the Word of God that the Spirit of God gives to him.

2:25—The Servant

> *Yet I supposed it necessary to send to you Epaphroditus, my brother, and companion in labour, and fellowsoldier, but your messenger, and he that ministered to my wants.*

There are five expressions in the verse that are used to describe this man and his ministry.

I. My Brother "Because of his Birth at Salvation"

A beautiful relationship is established between believers the moment we are saved, as we are brought into the family of God. In the Roman epistle 16:23, the Apostle speaks of *"Quartus a brother."* He would also say the same of Onesimus the runaway slave, when commending him to Philemon and desiring that he will receive him again, *"not now as a servant, but above a servant, a brother beloved" (Phmn. 16).* It is interesting that when Paul speaks of Epaphroditus, he does not call him "a brother" but *"my brother."* Evidently he had become very dear to the Apostle, and he appreciated such a man as this being in the same family. There is a lovely comment by G. Christopher Willis in his exposition of Philippians saying "'A brother is born for adversity'. And it was surely in a day of adversity that Epaphroditus came and proved himself to be a true 'brother' to Paul" (*Sacrifices of Joy*, page 193).

II. Companion in labour "The Burden of Service"

Another trait that marked Epaphroditus was his unstinting toil in the service of God. Paul calls him *"my companion in labour."* This is but one word in the Greek text (*sunergos*). It is from the preposition *sun*, which carries the thought of being "one with," and *ergon*, speaking of hard work. The word speaks volumes of Paul's appreciation of the labours that were put into the work of God by Epaphroditus. The Apostle is very quick to voice his approval of many who gave themselves to the service of God, and to express the toil and energy that saints put into their labours for God (see Rom. 16:3, 9, 21, Phmn. 1, 24).

III. Fellow soldier "The Battle as Soldiers"

Another feature of this dedicated life is that, unlike Demas, he did not shun the battle to which he had been called. The Apostle exposes Demas as one who *"hath forsaken me, having loved this present world" (2 Tim. 4:10)*. One has said, "the jangling of the chain got on his nerves" (J. Douglas). While Paul had *"fought a good fight" (2 Tim. 4:7)*, Demas had removed himself from the battlefield, and his heart is exposed. He did not love the appearing of our Lord Jesus, otherwise he would have stood by Him "who had chosen him to be a soldier," instead of looking for an easier path in this world.

The Apostle also writes of Archippus as a fellow soldier (Phmn. 2). Though again it would seem that a little carelessness would mark this cavalry captain (such is his name), for he is encouraged to *"Take heed to the ministry which thou hast received in the Lord, that thou fulfil it" (Col. 4:17)*. There does not seem to be anything in the life of Epaphroditus that would have caused him to be a deserter, or to lay down his arms before the enemy.

IV. Apostle "As the Bearer of Support"

The translators were in some way careful to use a word that rightly conveys the business that Epaphroditus had, as he was chosen by the church at Philippi to bear the gift that they desired to reach Paul, to help to relieve him during the days of his imprisonment. Nevertheless we must again draw attention to the fact that the word used is *apostolos*, the word that is consistently used of the twelve Apostles. But as we taught when looking at 1:1, there is a distinction between those who are chosen by Christ, and those who are chosen by the church. Epaphroditus is "your Apostle"; that is, they had chosen him for this ministry of bearing the gift to the Apostle Paul. Once again, it is evident that his labours in travelling the many miles to Rome were held in very high esteem.

V. Priest "In the Fragrance of the Sanctuary"

The word "ministered" is that used of priests as they minister before God (Heb. 8:2). It is beautiful to know that the ministry of saints to each other is seen as being a spiritual work God-ward. That ministry of not looking upon our own things, but on the things of others, rises as a sweet odour to God. What pleasure the whole life of the Lord Jesus must have given His Father, and how blessed to see the mind of Christ in believers as they do the same things. The word is used of Paul's service in the gospel as he sought to win sinners for Christ. Romans 15:16 records Paul's ministry as a priestly ministry, "*that the offering up of the Gentiles might be acceptable, being sanctified by the Holy Ghost.*" If Epaphroditus acted as a priest as he fulfilled the mission that was given to him, the service of the saints at Philippi is seen also as a priestly exercise in 2:30, where again the word *leitourgia* is used.

J. A. Motyer sums up Paul's feelings well when he writes, "He expresses ungrudging praise when he heaps word upon word in his appreciation of Epaphroditus whom he loves as a brother, acknowledges as a colleague, and welcomes as a minister" (*Philippians*, page 142).

2:26—HIS SORROW AND SENSITIVITY

For he longed after you all, and was full of heaviness, because that ye had heard that he had been sick.

If the commitment of Epaphroditus to the service of God is revealed in verse 25, we are now shown something of his character. What a delightful man he must have been. Once again, the mind of Christ is fully seen in him, as still further he looks not on his own things but on the things of others. It would be very natural to expect those who commissioned him to carry their fellowship to the Apostle to grieve when they heard that such a one had taken seriously ill along the way, but the very thought that the news had reached his home assembly brought great sorrow to Epaphroditus. The words that are used to describe his feelings are very strong in exposing the feelings of his heart. We have already spoken of the word "longed," and its meaning to intensely crave for, to dote upon (see 1:8). The fact that he may have brought concern to the believers at home caused him to feel very strongly for them.

He is also said to have been *"full of heaviness."* The word is only found here and in two other places, where it is used to describe the burden that was upon the Lord Jesus as Calvary approached. Matthew 26:37 and Mark 14:33 both tell us that the Lord was very heavy, the same word that is used here. The burden of Calvary was upon the Saviour, whilst a burden of care was upon Epaphroditus. The Received Text translates the word as "deeply depressed"; such were his feelings for the church that their knowledge of his illness caused him to have another burden besides the illness itself.

2:27—THE SICKNESS

> *For indeed he was sick nigh unto death: but God had mercy on him; and not on him only, but on me also, lest I should have sorrow upon sorrow.*

The Apostle reveals the extent of the illness as one that brought Epaphroditus *"nigh unto death."* He was like others who had hazarded their lives for the name of the Lord Jesus (Acts 15:26). His restoration to health was evidently by divine intervention for *"God had mercy on him."* It must be noted that it was a mercy, not a miracle by which he was raised up. Without going into controversy in our day of looking for an experiential gospel, it would seem at this period in the church's history that this sign gift to Israel had already ceased to function as it once did in early apostolic times. The fact that Paul has to encourage Timothy to *"use a little wine for thy stomach's sake, and thine often infirmities" (1 Tim. 5:23)* is evidence that the gift of the miraculous had ceased. He also says that he left Trophimus at Miletum sick (2 Tim. 4:20). Both these cases are very strange if the power to heal was still available to the Apostle. Let none dare to say that Paul had not the faith to heal in these cases, as certain would propound when healings fail to be effective in their meetings.

The kindness of God not only affected Epaphroditus, but extended to Paul. He realizes that God had mercy on him also *"lest I should have sorrow upon sorrow."* The Lord was not going to add to the burden of imprisonment, the sickness of Epaphroditus. Had Epaphroditus died whilst he was fulfilling his ministry to bring relief to Paul, it would have added to the sorrow he knew.

2:28—HIS SENDING

> *I sent him therefore the more carefully, that, when ye see him again, ye may rejoice, and that I may be the less sorrowful.*

There was a dual purpose in the diligent sending of Epaphroditus back to the saints at Philippi. First of all, it would rejoice their hearts to know that his recovery was complete, and that the severe sickness did not leave him impaired. There was also the effect that it would have on Paul as they knew of his restoration and preservation; this would continue to relieve the grief and heaviness that Paul had endured during the illness.

2:29—HIS STANDING

> *Receive him therefore in the Lord with all gladness; and hold such in reputation:*

Epaphroditus is put at the forefront of those brethren who serve the Lord. Such saints should be heartily received with all joy. We should hold such in reputation, that is, give them the honour that is due to such as are so faithful in the service of God. The word "reputation" (*entimos*) is used of the Lord Jesus in 1 Peter 2:4, 6 and is translated "precious." How precious to any company of believers is a brother who is like Epaphroditus. The word is also used of the centurion's servant in Luke 7:2, who was *"dear unto him."*

2:30—His Selflessness

> *Because for the work of Christ he was nigh unto death, not regarding his life, to supply your lack of service toward me.*

The esteem that he should be held in is emphasised because of what he suffered for the work of Christ, which was carried on with no thought of his own life. Do we not see that the work of Christ exceeds in importance everything else in this life? It matters not the character it takes, all who are engaged in it are promoting the Lord's glory, and this should be recognised by believers. The final clause of the verse would again stress the priestly ministry of bearing the gift, and how that Epaphroditus was representing the whole assembly, who were not able themselves to bring their fellowship to Paul.

3

THE SPIRITUAL MIND

As we approach our present chapter, one feels that here we have the highest truth there is to be known in Christian experience, that is, to be so like Christ this side of heaven that we have reached the goal for which God saved us. We know from many Scriptures that the day will dawn as the rapture takes place, when we are going to be *"conformed to the image of his Son" (Rom. 8:29)*. We shall also *"bear the image of the heavenly" (1 Cor. 15:49)*, when we shall be pure *"even as he is pure" (1 Jn. 3:3)*. This chapter would instil in us the thought that our future destiny should be our present desire.

The chapter has four basic divisions to it:
1. In verses 1-8, we have Paul's past, in which he says, *"I count" (3:8)*.
2. From verse 9-16 it is Paul's present, where the dominant theme is, *"I press" (3:14)*.
3. In verses 17-19, we have Paul's pain as he sees evil men who walk not well and says I *"mark" (3:17)*.
4. The final section brings before us Paul's prospect where we hear him saying I *"look" (3:20)*.

We see Paul:
- Losing (3:1-8)
- Longing (3:9-16)
- Lamenting (3:17-19)
- Looking (3:20-21)

There are also four types of people that he will refer to, and correct the errors that some of them propound:
3:1-8   The Legalist
3:9-16 The Perfectionist
3:17-19 The Sensualist
3:20-21 The Optimist

3:1-8—Paul's Past: Losing

Finally, my brethren, rejoice in the Lord. To write the same things to you, to me indeed is not grievous, but for you it is safe.

Beware of dogs, beware of evil workers, beware of the concision. For we are the circumcision, which worship God in the Spirit, and rejoice in Christ Jesus, and have no confidence in the flesh. Though I might also have confidence in the flesh. If any other man thinketh that he hath whereof he might trust in the flesh, I more: circumcised the eighth day, of the stock of Israel, of the tribe of Benjamin, an Hebrew of the Hebrews; as touching the law, a Pharisee; Concerning zeal, persecuting the church; touching the righteousness which is in the law, blameless.

But what things were gain to me, those I counted loss for Christ. Yea doubtless, and I count all things but loss for the excellency of the knowledge of Christ Jesus my Lord: for whom I have suffered the loss of all things, and do count them but dung, that I may win Christ.

3:1-3—The Exposure of Judaisers

In verses 1-3, the Apostle brings to bear upon the minds of the saints those who would hinder their walk with God, and who would add Jewish practices to Christian doctrine with a view to perfecting the lives of the saints. From the very outset of his missionary activity, these Judaisers were never far behind the movements of the Apostle as they sought to introduce a false brand of Christianity. The epistle to the Galatians was written to address this great problem. These men left Jerusalem as recorded in Acts 15:1, and taught that the work of Calvary was not enough to save a soul, but that circumcision and observance of certain Mosaic laws were needed to complete one's salvation. Paul will have none of their teaching; he exposes them as bringing *"another gospel" (Gal. 1:6-10)*. Such a gospel, rather than adding to the blessing of the redeemed, causes Paul to doubt if there had ever been a true work of grace in them, *"I stand in doubt of you" (Gal. 4:20)*. Nor is he going to leave this teaching unchallenged, *"To whom we gave place by subjection, no, not for an hour; that the truth of the gospel might continue with you" (Gal. 2:5)*. He is even prepared to withstand Peter and Barnabas, who feared the face of man as they were carried away with the dissimulation (Gal. 2:13-14).

3:1—REPETITION OF MINISTRY

> *Finally, my brethren, rejoice in the Lord. To write the same things to you, to me indeed [is] not grievous, but for you [it is] safe.*

The chapter opens with *"finally"*; some would assume that he considers drawing his letter to a close, though such a thought is lacking in this expression. It seems to carry the thought, "for the rest" or "henceforth." The Century Bible puts it as, "It seems to have been used by Paul as a connective when passing on to some new subject. It cannot in itself be taken as a certain indication that he meant to close his letter forthwith" (page 169).

As we have already noticed, he now brings before the saints the highest form of joy. It is to *"rejoice in the Lord."* How thankful we are that this does not depend upon our circumstances; often these can bring us very low and cause us to be dependent upon God. Peter catches something of this as he speaks of the trials that confront the believer. In verses 5-9 of 1 Peter 1, he recalls how believers can rejoice in their salvation, and also in their Saviour, but when it comes to their suffering it is *"though now for a season, if need be, ye are in heaviness through manifold temptations" (v. 6).* The trials a believer is called to pass through are not indefinite; they are always *"for a season."* Nor are they indiscriminate; there must be a reason, *"if need be."* We can be sure that our God, who knows the end from the beginning, *"will not suffer you to be tempted above that ye are able"* (1 Cor. 10:13). One thing is sure, whatever the circumstances we can *"Rejoice in the Lord."* It is a blessed thing to have a measure of appreciation for the purpose of God, and of His desires for us in that purpose, for then we would know that *"all things work together for good to them that love God, to them who are the called according to His purpose" (Rom. 8:28).*

The fact that he writes concerning the *"same things"* does not mean that he is taking the easy way out, by just taking up well trodden paths, either because he has nothing else to say, or because it is a favourite topic in which he is well versed. No, he is thinking of the spiritual welfare of the saints of God. The word "grievous" (*okneros*) is found three times: Matthew 25:26; Romans 12:11 and here. In the two previous passages, it is translated "slothful," and Paul insists that he is not being slothful in writing the same things, but he is being "safe." One brother has said "same things are safe things" (John Douglas). There is a need to fasten the nails of truth with the hammer of repetition. We are living in a day when the majority are looking for something new to bolster their faith, but there is enough in the unchanging Word to keep and bless every believer, if we will but do it. The Apostle Peter would also confirm the strategy of Paul in teaching the same things as he writes, *"This second epistle, beloved, I now write unto you; in both which I stir up your pure minds by way of remembrance"* (2 Pet. 3:1). He would also confirm that the Word of God spoken by the holy prophets, and by the Apostles of our Lord and Saviour, were enough to preserve our lives for God. But how blessed to be put in mind of them, even though they are known (2 Pet. 3:2).

The Apostle Paul knew that the Judaisers were never far away, and with their fair speeches they could beguile the hearts of the simple, so he will remind the saints to be on their guard against them.

3:2—REVEAL THE EVIL MEN

> *Beware of dogs, beware of evil workers, beware of the concision.*

Such is the fear for the safety of the saints that three times over in this verse he warns them to *"beware."* The word literally means "to keep your eyes on." We must be on our guard against false teachers at all times. The Apostle describes them in a threefold way. They are dogs, evil workers, and the concision. Of course, they once taught what was divine in origin, and was a vital necessity to any Jew who desired to maintain fellowship with God. But now these things are of no value to the salvation of a soul and they will only bind a man to Jewish legalism which has proved that it cannot benefit any who would desire to draw nigh to God. The distinct character of Christianity now becomes apparent, that is not a continuation of Judaism, but God's means of delivering men from its bondage. In Galatians 3:24, the Law is set forth as a schoolmaster unto Christ. It taught lessons, but, when Christ came, the classroom was closed; it could teach no more. Those who now sought to continue to use the Mosaic Law as a way of approach to God are now exposed, not as holy men, but as the kind of people that the Law declared would bring defilement.

They are first brought before us as "dogs." That is, their **character** is brought before us. Dogs were unclean beasts, and to be called a dog was very derogatory. Goliath chided David in his approach as one who came against him as if he were a dog (1 Sam. 17:43). David also called to Saul after he spared his life in the cave, as one who came out to destroy *"a dead dog, a flea"* (1 Sam. 24:14). The nation of Israel was warned that they must not *"bring the hire of a whore, or the price of a dog, into the house of the Lord thy God for any vow"* (Deut. 23:18). It is evident that these men had become unclean, and the Christians were not to contaminate themselves in association with them.

They were not only unclean but they were also unrighteous, as they are further defined as being *"evil workers."* This would also describe their **conduct**. They were not like Tychicus, who in Colossians 4:7 is described as a *"fellowservant in the Lord."* Or as others mentioned in the same chapter who are said to be *"fellow-workers unto the kingdom of God"* (4:11). It is also said of Timothy, *"he worketh the work of the Lord, as I also do" (1 Cor. 16:10)*. But there is nothing to recommend in these men; their ministry was destructive, they are said to be *"evil,"* that is, intrinsically worthless—depraved.

The final thing he says of them is not regarding their **conduct** or their **character**, but it involves their **creed**. They are not only unclean and unrighteous, but they are also exposed as being unlawful. They disturbed the believers with their false teaching, insisting on the rite of circumcision being practiced for salvation, the Apostle exposes circumcision as being mere flesh cuttings; that is, it was like the practice of flesh cutting in the religious ceremonies of the heathen as they worshipped idols. We will remember the actions of the prophets of Baal on Mount Carmel; when confronted and challenged by Elijah to prove the validity of their God, they *"cut themselves after their manner with knives and lancets" (1 Kgs. 18:28)*. The Law forbade the Israelites such practice (see Lev. 19:28 and 21:5). Though these men professed high moral ground, they had degenerated into idolatrous flesh cutters; there was no spiritual value in it, merely an act of physical mutilation.

3:3—REASSURING THE SAINTS

> *For we are the circumcision, which worship God in the spirit, and rejoice in Christ Jesus, and have no confidence in the flesh.*

If three things are brought before us to expose the true character of the false teachers in verse 2, Paul now adds three blessed truths that will establish the saints in their faith. He brings before them:

THE SPIRITUAL MIND

THE REALITY OF THEIR POSITION

"We are the circumcision, which worship God in the Spirit."
How full this statement is, and what a contrast to the teachings of the Judaisers.

The Apostle affirms that we are not mere flesh cutters, but we are *"the circumcision."* He makes no room for any other form of circumcision but that which is spiritual in nature. The Judaisers would insist on the Law of Moses (Acts 15:1) as the ground for their doctrine; the Apostle Paul will take us back to the origins of circumcision, which was 430 years before the Law was given (Gal. 3:17). We have entered by faith into the good of all that was covenanted to Abraham in Genesis 17, and linked to that covenant was the sign of circumcision:

> *"In whom also ye are circumcised with the circumcision made without hands, in putting off the body of the sins of the flesh by the circumcision of Christ: Buried with Him in baptism, wherein also ye are risen with Him through the faith of the operation of God, who hath raised Him from the dead. And you, being dead in your sins and the uncircumcision of your flesh hath He quickened together with Him, having forgiven you all trespasses"*
> —Colossians 2:11-13

"When Paul says 'we are the circumcision' he is claiming for himself and for the Philippians the privilege of being the undoubted heirs of this age-long divine program of salvation" (Motyer, page 149).

Again, he links this circumcision with the true worship of God. Twice over in the Abrahamic covenant, God said He would be a God unto them (Gen. 17:7-8). We are now encouraged as to the true character of our worship. We are not looking to the many ceremonies of Mosaic Law and ordinances; our worship is in the Spirit. The Lord Jesus taught the Samaritan woman that the time had now arrived when worship was not in a place, be that Jerusalem for the Jew, or Mount Gerizim for the Samaritan, but it must be in spirit and in truth. We are told that this is the happy position of all those saved by grace.

REJOICING IN CHRIST JESUS

The second point that Paul touches is in what we boast or glory, for that is the thought behind the word "rejoice." If the Jewish adherents boasted and gloried in the Law, how blessed to be able to lift our eyes far above it, finding all our glorying in the blessed Man who has delivered us from the curse of the Law.

REJECTION OF THE FLESH

Again, the Apostle embraces all the believers with him in the renunciation of the flesh. We have already drawn attention to the word "confidence," to be persuaded, trust. To turn again to Jewish observances would have made much of the flesh, and would have produced the condition of Galatians 3:3, "*Are ye so foolish? Having begun in the Spirit, are ye now made perfect by the flesh?*" In the following verses Paul renounces all confidence in the flesh, be it for religious observance or moral character.

3:4-8—HIS EXAMPLE AS A JEW

> *Though I might also have confidence in the flesh. If any other man thinketh that he hath whereof he might trust in the flesh, I more: Circumcised the eighth day, of the stock of Israel, [of] the tribe of Benjamin, an Hebrew of the Hebrews; as touching the law, a Pharisee; Concerning zeal, persecuting the church; touching the righteousness which is in the law, blameless. But what things were gain to me, those I counted loss for Christ. Yea doubtless, and I count all things [but] loss for the excellency of the knowledge of Christ Jesus my Lord: for whom I have suffered the loss of all things, and do count them [but] dung, that I may win Christ,*

If there needs to be any qualification regarding the futility of the Law to give acceptance with God, then Paul can provide it. He will now scan over his life, a life that was dedicated to a strict adherence of all that the Mosaic Law spoke of. He will produce seven features of his former life as a Jew, all profiting him nothing as far as finding acceptance with God.

As he challenges the teachings of the Judaisers, it is as if he throws down the gauntlet of personal righteousness to expose their attempts to seduce the believers from the truth. His former life far outstripped any of his nation in attempting to find acceptance with God by legal observance. There was ground to have confidence in the flesh if there was any value in it. In fact, he has more cause than others to "think" that his activities as a Jew exceeded all that these Jewish teachers could set forth. The word "think" means, to seem, to appear, to seem to one's self, to form an estimate or opinion which may be right (John 5:39; Acts 15:28; 1 Cor. 4:9; 1 Cor. 7:40), but which may be wrong (Matt. 6:7; Mark 6:49; John 16:2) (*Critical Concordance*, E. W. Bullinger). It is evident that Paul had come to a right estimate of the activity of the flesh, whereas these Judaisers had missed the mark. He traces the seven steps of religious achievement in verses 5 and 6.

3:5—The Token of the Covenant

> *Circumcised the eighth day, of the stock of Israel, [of] the tribe of Benjamin, an Hebrew of the Hebrews; as touching the law, a Pharisee;*

The men who originally were circumcised, Abraham, Ishmael, and all the men born in his house, as well as those bought with money, were all outside the eight day limitation. Abraham was 99 and Ishmael 13 when they obeyed God. There would be many who passed through the wilderness during the journey to the Promised Land who were not circumcised. Those who were born in the wilderness were circumcised at Gilgal. I suppose they typify the true character of the wilderness experience of Israel, when the flesh was not dealt with. Moses also failed to circumcise his firstborn and it caused the Lord to act against him. It is evident that his wife,

Zipporah, was not in sympathy with the truth, but before God could use Moses, the will of God had to be fulfilled. There would also be Gentile proselytes who would not know circumcision until they were converted to Judaism. Paul stands apart from all such. He was circumcised according to the covenant on the eighth day (Gen. 17:10-12). The eighth day is the day linked with a new beginning; such is the resurrection morn. Perhaps God's decree to circumcise all male children on this day was to teach that, through the covenant of Genesis 17, they would be entering into a new life.

HIS TITLE OF HONOUR

Paul counted it no small thing to have his origins in the stock of Israel. His appreciation of what that nation is to God is graphically portrayed in Romans 9:3-5, where he speaks of the **people**—Israelites; their **prospect** as the adoption; knowing the **presence** of God as His glory is among them; the **pattern** and **privilege** that belonged to them in the covenants and the giving of the Law and the service of God; he knows that the **promises** are bound up in Israel, and he delights in the **parentage** *"whose are the fathers"*; finally, they have the **person** of Christ in all His glory as *"God over all,"* and *"blessed for ever."* What an honour to be an Israelite!

HIS TRIBE WITHIN THE NATION

Paul was not like those who could not reckon their genealogy, as recorded in Ezra 2:61-63. These people, because of their association with Babylon, could not prove that they belonged to the tribe of Levi and, as a result, they were put away from the priesthood as being polluted. There are many Jews today who would not be able to prove which tribe they descended from. Paul had no doubts; he belonged to the tribe of Benjamin, Jacob's youngest son by Rachel. It was after Jacob had returned to the land, and was told by God to go up to Bethel (Gen. 35), that Benjamin was born. It is as if, being in the will of God, he knows the blessing of God for it. The birth of Benjamin caused the death of his mother, and she cried out in departing, Ben-oni—son of my sorrow. His father reversed her

THE SPIRITUAL MIND

choice, calling him Benjamin, son of my right hand. Benjamin is a lovely picture of Christ, who began as the Man of sorrows, but became the Son of the right hand as He was exalted by the Father.

It is fitting that God called Paul, who came from this tribe. There is no writer in the New Testament who speaks as vividly as Paul on the three subjects his fore-father was linked with. Paul delights to speak of the house of God and sees it as the place where the Lord's honour dwelleth. 1 Timothy 3:15-4:7 brings before us just one aspect of that which Paul loves to dwell on. In Genesis 35:7 the Lord's presence is known at Bethel, whilst in verse 14 we have the stone of testimony, the drink offering of joy, and the oil poured on it, a fitting emblem of the power of the Spirit. These are lovely types of the present character of the church of God. All are beautifully seen in 1 Timothy 3. I notice too, that, when Jacob was called to go up to Bethel, adjustments had to be made in the house, as they were bidden to *"Put away the strange gods that are among you, and be clean, and change your garments" (Gen. 35:2)*. Perhaps there is something of this in Paul's mind when he says, *"how thou oughtest to behave thyself in the house of God, which is the church of the living God, the pillar and ground of the truth" (1 Tim. 3:15).*

He also loves to dwell on the Lord Jesus in his epistles, and I am sure that we could draw upon many passages where the Lord Jesus is seen as the man of sorrows. Paul also makes much of Christ at the right hand of God. He is a true son of Benjamin.

HIS TONGUE—A HEBREW

When the Apostle recalls his parentage, he knows that they were pure and unmixed in their descent. Not only were they of the stock of Israel, but they were also Hebrew in the language that they spoke. He did not come from an Hellenistic family that had Greek culture as its background, and spoke Greek as its first language. The prime thought behind being *"an Hebrew of the Hebrews"* is the fact that he was raised in the Hebrew language, and that the family maintained Hebrew customs. At his conversion, the Lord Jesus spoke to him in the Hebrew tongue and said, *"Saul, Saul, why persecutest thou me?"*

(Acts 26:14). It was in the *"Hebrew tongue" (Acts 21:40)* that Paul addressed his fellow-countrymen after the uproar in the temple which led to his captivity and now found him in the prison cell in Rome. That there was a difference between the Hebrew and Hellenistic Jews is recorded for us in Acts 6 when there arose a murmuring of the Grecians against the Hebrews (v. 1). There were very definite cultural differences that caused this early dispute in the church, where Hebrew speaking believers seem to have been favoured. Paul links himself with this favoured clan; he will boast of his pure links with the nation.

His Teaching—A Pharisee

Up to this point Paul has touched on four things as to his birth: he now draws out three things in relation to his life:
 i. His Sect—a Pharisee;
 ii. His Service—zealous persecution;
 iii. His Standing—righteous and blameless.

His links with the Pharisees are based not so much on his belonging to that sect, nor on his father also being a Pharisee (Acts 23:6). It is rather that he abode by the traditions that marked them in their strict adherence to the Law, *"as touching the Law, a Pharisee."* Did not the Judaisers seek to make the Christians observers of the Law? The Apostle will boast that he himself endeavoured to walk in its ways, but it was of no value to him for salvation.

The word Pharisee comes from the Hebrew word *Perushim*, the separated (*Critical Concordance*, E. W. Bullinger). "As a sect, they seem to have arisen after the captivity with a desire to preserve the purity of the nation that, before the captivity, was always slipping into idolatry. To know the Law, to have the most minute and accurate acquaintance with it, was, according to Josephus, the distinguishing aim and ambition of the Pharisees" (*Imperial Bible Dictionary*). They are called by Paul *"the most straitest sect of our religion" (Acts 26:5).* In the same passage, he says how he lived by their decrees. This would correspond with his claim here that, as touching the law, he lived as a Pharisee.

3:6—His Testimony

Concerning zeal, persecuting the church; touching the righteousness which is in the law, blameless.

The testimony regarding his former life as a Pharisee is twofold:

His Loyal Opposition
The Pharisees, from the outset of the Lord's ministry, moved in opposition to it. They also were the chief instigators of His crucifixion and rejection by the people. As soon as the gospel and the name of Christ were spread abroad after His resurrection, they were again instrumental in seeking to eradicate Christianity from the land. It was with their sanction that Saul oversaw the stoning of Stephen and, emboldened by this, in spite of the conviction of the Spirit as goads to his conscience, he kicked against them as a stubborn mule. On receiving letters from the Pharisees, he continued to cause havoc to the church. Well might he boast of his loyal opposition to a salvation found in Christ alone, as he followed the dictates of his superiors.

His Legal Observance
His manner of life was consistent with his religious zeal. It was like the Pharisee spoken of in the parable of Luke 18:11-12. It is evident that as a group they were full of pride as to the outward observance of the Law. It is noticeable that in the parable the man had such a high estimation of himself, that he put himself in the place of God, and was judge and jury of his own attainments, for he prayed *"thus with **himself**, God, I thank thee, that I am not as other men are" (v. 11);* he was to himself, **God**. He was like the certain ruler of Luke 18:18-21, who would glory in his observance of the Law. It took the probing of the Lord Jesus to expose his moral failure, and for him to be brought low as one who, offending in one point, is guilty of all (Jas. 2:10). The Lord proved this man's guilt by asking him to *"sell all that thou hast, and distribute unto the poor" (Luke 18:22).*

He failed in the last commandment, *"Thou shalt not covet."* His heart was exposed and, like Adam before him, he must go out from the presence of the Lord.

As a Christian, Paul is going to recognise the folly of his Pharisaical days, and he will confess, *"that in me (that is, in my flesh), dwelleth no good thing" (Rom. 7:18).* He is also going to acknowledge that what he might boast in as a Pharisee caused him only grief as a child of God, and should have debarred him from holding such high office among the saints as an Apostle. *"I am the least of the apostles, that am not meet to be called an apostle, because I persecuted the church of God" (1 Cor. 15:9).* It is interesting that the zeal marked him before his conversion continued after it. There are many who show a remarkable energy in propagating false doctrine when linked to a cult, but, on finding Christ, fail to have the same desires in bringing sinners to the Saviour.

3:7—THE TRANSFORMATION OF HIS THOUGHTS

But what things were gain to me, those I counted loss for Christ.

Paul has been taking account of his life like a book-keeper. Having added up those things that were seen as virtues under Judaism, he now considers the loss column. In it we see the transformation that has taken place in his life, as he reckons those same things now of no value in Christ. There is no doubt that, as far as this world was concerned, all that marked him under Judaism was to his advantage—he calls them *"gains"*; he also calls them *"things."* He has come face to face with a person, and what are things compared to Him? It is a sad fact that we can be taken up with many things and attainments, and lose sight of the Lord Jesus, but Paul lost sight of everything else since he got a glimpse of Christ.

> "Turn your eyes upon Jesus,
> Look full in his wonderful face,
> And the things of earth will grow strangely dim
> In the light of his glory and grace."

All these things were *"counted"* loss by Paul. There are six references to the word throughout the epistle.
   1. In chapter 2:3, it is a call to the *Saints* to *esteem* other better than themselves
   2. The *Saviour* is the subject of 2:6, who *thought* it not robbery to be equal with God
   3. When we look at chapter 2:25, the background is the *Servant*, Epaphroditus, whom Paul *supposes* it necessary to send back to Philippi
   4. We now find the word three times in these two verses 7-8, as Paul *counts* his past *Service* of no value as regards his acceptance with God

The word "count" is in the perfect tense. Wuest says it "speaks of a process completed in past time having present results" (*Philippians*, page 90). Whereas the word "gain" is a plural word embracing all that Paul once held dear, the word "loss" is in the singular. It brings before us that everything has been gathered up and thrown overboard, for it carries the thought of a loss at sea. I remember hearing someone say many years ago, that Paul then put up the sign, "No Fishing." The root of both words, "gain" and "loss" is found in Matthew 16:26 where the Lord Jesus says, *"For what is a man profited, if he shall gain the whole world, and lose his own soul?"* The Apostle has made his choice; all that was gain to him he will lose, that he might be saved.

There is something that has caused Paul to make such a choice. He is not renouncing everything that he might take a stoical stand against all that this world offers; no, but he has found One that surpasses all the glory of this world, and his heart is now full of Christ.

3:8—THE TOTALITY OF HIS LOSS

> *Yea doubtless, and I count all things [but] loss for the excellency of the knowledge of Christ Jesus my Lord: for whom I have suffered the loss of all things, and do count them [but] dung, that I may win Christ,*

PHILIPPIANS: THE MIND OF CHRIST

When it comes to what Paul is prepared to count loss, there is nothing treasured that he would want to hold back. He is emphatic in his desires. If one might ask, "What things, Paul?" he would immediately reply, **"All things."** With Paul, there were no regrets, no remorse. That which he had found in Christ caused everything else to lose its appeal. All that would have meant much to an orthodox Jew has no value compared to all that there is in Christ.

It is interesting how Paul begins to speak of the totality of his loss, when he says, *"Yea, doubtless."* I am thankful to the Lord for giving me a love for words, especially those the Holy Spirit uses. I discerned many years ago that Greek expositors usually came to their conclusion as to the meaning of a word by its usage in the New Testament. This caused me to take an interest in the likes of the Wigram concordance, where every use of a Greek word is set out. The present editions, with a record of how many times a word is used and the root from which it comes, are a great help in ascertaining the mind of God. The present word *menounge* occurs but four times. It is found in Luke 11:28 where the Lord would pronounce a blessing on those who are **obedient** to the Word of God, *"Yea rather (menounge), blessed are they that hear the Word of God, and keep it."* In the book of Romans, Paul uses it on two occasions: Romans 9:20, where he exposes the **opposition** of some to God, *"Nay but (menounge), O man, who art thou that repliest against God?"* Also, in chapter 10:18, when Paul is speaking of the **outreach** of the gospel he says, *"Yes verily (menounge), their sound went into all the earth."* In our present passage, he will leave no **obstacle** in the way of his appreciation of Christ.

We noticed in verse 7 that the words *"I counted"* were in the perfect tense, indicating an event in the past that still holds good. His use of the word in this verse is in the present tense; "what he has done in the past he continues to do" (Wuest). How blessed when all that we put away for Christ in a former day, we still have no longing for. Dear believer, do not lose your love for Christ, and if God caused you to see something in a former day as of no value to your Christian life, then remember, it will still be of no value now. Like Paul, count it a loss.

There was something supreme to Paul that surpassed anything he might have obtained through Judaism. There was something that far outshone the legal observance of the Law. It was He of whom the Law spake, *"Christ Jesus my Lord."* The word "excellency" has the thought of that which is better. How often is Christ seen as better in the Hebrew epistle! For that which surpasses and is supreme, it is little wonder that Paul will count all a loss when he has found Him who is *"altogether lovely" (Song 5:16).* The one who surpasses and is supremely better than all else in which he sought to find acceptance with God, he calls *"my Lord."* This is the only occasion that Paul speaks of the Lord Jesus as *"my Lord."* He often uses the expression *"my God."* Now having met the resurrected Christ on the Damascus road, he can say like Thomas when he saw Him in resurrection, *"My Lord and my God" (John 20:28).*

Who is this one for whom he will cast all his attainments aside? It is *"Christ Jesus my Lord."* In this beautiful title of the Lord Jesus is found all the hopes of the Jews based on the promises made to them, as Jehovah revealed Him as the one in whom those promises would be realized.

As "Christ" we are brought face to face with the anointed one; He is the one all Israel hoped for to bring in the promises of God. John the Baptist confessed to men that he was not *"the Christ" (John 1:20; 3:28).* The Samaritan woman knew that *"Messias cometh, which is called Christ" (John 4:25),* that the Christ was the Messiah. In His trial and crucifixion the Lord was mocked as the Christ, but when put to the test on hearing the voice of adjuration (Matt. 26:63; Lev. 5:1), He must confess in the affirmative, *"Thou sayest,"* or *"Thou hast said."* The record is true, He is the fulfilment of all that Israel hoped for, and Paul has found *"the Christ."*

The Messiah, Christ, is also Jesus. We need to go no further than Matthew 1:21 to discover what this meant to Paul. Not only is He the fulfilment of all Jehovah's promises, but He is also "the Saviour." The angelic message, bringing assurance to Joseph regarding the condition of Mary, also revealed by what name He should be called, and the reason for it, *"Thou shalt call his name JESUS, for he shall save his people from their sins."* His people are of course Israel in the context of Matthew's gospel. His name simply means "Jehovah the Saviour." It is Jehovah Himself who has come down to save His people. The name Jesus corresponds to the name Joshua, and we can remember how, in the Old Testament, the nation was dependent upon a Joshua to bring them into the promised land. So we now find another Joshua is needed, not only to bring them in, but also to establish their place in it. Could I remind my readers that Paul used the full title of our Lord Jesus Christ? There are many today and, sadly, even among expositors, who are very slipshod and minimize the glory of the Son of God by referring to Him only as Jesus. It is a favoured appellation of many in the charismatic movement, for what reason, it leaves me mystified. Let His names that are Spirit-taught even to His brethren and the Apostles, be those we love to use as we acknowledge the glory of His person, the Lord Jesus Christ. The Lord is never **spoken to** directly in the gospels as "Jesus" except by demons or those who were possessed by them. Otherwise He is only **spoken of** as "Jesus" in reference to Him, but never addressed as such (Matt. 21:11; 27:17, 22).

When we come to His title as "Lord," it is His sovereignty that is set forth. It is evident that Paul recognised the place God had given Him, and bowed to His sovereignty and would confess, He is "my" Lord. This would mean that every claim of the Lord Jesus, all He asked from His own, was put into practice by the Apostle. One day He will be manifested as *"Lord of lords" (Rev. 19:16),* and then *"every knee will bow and confess that he is Lord, to the glory of God the Father" (Phil. 2:11).*

Paul has come to the "knowledge" of such a one, as W. E. Vine expresses it, "Ginosko frequently indicates a relation between the person knowing and the object known; in this respect, what is known is of value or importance to the one who knows, and hence the establishment of the relationship" (Vine, *Expository Dictionary*). Ever since meeting with the Lord Jesus on the Damascus road when the cry of "Lord" first came from his lips, the intimacy of his knowledge of Christ caused Paul to be subject to His claims. We shall see as we continue to peruse these verses that the Damascus road experience was not enough for Paul. He wanted the seed to produce a hundred-fold, and he wanted to know the Lord in a greater way until he was just like Him. Many of us are content with our initial salvation experience and seem to go no further in our quest to appreciate the man who saved us.

The final clauses of the verse would again express Paul's thoughts toward those things that a religious Jew would have been proud of; for Christ's sake, he suffers the loss of all these things. The words "suffered loss" are but one word in the Greek text, and signify to "cast away." It is used by the Lord in Luke 9:25, *"For what is a man advantaged, if he gain the whole world, and lose himself, or be cast away."* The world that Judaism offered has lost its charm, and he has cast it away from himself. The popularity, prestige and prospects that it offered, Paul now counts as dung. What was a gain in the eyes of men in verse 7 has now become loathsome to him. He places himself before the Judgement Seat of Christ, where those things that have been of no value to further the glory of God will be burnt up, and he will "suffer loss"—the same word again as in this verse. Paul would rather suffer loss here, than in the day when rewards are given to those who have served the Lord according to His Word.

There is a gain that far surpasses that which men esteem highly; that gain is Christ, and Paul will renounce everything that he might win Christ. The word "win" is the word "to gain." To die and be with Christ is a gain in chapter 1:21. Now it is not a gain in death, but a gain in life.

1:21   It is a gain in the future, *destined*
3:7   A gain *despised*
3:8   A gain *desired*

3:9-16—Paul's Present: Longing

And be found in him, not having mine own righteousness, which is of the law, but that which is through the faith of Christ, the righteousness which is of God by faith: That I may know Him, and the power of His resurrection, and the fellowship of His sufferings, being made conformable unto His death; if by any means I might attain unto the resurrection of the dead.

Not as though I had already attained, either were already perfect: but I follow after, if that I may apprehend that for which also I am apprehended of Christ Jesus. Brethren, I count not myself to have apprehended: but this one thing I do, forgetting those things which are behind, and reaching forth unto those things which are before, I press toward the mark for the prize of the high calling of God in Christ Jesus.

Let us therefore, as many as be perfect, be thus minded: and if in any thing ye be otherwise minded, God shall reveal even this unto you. Nevertheless, whereto we have already attained, let us walk by the same rule, let us mind the same thing.

3:9-16—THE EXERCISE OF HIS HEART

If Paul has dealt with his past in the former verses, he now speaks of his present desires. We are approaching what I consider possibly the highest truth in the Word of God, that is, to endeavour to be like Christ this side of the Rapture. I recently heard a brother in Christ speak scathingly of, "doctrine and church practice; as long as you love your fellow Christian that is all that matters." Beloved, doctrine and church practice are vital to every believer, for if I do not know the mind of God, I cannot do it. The Lord has not left these things on the page of Scripture for me to ignore them or to treat them with contempt. Obedience to the revealed will of God is a proof of our love for Him (John 14:23-24). Though we are thankful for all that God has revealed, nevertheless one thing rises above all else; it is to be like Christ.

There are many beautiful things to consider in the following verses. Attention has already been drawn to Old Testament characters illustrated in these verses, to which others could be added. It is also good to see glimpses of the epistles throughout verses 9 and 10.

In verse 9, the truth of the book of Romans is set forth. In that declaration of the doctrine of the gospel, it is clearly demonstrated that no righteousness of man can avail to save a soul. It must be by the righteousness of God in Christ. The opening expression sums up the truth of Colossians, where Christ is the theme of the book. The book of Ephesians is the book of the power displayed in a resurrected man (Eph. 1:19-20), as seen here in verse 9. Peter in his first epistle dwells on the fact that the sufferings that the believers are passing through give them fellowship with the Lord's sufferings. And finally, to be *"made conformable to his death"* is brought before us in the book of Galatians. As the sufferings of Christ dominate every chapter of 1 Peter, so the death of Christ is found in every chapter of Galatians. If we desire, as Paul did, to be like Christ in everything, then a study of the epistles and a desire to practice them will provide fruit for God.

As we take a closer look at these verses, we will find that Paul wants a personal experience of the positional truth into which God has brought him.

There are two things that Paul brings before us in verse 9; he desires a place in Him and a position enjoyed through Him.

3:9—A Place in Christ

> *And be found in him, not having mine own righteousness, which is of the law, but that which is through the faith of Christ, the righteousness which is of God by faith:*

Every believer is *"in Christ Jesus."* This is a dispensational term and is the dominant theme of Paul's writings. The expressions *"in Christ," "in Christ Jesus," "in the Lord," "in Him"* occur over one hundred times in his writings, and the only epistle where this blessed truth is not found is that of Titus. As far as Old Testament believers are concerned, they are said to *"be Christ's,"* but are not said to be "in Christ" (see 1 Cor. 15:23).

The mighty Apostle has come to know the unique position of those who form the church, as it reveals the closeness of the relationship that we now enjoy, for "In the person of the Son we are as near as He."

These expressions are not found in the epistle to the Hebrews where the hopes that have been promised to Israel are unveiled and anticipated. The fulfilment of those promises is seen in the expectation of the Kingdom, where Christ will sit on His throne as God in chapter 1:8 and 9; and will establish God's initial purpose as seen in Genesis 1:26, that a man will govern this world, Hebrews 2 unfolds the purpose of God to see that the second man the Lord Jesus will take the responsibility of bringing this to pass. In chapters 3 and 4 the promised rest that has not been enjoyed since Genesis 2:1 will be introduced; and the promises to the Patriarchs of a land will be enjoyed, as seen in chapter 11:8-16. The present enjoyment of the nearness of the saints as the church of this dispensation is not the teaching of this very precious book. It must be added that Peter and John make scant use of these terms that Paul loves to use, but as it was given to Paul to make known the truth of the church (Eph. 3), it is fitting that he will dwell on the present place of the Church.

In this verse, Paul is once again renouncing all that he once gloried in to find acceptance with God. He no longer desires to trust in his family record, or in his faithful adherence to the many tenets of Jewish Law. There is only one place where he wants to be found, and that is *"in Him."*

The word "found" carries the thought of finding by search or by accident, but when found it is a concrete discovery that cannot be denied. Figuratively it means "to gain perception or insight" (Kittel). On the way into Damascus, the then Saul of Tarsus had a vision unsought. It revealed the Lord Jesus to him, and as a result Judaism, like himself, fell to the ground, and he now wants no other place than that into which he has come, into the security and safety of being *"in Him."*

Robert Rainy on Philippians in the *Expositor* series writes concerning this, "A similar remark applies to the expression 'In Christ' so frequently occurring in the Pauline writings. This

THE SPIRITUAL MIND

is usually explained by saying that the Apostle sets before us Christ as the sphere of his spiritual being—in whom he lived and moved—never out of relation to Him, and not so related to any other. Such explanations are true and good: only we may say that the pregnant strength of the expression seems to be weakened even by the best explanations. The relation in view is too wonderful ever to be adequately described. The union between Christ and His church, between Christ and the believing man, is a mystery; and, like all objects of faith, it is dimly apprehended by us for the present" (*Philippians*, page 212).

3:9—A POSITION THROUGH HIM

> *And be found in him, not having mine own righteousness, which is of the law, but that which is through the faith of Christ, the righteousness which is of God by faith:*

The thought of being *"found in Him"* leads the Apostle to think of the moral standing this gives him in the sight of God. The ground of righteousness he now enjoys is vastly different from that known in Judaism. What a contrast there is between them. The former was of self, *"mine own righteousness"*: the latter is of God. The first found itself in the Law, whereas this is of Christ. Again, all that was of self and the Law was by works: this righteousness is by faith. The end results are far greater than anything he could have gained in his former manner of living. This righteousness has for its *source*, God. The closing expression of the verse simply states *"which is of God."* This righteousness is not God's righteousness, but it is that which comes from Him. It is that which is imputed to Abraham (Rom. 4:3), and that David speaks of as being "blessed." The blessing is enjoyed in the knowledge that our sins have been covered, and that *"the Lord will not impute sin"* (Rom. 4:7-8).

If the source is God, it is **secured** by faith, and that faith looks to another—Christ, whom *"he hath made him to be sin for us, who knew no sin; that we might be made the righteousness of God in him"* (2 Cor. 5:21). This is emphasised in Romans 10:9-10, where

139

the *"righteousness which is of faith"* (v. 6) is a confession of His person and a belief in His resurrection, resulting in *"For with the heart man believeth unto righteousness."* How thankful we are for the word of faith that was preached, and the blessing of righteousness that it has brought to us.

If the source of this righteousness is God, and it is secured by faith, we are thankful it is **sealed and safeguarded** by the work of Christ. *"To declare ... at this time his righteousness: that he might be just, and the justifier of him which believeth in Jesus"* (Rom. 3:26) can only be enjoyed by those who have put their faith in the one *"Whom God hath set forth to be a propitiation through faith in his blood, to declare his righteousness for the remission of sins that are past"* (v. 25). Our present standing of righteousness is based on the reality of that which God accepts in the work of His Son.

3:10—A Person to Know

> *That I may know him, and the power of his resurrection, and the fellowship of his sufferings, being made conformable unto his death;*

Having expressed a desire to be found in Him, that is to enter into the fulness of the positional truth that God has brought him to, he now expresses how he would long to have a deeper appreciation of the person and work of Christ. It is plain to see that he begins with a man on the throne and ends with a man in resurrection. The Apostle, as do we all, came to know Christ as an exalted man; he was not acquainted with His walk on earth. In these verses, he wants to become identified with Him in the deep sufferings He passed through, and then to be linked to Him, on this side of eternity, in resurrection life.

The word "to know" (*ginosko*) means "to be taking in knowledge, to come to know, recognise, understand" (W. E. Vine). He is not content with the knowledge he had of Christ the day he was saved. He wants a deeper experience of His person. It is not merely an intellectual conviction regarding

Christ, but a personal appreciation of all that is found in His blessed person. One has said, "For the knowledge here spoken of is a personal knowledge gained, not by hearing or reading, but by direct personal communion with the Lord" (*Pulpit Commentary, Philippians*, page 113). May we desire such communion, so that we also can attain to knowing Him.

A Power to Experience

Again, the Apostle Paul wanted to experience in his life the power that raised the Lord Jesus from the dead—the power that is inherent in all persons of the Godhead, for all were involved in the resurrection of the Lord Jesus (see John 10:17-18; Acts 2:24; 1 Pet. 3:18). He desires that all believers will enter into the good of it in Ephesians 1:19-22. Do we need power for Christian living? Do we feel weak, always being overcome by evil? Well, here is a power that God wants us to know is at our disposal. That dynamic power which brought a man out of the realm of death and took Him to the highest place in the universe, that same power is available to all God's children. The Ephesian epistle speaks much of this power. In chapter 1, it is a power to live; in chapter 3:7, it is a power to serve; in chapter 3:16, it is by this power that the inner man is strengthened. The knowledge that this power is available to us will encourage us to supplicate the throne of God (3:20). This is the power that will enable us to stand against every onslaught of the devil (6:10). Paul knew much about this power; now he longs to feel the effects of it.

A Pain to Endure

Coming now from the man in the glory, exalted there by the Father's power, he speaks of having fellowship in the deep sufferings that the Lord Jesus passed through.

Three times in this epistle Paul spoke of fellowship, a word that means, to have in common, a sharing:

In chapter 1:5, it is fellowship with the **Servant in his Ministry**. As we noticed when expounding that verse, the generous nature of the assembly toward Paul made them partakers with him in the great work of God to which he was called.

PHILIPPIANS: THE MIND OF CHRIST

In chapter 2:1, it is fellowship with the **Spirit, seen in the Unity** of saints. Again, attention has been drawn to the central theme of Paul's ministry to them: to walk in unity.

Here in chapter 3:10, it is fellowship with Christ's **Sufferings and Agony,** which sufferings He endured on account of His rejection. The Apostle's desire to be like Christ in everything causes him to know that this is no easy path, and there are no short-cuts to its goal. To attain the out-resurrection he must be completely identified with the Lord Jesus, and this will involve (to have in common, to share in) the sufferings He endured here.

A Passion to be Conformed to

The Apostle Paul knows that to attain to being like Christ here in this present world, he is going to have to finish with the world in everything. Not only must he finish with it, but he must be identified with the Lord Jesus in His death, for His death is God's only remedy to eradicate evil from the world. For the life of the believer to be completely free from the evil that would keep us from being like Christ this side of glory, is to be so linked with the death of Christ that that evil is finally judged and we are delivered from it. The word "conformable" is a compound word formed by the preposition *"sun"* and *"morphee." Sun* indicates we are one with, and as we saw in chapter 2 where the Lord Jesus is in the "form" of God, and took the "form" of a servant, *morphee* means to be completely like. Vine says the word here is "in the passive participle of the verb, 'becoming conformed'." As in all his desires to attain to this conformity, it is something he has not reached as yet.

The doctrinal truth of what is taught here is the constant burden of Paul's ministry. The teaching of Romans 6, that we should not continue in sin, is answered by the fact that *"our old man is crucified with Christ,"* and dead men cannot sin. His answer to those who would set forth the Law as a means of perfecting man is seen in Galatians, all that Paul can propound to accomplish it is *"I am crucified with Christ" (Gal. 2:20).* Speaking to those who would desire the rudiments of the world in Colossians, he reminds the saints that they are *"dead and your life is hid with Christ in God" (Col. 3:3).* Paul is looking for far more than a doctrinal thesis; he wants to know it experientially, for it to be put into practice, and for him to know it as a transforming power in his life.

3:11—A Prospect to be Enjoyed

> *If by any means I might attain unto the resurrection of the dead.*

The reason Paul desired to have a personal identification with Christ, to be associated with Him in His humiliation and crucifixion, is that he might attain to the greatest experience of Christian living: to be, this side of resurrection, what he will be after the coming of the Lord—perfect!

Though many expositors link the verse with the future resurrection of believers at the coming of the Lord Jesus, to me they have missed the whole point of what Paul is expressing in this text. John MacArthur, to get around a difficulty with this view, says "The Greek phrase the NASB translates **'in order that'**, actually reads 'if somehow'. However, that does not express doubt on Paul's part, but rather humility. Paul's sense of unworthiness never left him" (*Philippians*, page 240). Alex Motyer who interprets the verse in the same way—that of the future resurrection, says, "We could be misled by *'if possible'*, which seems to suggest that, after all, Paul was not sure of final salvation. If this verse meant this, it would not only be discordant with verse 9, but flatly contradict 1:23, and many other passages in Paul's writings. Yet this verse does express uncertainty, not of the goal but of the way. The resurrection is certain; the intervening events are uncertain" (*Philippians*, page 170). The value of the written ministry of these brethren in Christ is unquestionable, even though we have divergent views on this verse.

The context of verses 9-16 must bring verse 11 within the orbit of the believer's present, not future, experience. He is longing to be, this side of resurrection, what he will be at the coming of the Lord Jesus, to be so conformed to Christ here and now, that he will enjoy the power and blessedness of a victorious life where sin will not dominate him. This is the answer to the problems expressed in Romans 7, *"for what I would, that do I not; but what I hate, that do I" (v. 15)*. The Apostle feels the wretchedness of his own flesh and cries out, *"For I know that in me (that is, in my flesh,) dwelleth no good thing" (v. 18)*. Again, in verse 24 he exclaims, *"Oh wretched man that I am! Who shall deliver me from the body of this death?"* The only deliverance the believer will know is in the resurrection, when the seat of the problem, the body, will be changed. The desire of Paul's heart is to experience it this side of that glorious day and, "if possible" to live a resurrection life whilst waiting for the Rapture. He wants to be so like Christ here and now that he will never sin again.

He says *"If by any means I might attain unto."* As the good brethren quoted agree, as far as those who have died in Christ are concerned, their destiny is secure. That resurrection is dependent on the work of the Lord Jesus, and in no way rests upon the meritorious efforts of Christians to attain to it. The phrase *"might attain unto"* carries the thought of to reach, to arrive at. It is used:

- of people arriving at a destination (Acts 16:1; 18:19, 24; 20:15; 25:13);
- of the twelve tribes in their service before God in the expectation of the arriving of the messianic hope (Acts 26:7);
- also of the ministry of the Word of God through the gifts provided by the risen head, causing all believers to arrive at *"the unity of the faith" (Eph. 4:13)*.
- The ultimate purpose of Israel's journeys through the wilderness was for believers of the present church age, because God ordered all things for us *"upon whom the ends of the world* [age] *are come" (1 Cor. 10:11)*.
- The Apostle Paul rebukes the Corinthian church for their carelessness with divine revelation as to their church gatherings, as if God had revealed truth to them alone and not through apostolic men, and not seen in

other churches. *"What? came the Word of God out from you? or came it unto [arrived at] you only? (1 Cor. 14:36).*

In our present verse, Paul has a desire to reach, to arrive at a Christian experience of being so linked to Christ and enjoying the fruits of His person and work, that he will live the life of a resurrected man.

The resurrection spoken of here is unique in that the word used occurs only here. It is an "out-resurrection" (*exanastasis*). Paul is looking for the ultimate experience of Christian living, that, having been conformed to "his death," the flesh has been dealt with, and he now wants to live this out by an out-resurrection life.

3:12—A Pursuit to Seek After

> *Not as though I had already attained, either were already perfect: but I follow after, if that I may apprehend that for which also I am apprehended of Christ Jesus.*

The expressions in this verse confirm that Paul has a present experience in view in verse 11, not a future possibility. As in verse 11 he writes *"if by any means,"* so now he records his desires as something yet to be attained and still beyond his grasp. He is not like many who, as a result of the Oxford movement during the 1800s, professed to have reached what Paul desired. The Keswick Convention was born out of the Holiness movement, and its founder Canon T. D. Harford Batterson, vicar of St. John's, Keswick is reputed to have professed that "he had not sinned for 22 years." This was after a sanctification experience at an Oxford meeting. It is said that once Mr. Spurgeon deliberately spilled a drink down him that brought forth a display of temper, to which Spurgeon said, "Where is the old man now of whom ye speak?" Dear fellow-believer, how we all ought to seek after conformity to Christ and inner holiness. Yet like Paul we will have to confess, *"not as though I had already attained."* There are four prime thoughts in the verse:

PHILIPPIANS: THE MIND OF CHRIST

THE PROSPECT
When Paul says *"not as though I had already attained,"* he is exposing the fact that although this is the ambition of his life, as yet he had not reached it. The word "attained" (*lambano*) has the thought of, *to take; to receive*. It is used frequently in the New Testament (263 times) in such verses as Matthew 13:31 of a man who *"took seed"* and sowed it in his field, and of the Lord Jesus who *"took bread, and blessed it"* (Mark 14:22). It is also used in Acts 1:8 regarding the coming of the Holy Spirit when the Lord said, *"Ye shall receive power."* W. E. Vine comments, "*Lambano*, incorrectly translated *attained* in the A. V. of Philippians 3:12, means *obtained* (R. V.)." Paul had not yet reached the fulfilment of his desire, as he longed to be like Christ.

THE PERFECTION
He adds *"either were already perfect."* Once again he has to admit that the goal which is before every believer has not yet been reached. Now he longs to obtain that for which God saved him, and he sees it as the consummation of Christian experience. The Apostle uses the word on three occasions of himself.

I. RELATING TO HIS SERVICE—ACTS 20:24
In his address to the Ephesian elders, Paul will let nothing move him from the ministry that had been committed to his trust. His desire is to *"finish my course with joy, and the ministry, which I have received of the Lord Jesus, to testify the gospel of the grace of God."*

II. RELATING TO HIS SUFFERINGS—2 CORINTHIANS 12:9
Those sufferings were ordered by God lest His servant should be exalted above measure, God sending a thorn in the flesh. This experience was because of **spiritual revelations**, and God sent the **physical affliction** through a messenger of Satan. It was a **diabolical assault** as he was buffeted, that is, "beat with the fist." Yet through it all he could write *"my strength is made perfect in weakness."*

III. RELATING TO HIS SENTIMENT—PHILIPPIANS 3:12

As Paul thinks of his ministry and his frailty in the former verses, he continues with his desire for conformity in this statement. Realizing that the quest was not yet complete he adds to his sentiment the fact that he is making a determined effort to be like the Lord Jesus *"I follow after."* The intensity of the pursuit is seen in the word that he uses, *"lambano."*

THE PERSECUTION

This is what is behind the expression *"I follow after."* The word "follow" is translated *persecute* or *persecuted* over thirty times in the New Testament, and is found three times in this chapter (vv. 6, 12, 14). It has the thought of chasing with a view to bringing down. Before his conversion, and even up to his conversion, this was the pattern of his life as he *"persecuted the church"* (v. 6), so that *"if he found any of this way, whether they were men or women, he might bring them bound unto Jerusalem"* (Acts 9:2). How blessed it is that after he was saved his zeal remains, but the object of his chase is so different now. His object is the man whose glory he saw on the Damascus road, and he desires to bring that pattern of life, as seen in Christ, into his own being. He will *press* (same word) toward this in an endeavour to be like Christ.

HIS PURPOSE

There was but one purpose in life for Paul, and that was to *"apprehend that for which also I am apprehended of Christ Jesus."* He wanted to, "lay hold of so as to possess as his own, to appropriate" (Vine's *Dictionary*), that for which the Lord Jesus had laid hold upon him. It must be noticed that the same Greek word is used three times in verses 12-13, each time carrying the same thought. Do we look, beloved child of God, beyond the fact that our sins are forgiven, and our eternal destiny is secure? The day we were brought to faith in our Lord Jesus, God had far more for us than just to save us from the judgement to which we were heading. It is evident from this verse that divine persons laid their hands upon us, so that we might bear the features of Christ in our daily living. Evidently this must come by personal exercise of heart, for the Apostle sees it as a goal for him to achieve. All the practical sections of the New Testament teach that the responsibility for a life of godliness rests with each believer and it is obviously within the grasp of every true child of God to attain it.

3:13—HIS PERSISTENCE

> *Brethren, I count not myself to have apprehended: but [this] one thing [I do], forgetting those things which are behind, and reaching forth unto those things which are before,*

The fact that Paul was aware that he had not accomplished what he knew to be the mind of Christ for him, only increased his endeavour to reach out to be what God wanted him to be.

The opening statement of the verse introduces Paul's appraisal of the situation. He is quick to inform the brethren that as yet he does not *"count"* himself to have laid hold of this great truth. There are many things that Paul does value that are his in Christ, for the word used here is the word that is continually used in the epistle to the Romans relating to the believer's place in Christ as far as salvation is concerned. The word is used to express the positional truth that we are brought into by faith. In Romans chapter 4 the word is used 11 times:

4:3 where faith is *"counted ... for righteousness";*
4:4 salvation is not of works but *"reckoned of grace"*
4:5 again, *"his faith is counted for righteousness"*
4:6 the blessedness of the man *"unto whom God imputeth righteousness"*
4:8 the blessing when *"the Lord will not impute sin"*

These quotations are sufficient to describe what we have received by faith in Christ.

THE SPIRITUAL MIND

The Apostle also uses the word in relation to his service, which was being questioned by many at Corinth. He says in 1 Corinthians 4:1, *"Let a man so account of us, as of the ministers of Christ."* He counts it a small matter that he is judged of men. He will not judge his own service; that must be done by Christ at the coming of the Lord (vv. 3-5). It would be well for all who serve the Lord to keep these verses in mind. It is not our business to please men, but to *"be found faithful" (v. 2)*. How often is the work of God marred by the servants of God seeking to please men and not being faithful to the Lord? It is also a sad reality that those who, like Paul, seek to minister carefully often receive abuse as a result.

As far as his spiritual attainments are concerned, the Apostle is only too ready to confess that the purpose of God for him, and his desire to fulfil it, had as yet not been reached.

This does not diminish his **activity** for the *"one thing"* that now dominates his life. In pursuit of it he will, like Abraham, *"[forgetting] those things which are behind."* Hebrews 11:15 expresses this in Abraham's life, *"And truly, if they had been mindful of that country from whence they came out, they might have had opportunity to have returned."* Is the Apostle alluding once again to his attainments under Judaism as seen in verses 4-8? Or is he once again using the metaphor of the race, when his concern is not the other contestants, but the prize before him? He will use both his mind (forgetting), and his members (his hands and feet) to reach his objective.

The word for "reaching forth" is only used here in the New Testament and seems to be an intensified form of a word that means, to stretch forth the hand. He is reaching out for that which is before; that I take to be Christ-likeness.

3:14—HIS PRESSING

I press toward the mark for the prize of the high calling of God in Christ Jesus.

As we have seen, the word for "press" is that used in verse 6 and verse 12, where it is translated *"persecute" (v. 6)* and *"follow" (v. 12)*. Evidently Paul has a great desire to lay hold of that which God has purposed for him. He sees it as the final goal of Christian experience, for this is the thought behind the word "mark." It means, to keep your eye on. It comes from the same root as a word found in chapter 2:4, where Paul says, *"Look not every man on his own things."* There we have man's **preoccupation with things natural.** In the verse before us, we have Paul **looking for the prize in that which is spiritual.** As we come to 3:17, the Apostle desires that we *"mark,"* keep our eye on, **people who propagate that which is infernal.**

It would seem that he has his eye on the finishing line and the prize that awaits the victor. In 1 Corinthians 9:24, the prize is that which a believer will receive at the Judgement Seat of Christ in a future day. The incorruptible crown that will then be given is only for those who have been faithful to the Word of God, and have been temperate in all things. The prize here is Christ-likeness, and is spoken of as *"the high calling of God in Christ Jesus."*

What a blessed calling we have! 1 Corinthians 1:26-29 indicates that this calling should **humble** us, as we realize who it is that God chose: the foolish, the weak, the base and the despised of this world. And why has God chosen such? *"That no flesh should glory in his presence" (1:29).*

We are reminded in 2 Timothy 1:9 that it is a *"holy"* calling. The grandeur of this verse thrills the heart as we see the purpose and grace of God, which was given us in Christ Jesus before the world began. Our salvation is seen to be all of God in this verse, with its links to the past. In chapter 2:10, our salvation has links to the future, a *"salvation which is in Christ Jesus with eternal glory."*

Hebrews 3:1 speaks of our calling as being a *"heavenly"* one. The contrast is obviously to the calling of Israel as they came out of Egypt, when they were called to earthly privilege and earthly blessing. Our calling is linked with that which is heavenly in character, and spiritual in content.

Here in Philippians, Paul loves to dwell on a *"high"* calling. Is there anything higher than this? The divine purpose for which we were apprehended is to be like Christ. Some would translate this as "the calling from on high." Wuest says, "The word is not to be construed as meaning "a calling in life," but a call from heaven, to which the Apostle must ever give heed" (*Word Studies in the Greek New Testament, Vol. 2, page 98*).

I suppose we should add to this, the *"hope"* of our calling, as seen in Ephesians 1:18; 4:4. This seems to point back to verses 4 and 5 of Ephesians chapter 1, where God has brought us into His family, and made us His sons.

Another reference to the same word is found in 2 Thessalonians 1:11, where the **honour** of such a calling seems to be stressed. Here Paul is in prayer for the believers that *"our God would count you worthy of this calling, and fulfil all the good pleasure of His goodness, and the work of faith with power: That the name of our Lord Jesus Christ may be glorified in you"* (1:11-12).

3:15—PONDER GOD'S PURPOSE

> *Let us therefore, as many as be perfect, be thus minded: and if in any thing ye be otherwise minded, God shall reveal even this unto you.*

The Word of God calls every believer to have the same desires after holiness. In fact, it is the final goal of those who have reached a measure of maturity. The opening expression is something of an encouragement to this end. *"Let us therefore"* would prompt the heart to seek further the mind of God for us.

The appeal is to those *"as many as be perfect."* The word "perfect" signifies "mature, fully developed" (R. P. Martin). It is for such that Paul would desire that they continue to pursue those spiritual desires that are already formed in them. Is not this a word to all who have attained to a measure of devotion and likeness to Christ, not to become self-satisfied, but to remain Christ-centred?

As R. P. Martin has said on this verse, "Apparently in the Philippian church there were those who tended to be otherwise minded, i.e. to adopt a different viewpoint from that given in Paul's teaching and to act upon it. The use of the word *phroneo* shows that it was more than an intellectual difference; it betrayed a different outlook and affected the conduct of those whom Paul had in mind" (Tyndale, *Philippians*, page 155).

The word "otherwise" (*heteros*) would confirm the thought expressed by Martin, for it carries the thought of "those of a different kind." How sad when there are those who do not long to bear the image of the Lord Jesus in all its fulness, or think that it has been attained and they need go no further.

A word is perhaps needed on the thought of "as many as be perfect," for some would think that these must be older and experienced Christians. I feel that the Apostle is writing to all the saints irrespective of age, for there are many who are young in the faith who nevertheless show great maturity in their desires to apprehend the truth that God has for them. When the Word speaks of those who are babes, it is not referring to those who have newly come to the faith, but to those who have failed to grasp the truth of God when it has been set before them. The babes of 1 Corinthians 3:1 are those who are marked by **Carnality**. The fact they are following men, and by it causing division, is a mark of immaturity. How sad when there are those who still persist in making the clarion call *"I am of Paul; and I of Apollos"* (1 Cor. 1:12). It matters not how gifted a man is, we must learn, *"let no man glory in men. For all things are yours"* (1 Cor. 3:21).

The epistle to the Hebrews speaks of babes who are guilty of **legality**. They were in danger of drifting back into Judaism, as they viewed the temple, its priesthood and sacrifices. This beautiful epistle makes much of the glories of Christ, who is seen eight times over to be, not only the fulfilment of all the types, but also far better than all that went before.

In 1 Peter 2:2, believers are encouraged to be like babes. In this letter, it is a mark of **spirituality**, though it is the desire of babes for milk that is promoted. Anyone who has had any children, and it is our privilege to have been blessed of God with nine, knows that when the child wants milk it is not looking for substitutes like a rocking of the crib, or a soother. No, it wants its food. So says Peter, *"As newborn babes, desire the sincere milk of the Word."*

3:16—A PATHWAY OF UNITY

> *Nevertheless, whereto we have already attained,*
> *let us walk by the same rule, let us mind the same*
> *thing.*

The verse begins with *"nevertheless"* (*plen*), a word that occurs 31 times in the New Testament. John McArthur says, "Plen (however) could also be translated "one more thing." It is often used to express one final thought" (*Philippians*, page 250). It is found three times in this lovely book, and on each occasion, it carries the idea that McArthur suggests. In chapter 1:18, Paul adds to the list of advantages linked to his prison experience that it brought about the Preaching of the Faithful Word. In our present verse, it is his final appeal to seek for likeness to Christ; a Pathway to Follow. Once again, it is used in 4:14 concerning the gift that was sent to Paul as evidence of their Practical Fellowship with him in the gospel. The *Linguistic Key to the Greek New Testament* confirms the thought expressed by McArthur, saying "Nevertheless. The word is used at the conclusion of a section in order to bring out the main point of discussion. Just one more thing" (Fritz Reinecker, *Philippians*, 3:16).

The desire expressed is that as the saints had come (attained) to appreciate something of the truth that has been set forth, let us walk by the same rule. The desire of the Apostle is that all would walk (*stoicheo*) in a line, without deviation. It carries the thought of walking along with others, and of walking in step. Other words are used for walk in the New Testament:

- *Peripateo* carries the thought of our Disposition; to walk around. The habit of our life is in view (*"walk worthy of the vocation wherewith ye are called"* (Eph. 4:1); *"walk worthy of the Lord"* (Col. 1:10)).
- *Poreuomai* involves purpose and means to walk with Design—Determination (*"Go and search diligently"* (Matt. 2:8); *"I say unto this man, Go, and he goeth"* (Matt. 8:9); *"Go ye therefore, and teach all nations"* (Matt. 28:19)).

- *Stoicheo*, the word used here, means without Deviation (see also *"let us also walk in the Spirit" (Gal. 5:25); "as many as walk according to this rule" (Gal. 6:16)*).

How blessed when all walk with the same desire, having before us the thought of being like Christ. Paul longs that we will all have the same rule, the same measuring line. There should be a united front with one mind, as we all mind the same things. How different this was in practice at Philippi where we find *"all seek their own, not the things that are Jesus Christ's"* (2:21). The answer to this is not only the "things" that are Jesus Christ's, but Jesus Christ Himself. Well might they be encouraged to attain to this higher ground.

Paul's Pain: Lamenting
3:17-19

Brethren, be followers together of me, and mark them which walk so as ye have us for an ensample. (For many walk, of whom I have told you often, and now tell you even weeping, that they are the enemies of the cross of Christ: Whose end is destruction, whose God is their belly, and whose glory is in their shame, who mind earthly things.)

3:17-19—An Exhortation to Watchfulness

3:17—Example to Follow

Brethren, be followers together of me, and mark them which walk so as ye have us for an ensample.

The literal reading of the opening phrase is, *"Be ye followers of me, brethren."* It seems to have an appeal about it as he uses the lovely term "brethren." The desire of his heart is that there should be a united testimony to the transforming power of the

THE SPIRITUAL MIND

gospel. As one has said, "the gospel is found, not in books, but in boots." We do not look to the testament of the Law but to the testimony of lives. The supreme example is that of Christ, and elsewhere the Apostle says, *"Be ye followers of me, even as I also am of Christ" (1 Cor. 11:1)*. It is a blessed thing to imitate the lives of godly men who portray divine features. If the Apostle can set himself forward as a type of what Christian ideals should be, I notice in Hebrews 13:7 that elders should also have such character of life that it can be said, *"whose faith follow, considering the end of their conversation."* The use of the preposition *"sun"* in the word *"followers together"* indicates that we should all be "one with" the Apostle in displaying and desiring Christ.

He wants us to not only imitate him, but also to keep an eye on them. In verse 14, we must keep an eye on the prize. Now we are told to keep an eye on persons. There is a little difficulty as to whom Paul is drawing their attention. Is he speaking of those who imitate his manner of life, or is he contrasting himself with those he will expose in verse 18? The fact that he speaks of those to whom we should look as having a habit of walk that sets them forth as types (*tupos*), would seem to point to himself and his fellow-workers. Vincent endorses this when he writes, "imitate me and those who follow my example" (*Word Studies, Vol. 3*, page 451).

The word "ensample" (*tupos*) is from a root meaning "to strike, smite, to make an impression." It is used of the idols that Israel made during their wilderness journeys (Acts 7:43). It comes from a word that unveils the deep sufferings of the Lord Jesus at the hands of men when they *"smote him on the head" (Matt. 27:30)*. An imprint and impression has been left for us to follow. How blessed if we can follow the pattern left to us.

3:18-19—ENEMIES TO FACE

> *(For many walk, of whom I have told you often, and now tell you even weeping, [that they are] the enemies of the cross of Christ: Whose end [is] destruction, whose God [is their] belly, and [whose] glory [is] in their shame, who mind earthly things.)*

It is evident that not all believers do have the same longing to reach the goal for which God drew us to Himself, that is conformity to Christ. The sad exposure of this verse is that there are many who move in total opposition to the life of holiness to which believers are called.

Paul states, *"For many walk."* By this, he reveals that the sad practice seen here was not by a minority. The word "many" (*polus*) occurs 365 times in the New Testament and three times in this epistle:

1:23—Departure to Glory

This amazing statement, which has been a source of great encouragement to many saints of God as they pass through the valley of the shadow of death, speaks of being with Christ as *"far better."* It cannot compare with the present experience of knowing Christ; it far exceeds anything we have ever known.

2:12—Demonstration of Grace

For believers to put into practice the teaching of the Word of God is always something to encourage those who set truth before the saints. The Apostle values the application of truth *"much more"* when he is absent from them and yet they still respond to his teaching.

3:18—Damaging the Gospel

Such were the *"many"* here whose lives caused grief to the Apostle as he thought of the effect such would have on the testimony of the cross. Would that more servants of God were moved as they see the drift among evangelicals today, as many have lost Bunyan's evaluation of this world's pleasures and seem very happy in "Vanity Fair." O for men to make Paul's appeals to their congregations, *"come out from among them, and be ye separate, saith the Lord, and touch not the unclean thing; and I will receive you"* (2 Cor. 6:17).

There are three things marking these people that Paul now exposes:

THE SPIRITUAL MIND

THEIR CONDUCT

They are said to be *"enemies of the cross of Christ."* Please note, it does not say they are enemies of Christ; no! but of His cross. They are hostile to the truth of the cross, for the cross finishes me with this world. The call of the Lord Jesus is, *"He that taketh not his cross, and followeth after me, is not worthy of me" (Matt. 10:38)*. The same thought is echoed in Matthew 16:24; after the Lord Jesus had spoken of His own rejection and death in verse 21. If He reminded His own *"any man will come after me, let him deny himself, and take up his cross, and follow me."* In the gospels we are called to take up the cross; in the epistles believers are seen to be crucified with Christ (Rom. 6:6; Gal. 6:14). The cross teaches us that a man must deny himself, and it is evident that these lived a life of self-indulgence. A far cry from taking up the cross, they became enemies to the truth of it.

THEIR CONSUMMATION

For such there is no hope of eternal life. Like Eli's sons, they may wear the ephod, minister at the altar, stand by the ark as they take it into battle, but they will also perish. Their end is to know ruin and loss. Let all take warning from these solemn verses and remember *"by their fruits ye shall know them" (Matt. 7:20)*.

THEIR CHARACTER

There are three distinctive marks that make up their essential nature:

PHYSICAL: "WHOSE GOD IS THEIR BELLY"

Motyer has put it well when he states, "They worship themselves. Their God is their belly. They recognise no need and no authority outside personal satisfaction" (*Philippians*, page 185).

The attitude seen here is also exposed by Vincent in his quote of Cyclops in *Euripides*, "My flocks which I sacrifice to no one but myself, and not to the gods, and to this my belly, the greatest of the gods: for to eat and drink each day, and to give one's self no trouble, this is the god for wise men" (Cyclops,

334-338) (Vincent, *Philippians, Vol. 3*, page 452). This reminds us of Paul's ministry to Titus as he sent him to Crete, warning him of the character that marked them as being *"liars, evil beasts, slow bellies* [lit. gluttons]." There was need to *"rebuke them sharply"* *(Tit. 1:12-13).* If there is moral failure and a carnal spirit seen in these, then it is to be noticed that those who are guilty of doctrinal error, whom Paul would encourage us to avoid, are said to *"serve not our Lord Jesus Christ, but their own belly" (Rom. 16:18).* It is evident that the belly represents every natural desire that grips a man, be it in things moral or spiritual.

MORAL: "WHOSE GLORY IS THEIR SHAME"

It seems beyond belief that any, who in any way would profess links to the Lord Jesus, could have such written of them. The word "shame" carries the thought of disgrace, dishonesty; it seems to be open and public shame. It is used of false teachers as *"Raging waves of the sea, foaming out their own shame" (Jude 13).* It also reminds us of what the Lord Jesus bore when He *"endured the cross, despising the shame" (Heb. 12:2).* We are reminded of Zimri who took a Midianitish woman, Cozbi, into his tent in open defiance of the Word of God, and in the sight of Moses and all the congregation of the children of Israel. It took a Phinehas, a priestly man, jealous for the honour of his God, to take the javelin and thrust it through both of them to stay the plague of God (Num. 25). Absalom heeded the council of Ahithophel, and spread a tent on the top of the house for all to see as he went in unto his father's concubines (2 Sam. 16:20-23). They gloried in their shame.

The word "glory" appears six times in this letter:
- 1:11   a believer's *Life* lived for the glory of God
- 2:11   Christ's *Lordship* displayed to the glory of God
- 3:19   the *Lasciviousness* of those who glory in their sin
- 3:21   the *Likeness* of believers to the body of His glory at His coming
- 4:19   the *Liberal* hand of God to provide according to His riches in glory
- 4:20   the *Lauding* of God eternally. Glory for ever and ever

THE SPIRITUAL MIND

NATURAL: "WHO MIND EARTHLY THINGS"

The whole epistle is a call for believers to set their mind on the things of God and Christ, *"Let this mind be in you"* (2:5). How sad when some grovel in the mire of earthly things. There is nothing in the lives of these to cause them to appreciate the precious things of God. Like the woman of Luke 13:11-13, they were bowed together and could in no wise lift themselves up. Nor had they known the transforming power of the Son of God to liberate them.

PAUL'S PROSPECT: LOOKING
3:20-21

> *For our conversation is in heaven; from whence also we look for the Saviour, the Lord Jesus Christ: who shall change our vile body, that it may be fashioned like unto his glorious body, according to the working whereby he is able even to subdue all things unto himself*

3:20-21—EXPECTING THE LORD

The contrast between these lives of those Paul has now exposed and those of true believers is beautifully illustrated in the following verses:
- Their *"end is destruction"*: ours the coming of the Lord.
- Their *"god is their belly"*: our bodies will be conformed to His body of glory.
- They *"mind earthly things"*: our citizenship is from heaven.

In these last two verses of the chapter, we have the great truth that fills the Apostle's heart, that of being like Christ finally being realized. The day will dawn when we will be like Him, and that day will be when the Lord returns. The verses are full of great truths for us to grasp.

3:20—Our Habitation, "our conversation is in heaven"

For our conversation is in heaven; from whence also we look for the Saviour, the Lord Jesus Christ:

There are divergent views by many expositors regarding the word "conversation" (*politeuma*). It occurs only here but comes from the same word as the verb found in 1:27. It seems to be the word from which we get our word politics, and many would translate it "our citizenship." We must remember that Philippi, being a colony of Rome, had its citizenship there. They carried all the rights and privileges of belonging to Rome. They also bore the responsibilities of carrying the honour of being Romans. Paul takes up the thought and transposes the idea to teach what Christians are in this world. They are a colony of heaven representing God here. Their laws and interests are all linked with heaven. We live on earth as a heavenly colony.

The expression does not refer to our **destiny** but to our **domain**. Many seem to be confused as to the meaning of the phrase and link it to our future hope into which we shall enter at the coming of the Lord. Such teaching will miss the point of Paul's ministry. He is not anticipating our future home, but what believers are now as they bear God's mind in the place where they serve Him. There is a sense in which the words of the Lord Jesus are presently worked out in the life of the Christian community in any locality, that is, *"Thy will be done in earth, as it is in heaven"* (Matt. 6:10).

The fact that our citizenship, community, political society (the last two expressions quoted from *Bloomfield's Greek Testament, Vol. 2*, page 350) "is" in heaven confirms the present reality of our calling. It is the word *huparcho* which is found in chapter 2:6 where, speaking of the Lord Jesus, it states, *"who being in the form of God."* Both W. E. Vine and Kenneth Wuest state that it means **exists** as a present reality. It is our present centre of life; we are not earthly, like those of 3:19.

THE SPIRITUAL MIND

The Anticipation, "from whence also we look for the Saviour"

The Apostle continues to draw from the idea of Philippi being a colony of Rome, which would at all times be prepared for an unexpected visit from the emperor. In this way, he turns the eyes of the believers to the coming of our Lord Jesus Christ. There was no certainty that there would ever be an official visit from Nero, but we **"look,"** that is, wait with expectation. The word that is used (*apekdechomai*) only ever occurs in connection with the second coming of the Lord Jesus Christ. In Romans 8:19, 23, 25, we find both a groaning creation and a groaning Christian waiting for the day of deliverance at the coming of the Lord. The Galatian epistle (5:5) has but one reference to the coming of the Lord Jesus, written against the background of those who seek to obtain righteousness by the works of the Law. Paul writes *"For we through the Spirit wait (apekdechomai) for the hope of righteousness by faith."* Our righteousness is by faith in Christ, but it also instils a hope through the Spirit of God of a coming Lord. The word also occurs in 1 Corinthians 1:7 and speaks of the gifts God has provided for the church as we eagerly wait for the Lord's return. The seventh reference to *apekdechomai* is found in Hebrews 9:28, where those saved out of Judaism wait for the Lord Jesus to return, that He might establish the many promises that were made to that nation. They wait on the tiptoe of expectancy for the Lord to come; without that, there will be no hope for them as a nation. At His coming, Psalm 45 will be fulfilled as He sits upon His throne at Jerusalem (Heb. 1). Psalm 8 unfolds that a man must reign according to God's purpose in creation, as seen in Genesis 1:26. The second chapter of Hebrews sees Christ reigning as a man. The same epistle unfolds in chapters 3 and 4 how that a rest must be enjoyed. This was never known in Israel's history, but it remains (4:9). That rest, the rest of Genesis 2:2, will be enjoyed throughout the whole of the Millennium; it will be one long sabbath day. During the past 6000 years of human history, God has not enjoyed His sabbaths, but He will have them all together during the reign of the Lord Jesus. Finally in this connection, the Patriarchs were content to dwell in tents in the land promised to them whilst they saw the promises afar off, and were persuaded of them, and embraced them (Heb. 11:13).

3:21—Transformation

> *Who shall change our vile body, that it may be fashioned like unto his glorious body, according to the working whereby he is able even to subdue all things unto himself.*

If Hebrews concentrates on the fulfilment of Jewish hope, Paul now establishes what is very much his own hope and desire. In the former part of the chapter, his longing to be like Christ is the paramount thought. Now he sees the day when it will be accomplished, and through whom it will be done.

The great theme of the coming of the Lord is the effect that it will have upon the body of the believer. There will be a threefold change at that time—physical, moral and official.

Physical
Three things are linked to the change for believers:

1. Our Present Condition
Both here and in 1 Corinthians 15 we are confronted with the physical change that will take place in our mortal bodies when the Lord returns. The Apostle uses various expressions in 2 Corinthians 4-5 to describe the body of the believer as it is seen presently. It is an *"earthen vessel"* (4:7), the *"body"* (4:10), *"mortal flesh"* (4:11), our *"outward man"* (4:16), and in 5:1, our *"earthly house."* In Romans 8:10 the body is seen to be dead; it is not yet the object of divine life. In the verse before us, it is seen as a vile body, or a body of humiliation.

2. Our Purposed Change
The fifteenth chapter of 1 Corinthians reveals the change that will take place at the coming of the Lord. We are told that we will *"bear the image of the heavenly"* (v. 49). Many teach that this speaks of the Lord Jesus in resurrection. They imply, and some are dogmatic, that the Lord has a different body in

THE SPIRITUAL MIND

resurrection to the one He had in life, the one that was crucified. One cannot subscribe to such an idea; in fact, I would be totally opposed to it as it maligns the person of the Lord Jesus. It also implies that there was failure linked with His body similar to the failure and weakness that marks the rest of humanity. The Spirit of God is always careful when speaking of the humanity of the Son of God.

In Hebrews 10:5, it was a body prepared of the Father. The answer to Mary's question, *"How shall this be, seeing I know not a man?" (Luke 1:34)*, is given by Gabriel in verse 35; the Lord Jesus would be produced by the Spirit. It is little wonder that it is said regarding Him, *"that holy thing."* Regarding His sinless humanity, the Spirit is also careful to say He was *"in the likeness of sinful flesh" (Rom. 8:3)*. Good brethren taught us well when they said, "Not 'in sinful flesh' for that would be false, nor 'in the likeness of flesh' for that would be equally wrong. The Lord had flesh but not sinful flesh, nor did He have a body that was marked by the failure that touches fallen humanity." The Hebrew epistle chapter 4:15 confirms that though tempted in all points as we are, yet He was *"without sin."* Was not the Lord Jesus, God manifest in flesh when here? We know that *"God cannot be tempted with evil" (Jas. 1:13)*, and this must apply to the Lord Jesus in the days of His flesh.

The change is said to fashion us *"like unto his glorious body"* or "body of his glory" (Received Text). Some say this is His body from the tomb, His body in resurrection, whereas it is His body from the womb, His body from incarnation. 1 Corinthians 15:46-49, when speaking of the body we shall have, contrasts it with that which we presently bear, of the first man, earthy and natural. The body we will enjoy is linked to the second man. It is heavenly (as to its origin), and again, it will take on the character of that which marked the Lord Jesus as He walked in this world as *"the Lord out of heaven."* It was not out of the grave as many teach, but that which was prepared of the Father and produced by the Spirit.

What kind of body did the Lord Jesus bear? Once again, 1 Corinthians 15 is very helpful in this. Verses 42-44 describe the body of men in life and the body in resurrection. The body

163

in life is seen to be corruptible, dishonourable, weak, and a natural body. Such is the body of those linked with the first man, the earthly body. We are then told what will mark the body of resurrected saints. It will be a body of incorruption, a body of glory, of power, a spiritual body, that is, motivated by the Spirit, not by nature. Is not this the body that the Lord Jesus had while here? It was incorruptible, and well might Peter declare, *"Neither wilt thou suffer thine Holy One to see corruption" (Acts 2:27).* Death hastens the corruption seen in life, but as J. R. Caldwell has written, "It was love in ignorance that prepared the spices to anoint the body of the Lord Jesus to keep away the putrefaction, but these spices were just as fragrant on the resurrection morning as they were the day they were put in the tomb, for he saw no corruption."

The body of the Lord Jesus was also a body of glory; witness the scene on the mount of transfiguration. Power was associated with His body. Who else could have passed through a crowd eager to cast him from the brow of a hill? Who else could pass through those who would stone him, as they sought to do to Christ in the temple? His power is demonstrated as He walks upon the waves. The Lord did nothing on resurrection ground that He did not do before. His body was also a spiritual body. The thoughts, interests and impulses of the Lord Jesus were ever to do the will of His Father. The precious things of God will not be irksome to the believer in resurrection; they too will have their thoughts and actions motivated by moving eternally for God's pleasure.

If verses 42-44 in 1 Corinthians 15 relate to the body in resurrection, in verses 50-58 unveil that not all will die, but all will be changed. The change of the living believer will take place when the Lord returns, and this is confirmed in verse 21 of Philippians 3. The change is said to be two-fold; *"For this corruptible must put on incorruption, and this mortal must put on immortality" (1 Cor. 15:53).* The thought in corruption is of a body that is in decay, while the mortal body is subject to death. There will come a day when the believer will know neither decay nor death. It may be needful to remind our hearts that though we are not told the nature of the body of the wicked,

THE SPIRITUAL MIND

nevertheless we are told that the guilty sinner has his body in the Lake of Fire, teaching us that the body of a man is for eternity (Matt. 10:28; Rev. 20:13-15).

3. THE POWER CONTROLLING

Paul shows the source of the transformation that will take place. Paul's energy of verses 12-14 gives way to the enabling power of the Lord Jesus. As He is said to be the one who will change our body of humiliation, the transforming power must be His also. Three things are evident as we consider the change:

THE ENERGY, "ACCORDING TO THE WORKING"

The word "working" is that from which we get our word for energy (*energeia*). This is another lovely word that occurs eight times in the New Testament. They bring before us:

- **EPHESIANS 1:19—THE AUTHORITY OF CHRIST**
  This demonstrates the energy and power that raised the Lord Jesus and gave Him the place of supremacy, far above all.
- **EPHESIANS 3:7—MINISTRY OF PAUL**
  Divine service, to be effective, must be carried out in the energy that God gives. He who calls us to serve Him will both equip and empower us to fulfil our ministry.
- **EPHESIANS 4:16—UNITY OF SAINTS**
  The development of Christian unity is dependent upon the effort that is put into it, and every Christian should endeavour to supply that which will promote unity.
- **COLOSSIANS 1:29—THE ACTIVITY OF PAUL**
  Paul's toil in the service of God matched the energy that was supplied of God to do it. He was not like Archippus of chapter 4:17 who had to be encouraged to fulfil his ministry. Nor was he like Timothy in 2 Timothy 1:6 where he is exhorted to *"stir up the gift of God, which is in thee."*
- **COLOSSIANS 2:12—THE REALITY OF OUR POSITION**
  The new ground on which we stand, resurrection ground, is enjoyed by the saints because of the energy of God that has put us there.

- **2 THESSALONIANS 2:9— MASTERY OF THE DEVIL**
  This verse unfolds the power that will mark the Antichrist, the Man of Sin. It is *"after the working of Satan."*
- **2 THESSALONIANS 2:11—DESTINY OF HUMANITY**
  Here we are told of the power of God displayed in those who refuse to hear His word as the gospel of the kingdom is preached. At the rise of the Man of Sin in the midst of the Tribulation when he takes his place in the temple and sets himself forth as God, then God will send a working of error. Those who would not accept the Lord Jesus will bow to the Man of Sin in that day.
- **PHILIPPIANS 3:21—CONFORMITY TO CHRIST**
  Such is the mighty energy that will be wrought in the believers in the day of the coming of the Lord. Then we shall be what we should be, conformed to our blessed Lord.

THE ABILITY

There is not only energy, but praise God, He also has the ability to do what He has promised. The paean of praise in Ephesians 3:20-21 seems to sum up the appreciation that Paul had of the ability of God, *"Now unto him that is able to do exceeding abundantly above all that we ask or think, according to the power that worketh in us, Unto him be glory in the church by Jesus Christ throughout all ages, world without end. Amen."*

HIS AUTHORITY

The Lord Jesus is going to make a public manifestation of the place that has been given to Him by the Father. He has been carried to the Father's throne in exaltation, and the Father *"hath put (hupotasso) all things under him"* (Eph. 1:22). The day has yet to come when the promised *subjection* (*hupotasso*) of this world will be brought under a man (Heb. 2:8). That day will be seen when the Lord Jesus will bring all things *under (hupotasso)* His control (1 Cor. 15:27-28). The authority of the Lord Jesus will be fully manifested in that day, but for the believer, the power that will control the world will bring us into conformity with Himself. The word *hupotasso*, according to Vine, is "primarily a military term, to rank under." Kittel says, "In the New Testament the term has a wide range of meaning, centering on the idea of enforced or voluntary subordination" (Kittel, page 1159). What a glorious voluntary subjection when the change of believers is effected!

We can rejoice that there will not only be a physical change but there will also be a moral change.

MORAL

The moral change that will affect believers at the coming of the Lord Jesus is recorded for us in 1 John 3:1-3. Having expressed that the saints of God are the sons of God, John reveals that we are not what we shall be in the day when God has finished His work in us. The reading of verse 2 seems to be, not, *"when he shall appear"* but rather *"when it shall appear"* (compare New Translation, JND), that is, when it does appear what we shall be, we shall be like Him. It is evident that we must be like Him to be in His presence, and *"he is righteous"* (1 Jn. 2:29), *"he is pure"* (1 Jn. 3:3), and *"in him is no sin"* (1 Jn. 3:5). To have the hope of one day bearing such moral character set upon us as we look upon Him will have a practical effect; we will purify ourselves even as He is pure. In other words, we will long to be like Him now as we will be like Him morally then. What a glorious day is before us, when sin will no more touch us and the desires of the flesh will never again be known, when *"we shall be like him" (v. 2)*.

The Word of God also reveals that there will be a day when we will be like the Lord Jesus officially.

OFFICIAL

The Lord Jesus is set forth as a king and a priest, and in this way He will be revealed to wondering eyes at His manifestation in glory, but such is the link that has been forged by the work of redemption that, in the hour of His glory, we shall be revealed in exactly the same way.

The book of Revelation chapter 1:6 unveils how that He has *"made us kings and priests unto God and his Father."* All this is for His own supremacy, for the epistle to the Romans states in chapter 8:28-30 that the purpose of God in His dealings with us is *"that he might be the firstborn among many brethren."*

4

THE SAME MIND

As we come to the concluding remarks of Paul to the Philippian saints, he touches on a problem that still needs to be rectified, and on thoughts with which believers should be occupied. He follows this with a full expression of his appreciation of the fellowship that was sent to him from the assembly. The chapter has a very clear division where he brings before us:

1-7	God's Peace
9-9	God of Peace
19-19	Gift from the saints
23-23	Greetings to the saints

GOD'S PEACE
4:1-7

Therefore, my brethren dearly beloved and longed for, my joy and crown, so stand fast in the Lord, my dearly beloved.

I beseech Euodias, and beseech Syntyche, that they be of the same mind in the Lord. And I intreat thee also, true yokefellow, help those women which laboured with me in the gospel, with Clement also, and with other my fellowlabourers, whose names are in the book of life.

Rejoice in the Lord alway: and again I say, Rejoice. Let your moderation be known unto all men.

The Lord is at hand.

Be careful for nothing; but in every thing by prayer and supplication with thanksgiving let your requests be made known unto God. And the peace of God, which passeth all understanding, shall keep your hearts and minds through Christ Jesus.

4:1—STABILITY

Therefore, my brethren dearly beloved and longed for, my joy and crown, so stand fast in the Lord, [my] dearly beloved.

The chapter opens with a word that is translated in various ways even in this epistle, as:
"so that"   (1:13)
"wherefore"   (2:12)
"therefore"   in this verse

It is often translated "insomuch," and I must confess to enjoying the rendering of Willis, "so then." It links the words with what has gone before; it distinguishes the saints from those who are *"enemies of the cross of Christ" (3:18)*. He links them with the *"perfect"* of 3:15, and rejoices in the relationship enjoyed with them as brethren. He not only **relishes the relationship,** but also **recognises the responsibility,** that they have to *"stand."*

As we look at the verse a little more closely, we find that Paul had at least four things before his mind as he reflects upon them.

1. HIS AFFECTION FOR THEM

He calls them *"Dearly beloved."* It is the word that the Father used of the Lord Jesus, and the three occurrences of the word in Matthew's gospel all refer to the Father's love for His Son.
- Matthew 3:17—The Lord Jesus is separated from the worst of men as He fulfils all righteousness in Jordan, and the

THE SAME MIND

voice from heaven declares, *"This is My beloved Son."*
- Matthew 17:5 — Here the Lord is not distinguished from sinners but from saints. When on the holy mount the very best that the Law could produce (Moses), and that the prophets could show (Elijah) must pale before the glory of the Son. He through whom God speaks in these last days is *"My beloved Son."*
- Matthew 12:18 — Between these two events, that remind us of His Incarnation and coming Kingdom, we have the Pharisees accusing the Lord Jesus of being a sabbath-breaker (12:1-13), and guilty of sacrilege (12:22-37). In the midst of their evil council (12:14) the prophetic word of Isaiah 42 is quoted. This gives us the Father's estimation of the ministry of Christ as He is seen as Jehovah's servant, His chosen, His beloved (12:18).

The Father's appreciation of the Son is the same that Paul has for the saints. He has learned well that every believer is a love-gift from the Father to the Son (John 17:6). The love that the Father has for the Son is the love wherewith the Son loves us, *"As the Father hath loved me, so have I loved you: continue ye in my love" (John 15:9).* How lovely when the truth of this is owned by the saints. Paul is moving in the good of this in the opening verse where he uses the word twice. This is not mere sentiment, but heartfelt affection for the saints at Philippi.

2. His Absence from Them

The Apostle had such affection for these believers that he longed after them. The word "longed" only occurs here, but is that which means to desire greatly. It comes from the word, translated in 2 Corinthians 7:7 as *"earnest desire,"* and in verse 11 of the same chapter as *"vehement desire."* Gordon D. Fee has a footnote saying that the word used here "is one of the standard motifs in letters of friendship in antiquity" (Gordon D. Fee, *Philippians*, page 387). One could hardly believe that this was a mere cliché with Paul. The letter breathes with the deep longing he had for them.

3. His Anticipated Crown

Little wonder he has such desire for them as he realizes what they are, *"my joy and crown."* He sees them as a present satisfaction, my joy, and also as being to his future credit. It is a source of joy to all who serve the Lord to know that the Lord has blessed their ministry and that they have had the privilege of leading a soul to Christ. Whenever you think of them or see them, they bring joy to the heart, knowing that you have been instrumental under the hand of God in seeing them saved.

The country of Macedonia gave great pleasure to Paul in his extensive movements as he preached Christ, for what he says of the Philippians, he also says concerning the Thessalonians, to whom he went following his departure from Philippi (Acts 17). In 1 Thessalonians 2:19, he speaks of them also as being his *"joy"* and *"crown."* It is interesting that both assemblies of God's children were brought to birth as a result of much travail. Persecution was known in both places. In Philippi, it was the Gentiles who fomented the trouble, whereas in Thessalonica it came from the Jewish quarter who *"took unto them certain lewd fellows of the baser sort, and gathered a company, and set all the city on an uproar" (Acts 17:5).* The hatred of the world is fully manifested in both places but, through it all, souls were saved and Paul takes pleasure that from the sufferings there is both joy and a crown.

Crowns are promised to believers in a future day and will be received at the Judgement Seat of Christ. Every believer should live his life with that day in view. Paul speaks much of it and uses it as a means of motivating Christian living and Christian service.

The **gravity** of the Judgement Seat is expressed in 2 Corinthians 5:11, *"Knowing therefore the terror of the Lord, we persuade men."* Some would make it a friendly assignment rather than a final assessment of our service for Christ.

The **gathering** at the Judgement Seat. *"We must all appear"* (2 Cor. 5:10); *"Every man's work shall be made manifest"* (1 Cor. 3:13); *"So then every one of us shall give account of himself to God"* (Rom. 14:12). It is apparent from these verses that each of us has a personal responsibility to live with that day before us.

As we listen to the conversation of saints, it would seem that we think we are the judge and jury to whom believers give account, and not the Lord, for many like the Corinthians pass their judgement now upon the ministry of others, and Paul would remind us to *"judge nothing before the time"* (1 Cor. 4:5).

The **gladness or grief** at the Judgement Seat. The day will manifest our works of what sort they are, and we are to receive either reward or loss. If any man's work abides the test of the fire *"he shall receive a reward. If any man's work shall be burned, he shall suffer loss"* (1 Cor. 3:14-15). How sad to lose a reward that we should have received because of carelessness or disobedience regarding the will of God. *"[Let] no man take thy crown"* (Rev. 3:11).

The **grace** at the Judgement Seat. How gracious is our Lord! He not only saves and brings us into the family, but He also rewards our service with crowns, of which five are set before us:

JAMES 1:12—CROWN OF LIFE; FOR SALVATION

Some call this the martyr's crown, as the verse speaks of the present suffering of the believer, but in our suffering, we are encouraged by knowing that afterwards we shall receive the crown of life, which is given to those who *"love Him."* As all believers love Christ, and came into that love on the day of their salvation, this crown is not just for those who are brought into suffering unto death for Christ but for all who are saved by His grace.

1 CORINTHIANS 9:25—INCORRUPTIBLE CROWN; FOR OBEYING THE SCRIPTURES

The figure is that of the athlete, who must obey the rules if he is to receive the crown. 2 Timothy 2:5 could be linked to this, *"yet is he not crowned except he strive lawfully."*

1 THESSALONIANS 2:19—CROWN OF REJOICING; FOR SOUL WINNING

This is the theme of our present verse, and should encourage us to action in winning men for Christ.

2 TIMOTHY 4:8—CROWN OF RIGHTEOUSNESS; FOR STEADFASTNESS IN THE FAITH

Paul's journey is nearly over but he has been faithful to the end and, as a result, he is looking forward to receiving this crown from his blessed Saviour's hand. How sad to come across so many of whom it could be said, *"Ye did run well; who did hinder you?" (Gal. 5:7).* These crowns are for rule in the coming Kingdom. Let us all look to it that we shall have an abundant entrance at the coming of the Lord (2 Pet. 1:11). Sadly Demas seems to have lost this crown, for it is said of him that he *"loved this present world" (2 Tim. 4:10).*

1 PETER 5:4—CROWN OF GLORY; FOR SERVICE AS AN ELDER

The Word of God has much to say regarding those men He has raised up to be shepherds of the flock. For those who execute their ministry well, it will be worthwhile, for they receive this crown from the chief Shepherd's hand.

The crown that is before us in each of these verses is a STEPHANOS; that simply means "to wreathe." This is not the diadem of kings, nor can it be only that of the victor at the games. It is used of the honour that God bestowed both upon Adam and Christ in Hebrews chapter 2. Lightfoot says, "either (1) victory, or (2) merriment, as the wreath was worn equally by the conqueror and by the holiday-maker" (*Philippians,* page 155).

4. HIS ASPIRATIONS FOR THEM

The desires of his heart are found in this clause, *"so stand fast in the Lord."* With the legalist and the sensualist being exposed in the former chapter, and with the grandeur of their position as citizens of heaven having been revealed, they are urged to stand fast. This is once again a word that Paul uses to encourage believers in many assemblies to whom he writes, as in:

Romans 14:4 where he speaks of	Relationships
1 Corinthians 16:13	Receiving Truth
Galatians 5:1	Rejecting Error
Philippians 1:27	Refraining from Strife

THE SAME MIND

Philippians 4:1 — Resisting the Foe
1 Thessalonians 3:8 — Reassurance for Paul
2 Thessalonians 2:15 — Remember the Ministry

This word occurs elsewhere only in Mark 11:25 where the Lord says, *"and when ye stand praying, forgive."*

The *"last words of David"* recorded in 2 Samuel 23 recall the commendation of David for one, Shammah. This man fought when the Philistines gathered in a troop over a piece of ground that was full of lentils, a picture of Israel's inheritance. The people fled from them. The Philistines are always a type of religious evil that would continually seek to rob God's people of the blessings He has given them. In 1 Samuel 23:1, the Philistines fight against Keilah, and they rob the threshing floor. It is against these that others fled before, that Shammah *"stood in the midst of the ground, and defended it, and slew the Philistines: and the Lord wrought a great victory" (2 Sam. 23:12)*. We see what God can do with a man who cherishes his inheritance from God and who, in the face of great opposition before which others crumble, is prepared to stand and slay the enemy.

4:2—UNITY

> *I beseech Euodias, and beseech Syntyche, that they be of the same mind in the Lord.*

The arrival of Epaphroditus not only brought the welcome fellowship from the Philippian church, but also brought the sad news of the strife that had arisen among them. This strife was manifested in these two women to whom Paul now makes his appeal.

Often times **disharmony** between members of the assembly is treated as a minor disturbance, as in this case between two sisters in Christ. The Apostle looks beyond what might appear to be of no consequence to others beside themselves. As little foxes spoil the vine, so strife among saints has very sad repercussions. It not only **divides** saints, it also **disturbs** the assembly. This is the reason for Paul's call to help those women in verse 3. From this it is seen that women can cause great stress in the church; even sisters who take a subjective place need to watch their spirit in these matters. Such division **denies** our right to be worshippers, for Matthew 5:23-24 teaches that if I am not right with my fellow-believer then I am not right with God, and there is a need for reconciliation before we approach the altar of worship. It is also evident that it brings **distress** to the servant, as he knows that a quarrel has affected his converts. Such matters cannot be left to fester. Paul must expose and seek to rectify the problem. He does this in a number of ways.

1. THE ENTREATY

It is noticeable that he makes his appeal to both women when he writes, *"I beseech,"* in this both parties are appealed to. Paul will not take sides, and by this appeal, he does not apportion blame; he makes the fault mutual. It is as wrong to take offence as it is to give offence. As a young man I remember an older and wiser brother taking me aside when I felt I had been wronged and I was standing for my rights. He said, "Norman, it is easy to climb." Nothing more needed to be said to me at that time. I realized that I needed to act in humility to maintain unity. The Ephesians 4:1-3 teaches how we must maintain that unity into which we have been brought. We must walk worthy of such a vocation *"with all lowliness and meekness,"* our attitude before the saints, and *"with longsuffering, forbearing one another,"* our actions toward the saints.

The word "beseech" is used frequently by Paul and it is used to encourage to action. It is not so much the preacher's word, but that of the pastor as he draws alongside and puts his arm around you, seeking your compliance with the will of God.

2. THEIR ENDEAVOUR

Both had a responsibility to put an end to the difference that had come between them. They were to bow to the Lordship of Christ and not, like those of chapter 2:4, to look *"on their own things."* The call to be of the same mind in the Lord

THE SAME MIND

would see them put into practice the great Christological passage of chapter 2—to let the mind of Christ control them. How soon the discord between them would be settled if only they would apply the truth of this letter that was addressed to the assembly to their own hearts. I wonder if the call of Paul in 2:3, *"Let nothing be done through strife or vainglory; but in lowliness of mind let each esteem other better than themselves,"* affected them before he mentions their names and the division that marked them, in chapter 4.

Someone is reputed to have changed the names of these women when they were publicly reading this passage, to Odious and Soon-touchy. I suppose this would sum up the failure that characterised them.

4:3—THE MINISTRY

> *And I intreat thee also, true yokefellow, help those women which laboured with me in the gospel, with Clement also, and [with] other my fellowlabourers, whose names [are] in the book of life.*

THE ENTRUSTING

The dispute between these two sisters, who had been such a help to Paul in former days, obviously caused him great concern and added to his trial whilst in prison. Here is evidence of the truth he expressed to the Corinthians when he added to the many sufferings he endured as he served the Lord, *"that which cometh upon me daily, the care of all the churches" (2 Cor. 11:28).* The divisions at Corinth, the departure to legalism in Galatia and disputes between saints were a burden to his spirit. Hence the call to his true yokefellow to help these women.

The **intensity** of his desire to see reconciliation is seen in the words *"I intreat" (erotao),* which carries the thought of not only to ask, but to desire, to beg. This problem must not be allowed to simmer on. It needed someone to put out the fire that was burning.

The **intermediary** is called a *"true yokefellow."* The word "yokefellow" only occurs here, and some tell us that it is a proper name, *suzugos*. Much conjecture has gone into who this genuine (true) yokefellow is. Some agree with Ironside, who writes, "I take it that the third verse was spoken by Paul to Epaphroditus personally" (*Philippians*, page 107). This seems unlikely to me, for what was the point of putting this in a letter to the assembly when Epaphroditus was with Paul and probably carried the letter back with him? Surely, Paul would have made his appeal whilst he was still with him in Rome. Gordon D. Fee puts forth Luke as the likely yokefellow, drawing from the fact that the "we" passages of the book of Acts do not occur again after chapter 16 until we come to Acts 20:6, where it is recorded, *"and we sailed away from Philippi,"* implying that Luke remained in Philippi when Paul and the rest of his company left for Thessalonica. We could conjecture for ever who this person was; it is enough to know that his loyalty (true) and his links to Paul as one yoked together with him in the service of God, made him suitable to approach these sisters in Christ.

The **intimation** is to *"help those women which laboured with me in the gospel."* It seems to me as if this is an S.O.S., a call for help. The women appear to be oblivious to the gravity of the situation and its evident consequences. It is going to take another to rescue the situation from becoming a disaster.

The word "help" is *sullambano*, to join together. *"Lambano"* means to bring alongside and the preposition *"sun"* is to be in conjunction with. This is what the Lord desires, that we should be joined, and standing together as one in Him.

The **incentive** to help is seen in what these women had done along with Clement and others. There was a time when they laboured with Paul, which is to strive as athletes. Once they strove together to further the gospel; now they were striving against each other, and were becoming a hindrance to the work of God in Philippi.

The **inscription** of their names is in the book of life. There is no need for Paul to record the names of all who are faithful in their service for God. God keeps His own record and He has written them in His book.

The **inclusion** of these women among the names of those

who laboured with Paul displays the appreciation he had for the service of all the saints. Though he has taught that public, vocal ministry in the church is not permitted to women, nevertheless there is much that can be done by them to prosper the work of God, and Paul values highly all that is done for God. It is very apparent in our day that there are those who think that their own ministry alone is of value, and tend to decry the service of others. It is evident from the statements here that Paul had a high regard for all who served the Lord in any way whatsoever.

4:4—THE MELODY

Rejoice in the Lord alway: [and] again I say, Rejoice.

Disunity causes disharmony, and Paul knows that strife in any company of Christians can nullify the joy of the Lord among them. Disgruntled saints are like a virus that spreads its infection very rapidly in a heated, close-knit community. With this in mind Paul lifts their thoughts beyond the problem that should be rectified through the intervention of his true yokefellow to higher ground, *"Rejoice in the Lord."* As we have seen, there is a constant call to rejoice running through the letter. In this statement, the highest form of joy is found, it is in the Lord. Though all else fails, here is a sure resource for the child of God, particularly if the injunction *"always"* is heeded. In every circumstance, at all times, we are called upon to rejoice. Did not the Lord Jesus leave this with His own as He spoke with them in the upper room, *"These things have I spoken unto you, that my joy might remain in you, and that your joy might be full"* (John 15:11)? In spite of all that He was to suffer, and knowing all things that should come upon Him, the Lord can still speak of *"my joy."* With this in mind, Paul can lift their spirits and can re-emphasise the need to rejoice.

I notice that all is *"in the Lord"* in this section—*"Stand fast in the Lord; be of the same mind in the Lord; rejoice in the Lord."* Of Paul it is said, *"I rejoiced in the Lord greatly"* (4:10); and the book closes with *"the grace of our Lord Jesus Christ be with you all. Amen" (4:23).* Whenever there are practical exhortations, divine Lordship is stressed, and we are reminded that all practice is carried out because we are subject to the Lordship of Christ.

4:5—MODESTY

> *Let your moderation be known unto all men. The Lord [is] at hand.*

I choose this word to sum up the verse, for the definition of modesty is, unassuming, retiring, not over-rating one's qualities. Here is no proud, loud-mouthed charlatan, but a man who bears the dignity of Christ with a gentle spirit.

Alford says, "your forbearance, from *epi*, implying direction, and *eikos*, reasonableness of dealing" (*Greek Testament, Vol. 3*, page 188). It has been translated "sweet reasonableness," and Paul appeals to it as marking the Lord Jesus, and it is that which he sought to imitate in his dealings with the saints at Corinth (2 Cor. 10:1). Elders are exhorted to be controlled by it as they serve the Lord among the saints. In 1 Timothy 3:3, we are told they must be patient, which is the word used here. Three times over it is used as gentleness—in Titus 3:2; James 3:17; 1 Peter 2:18. What characterised Christ must not only be a feature in Paul's life, but also in every aspect of every believer's life. In Philippians, this trait must be seen among believers in the gatherings of the church. The same applies to elders in their ministry among the saints. In our relationships with those of the world, it is this spirit that should mark us before men, to speak no evil, not to be brawlers, but to be gentle (Tit. 3:2). The same word, gentle, is used for this Greek word when speaking of what the teaching ministry should produce in James 3:17, for that chapter deals with the tongue of the teacher. A teacher of the Word of God can so minister that his ministry is labelled *"earthly, sensual, devilish,"* bringing *"envying and strife,"* which is *"confusion and every evil work."* How much better when ministry is that which is from above and is *"first pure, then peaceable, gentle, and easy to be entreated"*

(Jas. 3:15-17). Every walk of life is covered by this word *epieikes*. Even in our daily employment as servants, we are exhorted to be subject to the gentle master. Even unsaved masters can bear this gentle nature.

The reason that gentleness in all our dealings is stressed is because *"the Lord is at hand."* Again, this has been written as "the Lord is at your elbow," speaking of the proximity of the Lord as we journey through life. His watchful eye watches over all our actions and should cause us to move with care at all times. The word, *eggus*, at hand, is used of events, such as the coming of the Lord; seasons and time, as "the summer is nigh"; and also of places, "John was baptising in Aenon near to Salim." All would indicate something not far away; such is the Lord with His own. In many ways, this is a comfort to know; in our verse, it is a challenge to living.

4:6—Anxiety

> *Be careful for nothing; but in every thing by prayer and supplication with thanksgiving let your requests be made known unto God.*

The life of every man can be fraught with care but, for the believer in Christ, the problems and even the perils that come our way should not cause great anxiety, for we have an omnipotent God who has promised never to leave us nor forsake us. It is evident from the ministry of the Lord Jesus in the Sermon on the Mount that there are a number of things we cannot change such as the height of our body (Matt. 6:27). If God, who says we are of more value than many sparrows, has determined that, we are encouraged to learn that He knows our needs for food and raiment, and these needful things will be provided for us (see Matt. 6:25-34).

Even in circumstances of persecution and trial, we are not to take matters into our own hands or to take thought of how we shall speak, *"for it shall be given you in that same hour what ye shall speak"* (Matt. 10:19).

Peter must have listened well to his Lord's words, and

seems to recall them when he says, *"casting all your care upon him; for he careth for you" (1 Pet. 5:7).*

The word that is used in these cases carries the thought of being drawn in different directions, to be distracted. The hymn writer expresses the truth when he wrote, "Take your burdens to the Lord and leave them there." This is what Paul now encouraging the believers to do as he says that we should not only be careful for nothing, but prayerful for everything.

In the circumstances in which this encouragement to prayer is found, it is fitting that we should be brought first to the **Range of Prayer.** The word is, *"but in everything"*; there is nothing that we cannot take to the Lord in prayer. Every situation that comes our way is an opportunity to approach the throne of grace. In prayer, we not only approach God, but we come with devotion and worship. The word that is used, *proseuche,* is "restricted to prayer to God, and marking the power of him whom we invoke" (*Bullinger's Lexicon and Concordance*). With diverse patterns of life that beset each of us, it is good to know that there is nothing the Father cannot deal with.

The **Requirement in Prayer** is brought before us in our supplications. The word carries the thought of want or need. There is obviously some particular need in mind when we supplicate God. The supplication of Zacharias and Elisabeth was for a child. It would seem that because of age their supplication had ceased, but the message of the angel was, *"thy prayer is heard."* The fact that we may be called to wait for God's answer is no indication that the Lord is not willing to grant our petition.

The **Rule in Prayer** is that we should be a thankful people. Even in days of adversity we are called on to give thanks, *"In every thing give thanks" (1 Thess. 5:18).* It was the constant practice of Paul, when writing to the various churches, always to begin with thanksgiving for them even when failure in testimony to God was apparent. The only exception was the churches of Galatia. Their departure was such that he feared if there had been a work of grace in them at all, and whether they had been truly born of God. It is a sad people who cannot thank God for His constant mercy toward us. So when we make our requests let us do it with a spirit of thanksgiving.

4:7—TRANQUILLITY

> *And the peace of God, which passeth all understanding, shall keep your hearts and minds through Christ Jesus.*

The exhortations that have been pressed in the former verses, if practiced, will have the blessed effect of causing us to know the peace of God. This peace and rest is in contrast with strife, and denotes the absence of strife. Like joy, peace was the state of the Lord's heart as He approached Calvary, and such peace He bequeathed to His disciples (John 14:27). Peace with God is what we entered into at salvation (Rom. 5:1). This peace is not merely an emotion, for it is based on a covenant; it is a peace that cannot be lost. We are now left with the peace of God—that of being untroubled and undisturbed as God protects our well-being.

This peace goes far beyond and excels anything we can ever bring our thoughts to, for the word "passeth" carries the thought of far outstripping that which our minds can grasp, or even think out.

The peace of God acts as a guard to the heart and mind. The heart is the seat of affection and controls the character of a man, whilst the mind relates to our intelligence. It is from these two spheres that our worries and fears arise. How blessed to have peace as a military guard, with power to protect us in every circumstance of life. The word "keep" is used in 2 Corinthians 11:32 of the governor who *"kept the city of the Damascenes with a garrison."* His desire was to apprehend Paul, but a basket let down through a window was enough to breach that garrison. There is no power that can break through the protective care of God for His own.

It is heart-warming what a simple word will do when uttered by the Spirit of God to the child of God. We could very easily skip over the word "shall" and miss its implications. There is no doubt, and no possibility of failure with God, and the power of God "shall" garrison our hearts and minds.

THE GOD OF PEACE
4:8-9

Finally, brethren, whatsoever things are true, whatsoever things are honest, whatsoever things are just, whatsoever things are pure, whatsoever things are lovely, whatsoever things are of good report; if there be any virtue, and if there be any praise, think on these things. Those things, which ye have both learned, and received, and heard, and seen in me, do: and the God of peace shall be with you.

4:8—VARIETY

These two verses would turn us away from the conflict and the things that are written for its correction which were seen in the former section, to that which should occupy our minds and thoughts.

We cannot help thinking, as one has written in his commentary on 1 Peter, "there is nothing more free-flowing than the mind" (W. Kelly). *"Wherefore gird up the loins of your mind" (1 Pet. 1:13).* Here we are encouraged to apply the mind to positive things and to be occupied with them. In verse 8 we have the provision, whilst in verse 9, the practice is brought before us.

THE PROVISION
The Apostle uses virtually the same language to open this part of his letter as he does in chapter 3:1, *"Finally brethren."* Here, just as in chapter 3, he is not seeking to draw his letter to a close as some commentators think. Rather, he is summing up the thoughts of verses 1-7, and as the words in chapter 3:1 can justly be written, *"for the rest,"* even so this is the point he is making here.

Of the many things he would draw their minds to in order to occupy them, six times over Paul uses the word "whatsoever," which is literally "as many things as." The word is embracive of everything that would come within the realm and orbit

THE SAME MIND

of the things spoken of here. It would make a great provision for everyone to be mindful of.

He begins by bringing before us what is true; he ends with praise. If everything we contemplate is true in every aspect, it will cause us to praise as we ponder such things.

"True" Anything that is true does not need to be hidden or done in the dark. The word carries the thought of unconcealment, what is seen, and what it really is. Everything that has truth for its basis can be an object of contemplation.

"Honest" The thought behind this word is rather different from our modern usage of the word. It actually carries the thought of that which is revered, grave, august, dignified. In the form that it is used here it only occurs four times and on the other occasions it is used of deacons (ministers) and their wives (1 Tim. 3:8, 11), and of the aged men (Tit. 2:2). On each occasion, it is translated as "grave." Yet how edifying it is to the mind to be occupied with whatsoever bears that lovely trait.

"Just" carries the thought of what is right or becoming. Again, this word is used of people such as Joseph *"being a just man" (Matt. 1:19)*, also of the Lord's judgement being just (John 5:30), and we are called on to be righteous in our judgements (John 7:24).

This is obviously a feature that marks the Godhead. Men recognised it in Christ, as when Pilate's wife who had a nightmare while she was daydreaming, having *"suffered many things this day in a dream because of him,"* said to her husband, *"have thou nothing to do with that just man" (Matt. 27:19)*. The Lord Jesus Himself addressed the Father as *"righteous (just) Father"* (John 17:25).

"Pure" Here we are brought face to face with that which is chaste, clean, uncontaminated, and free from defilement. As we pass through this present evil age in which we live, we are constantly confronted with much that contaminates our lives.

The advertisements we see, and the language we hear must affect us. It is a sad indictment if we deliberately place ourselves in a position where these things are commonplace in our homes and in our lives.

"Lovely" Here we have something that is dear to everyone. The word occurs only here, but it derives from *pros*, before and *phileo*, to love. There are so many lovely things for us to fix our eye upon and make them a theme for meditation.

"Good report" means exactly what it says, to be well spoken of, or well worded. It would remind us of the Queen of Sheba's exclamation when, having heard of Solomon's fame, she came to prove him with hard questions. The visit left her amazed, not only at his wisdom and the house that he had built, but also at the way it was ordered. This caused her to say, *"It was a true report that I heard in mine own land of thy acts and of thy wisdom"* (1 Kgs. 10:6). Remember that which was given to Boaz concerning Ruth, *"It hath fully been shewed me, all that thou hast done unto thy mother in law since the death of thine husband: and how thou hast left thy father and thy mother, and the land of thy nativity, and art come unto a people which thou knewest not heretofore"* (Ruth 2:11). There are many such instances, even among those we are contemporaries with. How blessed to think on these things.

"Virtue" is, as it sounds, a word meaning moral excellence, good quality. This is the only time this word occurs in Paul's writings, where it is something to peruse when we see it displayed. It is found three times in Peter's epistles. In 1 Peter 2:9, in the royal priesthood into which we have been called, we are to show forth the virtues of Him who hath called us. The word "praises" is that which we have here, and is literally "virtues." It is the responsibility of believers to make a public display of the moral excellence of God in our daily living. The word is found again on two occasions in his second epistle, where Peter is bringing before us the glorious prospect of being linked to Christ in His coming kingdom, and sets before

THE SAME MIND

us how God called us to it, *"by glory and virtue" (2 Pet. 1:3)*. The day of Christ's manifestation and the establishment of that kingdom will be a day when His glory will be seen, and moral excellence will cover the earth. It is fitting that, if we are called to it, God would call us on the ground that is going to mark that glorious day. Peter also desires that every believer will have an abundant entrance into the kingdom (2 Pet. 1:11), and encourages us to add to our faith, virtue. This is the first thing Peter looks for as he delineates those things that will enable us to have the abundant entrance. If God called us in moral excellence, then we should seek to portray it.

It is in connection with virtue that Paul changes from *"whatsoever"* to if *"there be any."* It would seem that virtue would be in short supply, and perhaps we can only find it in those who are truly born of God. One is appalled these days to hear the language of those even in high office, and those who seem outwardly respectable. Whilst in hospital recently, I was grieved to hear the gutter language of the patients as they spoke to each other. There was certainly nothing in their conversation that I could join in or "think on."

"Praise" has the thought of, to applaud or commend. The believer is going to be *"to the praise of the glory of his grace" (Eph. 1:6)* in a coming day when we are before Him as sons according to God's eternal counsel in Christ Jesus. We shall fully appreciate then the glory of His grace which made us sons, whilst in chapter 2:7 God is to display *"the riches of his grace"* to wondering worlds. The riches of His grace is that which reached us as sinners. Ephesians 1:12, 14 declare how both Jew (*"we"*) and Gentile will again be the cause of applauding the wonder of God's heart toward us as we become co-heirs with our Lord Jesus during His millennial reign, when all will be headed up in Him, that is, things in heaven and in earth. If Paul dwells upon the riches of God's blessings toward us that must generate praise, Peter would show the trials of life that we so often find difficult to bear, as that which God is using for our future good, that we *"might be found unto praise and honour and glory at the appearing of Jesus Christ" (1 Pet. 1:7)*.

Together these things make for good meditation for the mind of the believer. "To think" is to take an inventory, to count, indicating that these are the things we should be dwelling on continually and giving positive thought to them.

4:9—THE PRACTICE

> *Those things, which ye have both learned, and received, and heard, and seen in me, do: and the God of peace shall be with you.*

It would seem from this verse that Paul knew he lived the kind of life that is displayed in the previous verse; he has been an object lesson for them to think on. It is a blessed thing when a servant of God lives his ministry, when his walk matches his talk. How different the Pharisees were in the days of the Lord Jesus, as the Lord spoke of them as those that *"sit in Moses' seat,"* as the teachers of the Law. The people are exhorted, *"All therefore whatsoever they bid you observe, that observe and do; but do not after their works: for they say, and do not"* (Matt. 23:2-3).

The Apostle brings before us *first* of all things that will occupy the **mind**.

"Those things which ye have both learned." This would relate to the ministry that Paul had given them and, as all ministry must be to edification, exhortation, and comfort (1 Cor. 14:3), I am sure that Paul's teaching would be in accord with that which he exhorts the Corinthians when he takes examples from music (14:7), the military (14:8), and men (14:9). His ministry would have a distinct sound. Nor would not merely speak to the air. Not for Paul what someone said regarding the teaching of a certain brother, "he went down deep, he stayed down long, and he came up dry." The Lord preserve us from such.

Secondly, ministry must affect the **heart**.

The simple word *"received"* would indicate that they had taken to heart his former teaching. If their reception of his words in this letter were as acceptable as his former ministry, then peace would be brought again to the fellowship.

Thirdly, he brings before us the **ear**.

"*Heard*" would speak of a ready reception of all that he had brought before them. Let us not be like one young lady, who told me on one occasion when she realized that she had not been attentive to the Word of God, "I am not saying that I did not hear, but I did not listen." Would God we had a listening ear for the truth of God. We could draw attention to so many who heard but did not listen. We have to go no further than our first parents and the catastrophic consequences as a result of not obeying the Word. Nor can we find a greater example than the second man, the Lord out of heaven, who demonstrated the blessed results of fulfilling the will of God.

Fourthly, he draws attention to the **eye**.

"**Seen.**" Again, the Apostle could always set himself forth as an example of Christian living. In a day when the Word of God had not yet been fully written, Paul sets himself forth as a type for Christians to look to and imitate. On various occasions, he calls the Christians to be followers of him. Lincoln has written, "Paul evidently had the assurance that much of his own life and path had been according to God, as well as to his doctrine" (Lincoln, *Assembly Writers Library*, Vol. 2, page 147).

He exhorts the saints to be followers of him in:

HIS EXPOSITORY MINISTRY—1 CORINTHIANS 4:16
This is against the background of the Corinthians following men in their desire to follow certain types of ministry. They said, *"I am of Paul; and I of Apollos; and I of Cephas; and I of Christ."* Paul stood for liberty from the Law; Apollos evidently promoted learning (Acts 18:24); whilst, with Peter, perhaps legality was the aim of his followers. Those who followed Christ liked to show a spirit of independence. Paul rebukes this spirit in chapters 1-4, and reminds them that they should get the benefit of all who minister for God among them, *"all are yours"* (3:21-23). In chapter 4, he states that he is only using the names of these servants of God to illustrate the sad condition that had arisen in the congregation. Paul will not be judged of men and leaves all

to the coming Judgement Seat of Christ, and desires that they imitate him in this.

THE EATING OF MEATS—1 CORINTHIANS 11:1

The opening verse of this chapter really concludes chapter 10, where he has been exercising the saints to separate themselves from idol temples. The question of meats that are sold in the market is also raised, as some of this may have been offered to idols in the temple. Paul's advice is very sound, and none should give offence, *"neither to the Jews, nor to the Gentiles, nor to the church of God" (10:32)*. In this, they should be followers of him.

THE EXCELLENCE OF HIS MOVEMENTS—PHILIPPIANS 3:17

This has been covered in the previous chapter. The reminder of how we should live for Christ could follow that of Peter when he desired to *"stir up your pure minds by way of remembrance" (2 Pet. 3:1)*.

THE EVIL MALTREATMENT—1 THESSALONIANS 1:6

It is evident that the Thessalonian believers were subject to persecution on account of their faith in Christ. Paul would remind them that it is a path both for himself and his Lord. They were following a well-worn pathway that all saints are subject to if they live a godly life, for *"all that will live godly in Christ Jesus shall suffer persecution" (2 Tim. 3:12)*. There is a blessed promise to all who are called upon to suffer, *"if we suffer, we shall also reign with him" (2 Tim. 2:12)*.

Finally, Paul draws attention to the **feet**.

"Do." It is not enough to be cognisant of the will of God. Every believer is called upon to carry out that form of doctrine which is committed to us. It is only by the practice of the will of God that we will know His peace. In this verse, the presence of God is the prominent thought. It is good to know the peace of God, but how much better to know Him who is the source of it! The promise is sure, *"the God of peace **shall** be with you."* It is guaranteed to those who practice the truth of God.

THE SAME MIND

On five occasions, God is set before us as the God of peace:
Romans 15:33 emphasises   His Peace
Romans 16:20   the Prospect
Philippians 4:9   His Presence
1 Thessalonians 5:23   His Preservation
Hebrews 13:20   His Power

THE GIFT FROM THE SAINTS
4:10-19

> But I rejoiced in the Lord greatly, that now at the last your care of me hath flourished again; wherein ye were also careful, but ye lacked opportunity. Not that I speak in respect of want: for I have learned, in whatsoever state I am, therewith to be content. I know both how to be abased, and I know how to abound: every where and in all things I am instructed both to be full and to be hungry, both to abound and to suffer need. I can do all things through Christ which strengtheneth me.
>
> Notwithstanding ye have well done, that ye did communicate with my affliction. Now ye Philippians know also, that in the beginning of the gospel, when I departed from Macedonia, no church communicated with me as concerning giving and receiving, but ye only. For even in Thessalonica ye sent once and again unto my necessity. Not because I desire a gift: but I desire fruit that may abound to your account. But I have all, and abound: I am full, having received of Epaphroditus the things which were sent from you, an odour of a sweet smell, a sacrifice acceptable, wellpleasing to God. But my God shall supply all your need according to his riches in glory by Christ Jesus.

We now come to the section where Paul expresses his thanks, as he acknowledges the gift that was sent to him and tells of the circumstances that surrounded him when it arrived by the hand of Epaphroditus. To Paul, the pressing need had been the problems that beset the believers and evidently grieved his heart. Before he could speak about the gift, he must seek to help the saints rectify a serious problem among them. Having done this, he can now turn to show his appreciation and to give light by the Spirit of God on the value of giving to support those who serve the Lord by faith alone.

There are four main points that he draws attention to:
4:10	The Exercise of the Philippians
4:11-13	The Experiences of Paul
4:14-18	The Example of the Philippians
4:19	The Expression of Worship

Before looking at these verses in a little more detail, perhaps it would be good just to look at a few general principles regarding giving, as seen particularly in the New Testament, though giving has marked every generation of God's children. Great principles are set out in Exodus 35, where the redeemed of Israel gave to provide a tabernacle for God to dwell in. We also find in the days of Joash (2 Chron. 24) that the people gave to restore the temple which had been broken down. The temple was well provided for by David, as he desired to have a part in that which God precluded him from building because his hands were full of blood on account of the wars he had fought (1 Chron. 22:8). Yet in his provision for the temple that Solomon was going to build, he says of it, *"But who am I, and what is my people, that we should be able to offer so willingly after this sort? For all things come of thee, and of thine own have we given thee" (1 Chron. 29:14).* Malachi brings the Old Testament to a close with a call from God to a people who had robbed Him by not bringing their tithes and offerings to Him. They were obligated to bring a tithe, though an offering was entirely voluntary. Nevertheless, God still expected the people to offer to Him; it would be a cause of blessing if they were faithful. *"Bring ye all the tithes into the storehouse, that there may be meat in mine house, and prove me now herewith, saith the Lord of hosts, if I will not open you the windows of heaven and pour you out a bless-*

ing, that there shall not be room enough to receive it" (Mal. 3:10).

As far as the New Testament is concerned, a number of guidelines are set before believers as to our responsibility regarding giving. We are not committed to giving a tenth or tithe of our possessions to God. This originated with Jacob in Genesis 28:22 after his vision of God at what was to become Bethel. Each of us is asked to *"lay by him in store as God hath prospered him" (1 Cor. 16:2).* But can we give less under grace than Israel did under Law? Though a dear sister I know, whose husband gave her very little to run the home, found it impossible to give a tenth, she gave what she could.

Giving arises from devotion to God, "[they] *first gave their own selves to the Lord" (2 Cor. 8:5).* People who have little love for the Lord will give little. We are then taught that *"if there be first a willing mind, it is accepted according to that a man hath, and not according to that he hath not" (2 Cor. 8:12).* Again, in 2 Corinthians 9:6-8 we see that the hand of God is upon those who sow bountifully. When first commended to the work of God many years ago, a young couple gave us great help as they devoted all the summer months to helping us in our gospel tent outreach work. They gave not only their time, but their financial support was exceptional. On one occasion I protested as they passed another gift to me, to which he replied, "Norman, as I keep giving it out the Lord keeps shovelling it in. I have had many pay rises this year." We do not follow the prosperity gospel that nearly demands God must give you a hundredfold when you give to Him, but we do know that *"he which soweth bountifully shall reap also bountifully" (2 Cor. 9:6).*

We are taught of the **PERSONS** who gave to support the work of God in the New Testament. In 1 Timothy 6:17-19, it is the rich who are encouraged to be *"rich in good works, ready to distribute, willing to communicate."* The epistle to the Ephesians 4:28 brings before us one who would be poor, *"Let him that stole steal no more: but rather let him labour, working with his hands the thing which is good, that he may have to give to him that needeth."* So we see that both the poor and the rich should give to God.

The **PATTERN** concerning giving is that shown by God and Christ. When speaking of the Lord Jesus in 2 Corinthians 8:9 it says, *"though he was rich, yet for your sakes he became poor, that ye through his poverty might be rich."* The proof of the Father's giving is John 3:16, He *"so loved ... he gave."* No greater pattern of giving can be seen than this. Such giving is a proof that he will *"with him also freely give us all things"* (Rom. 8:32).

The **PURSE HOLDERS**, who handle the collective giving of the believers, are always seen to be spiritual men. When those who were wealthy in Jerusalem sold their possessions to help those who were poor, they laid the money at the Apostles' feet (Acts 4:34-37). Again, in 2 Corinthians 8:16-22, the collection made by the saints in Macedonia for the needs of those in Jerusalem was to be carried by spiritual men, chosen by the churches for this purpose. The business of funds is not for just any man, nor is it enough for one to be a banker or an accountant; it needs spiritual men to handle that which is given for the service of God. See also 2 Chronicles 31:11-15 where priestly men oversaw the offerings of the people that were given to sustain the priesthood in their service for God.

The **PURPOSE** of giving is also a very clear subject in the Word of God. It was not to be stored in the banks of men, just gaining interest, and to be left for the Man of Sin when the saints have been received to Christ. No, it was for the poor (2 Cor. 8-9) and for the servants of God, to enable the poor to live, and the servants to labour for God in undistracted service.

The principles set out here were carried out by the Philippian church and they are seen in the verses before us.

4:10—The Exercise of the Philippians

> *But I rejoiced in the Lord greatly, that now at the last your care of me hath flourished again; wherein ye were also careful, but ye lacked opportunity.*

THE SAME MIND

The gift that came through Epaphroditus gave Paul great joy. If one interprets the following verses correctly, then we must assume that Paul was in great need and perhaps feeling the strain of it somewhat. But what joy would rise in his heart as the need was met and the circumstances in which it came were revealed to him.

It is evident that they had had it in mind to provide for him for some time, for when he speaks of "your care," it literally means that they were "thinking" regarding it. The word that Paul uses is that which is so common in this letter, *phroneo*. It is that of which we have written much concerning the previous verses regarding being *"like minded,"* or *"let this mind be in you."* Thus the gift came out of an exercise of heart for him. God does not look for giving on an impulse. When the offering for the tabernacle was given, it was after Moses, having set out the need, sent the congregation home. It was in the confines of the tent that they purposed in their hearts what to bring to support this great work. He did not suddenly pass round the plate or, as we have heard with some, the buckets.

The exercise they had for Paul had finally *"flourished again."* Though having a great love for Paul, they had been hindered from supporting him for some time and the desire to help had lain dormant like a tree in winter that in the warmth of the spring sun started to shoot forth its buds; this is the thought carried by the words *"flourished again."* Paul was able to enjoy the warmth of that sun in the wintry blasts of his imprisonment as this gift arrived in Rome.

If the gift came out of exercise for Paul as a result of their thinking of him, it was also needful that there was opportunity given to them to fulfil their desires. There is no hint as to what enabled them to be able to send to Paul at this time. Perhaps Epaphroditus had reason to visit Rome and, if so, his travelling there gave opportunity for this gift to be sent with him. In reality, we have no way of knowing either what hindered them or how the opportunity arose to fulfil a long-standing desire. We do know that Paul was filled with great joy when desire and opportunity met. This is still the case today, and believers will never know what joy comes to those who depend upon God alone, when a gift comes to meet our needs when we are at wit's end corner. I remember on numerous occasions the Lord meeting our needs in a remarkable way. On one occasion, in our early days of service for God, a young couple in America sent us $500, which came when we had no money to our name. It gave us great joy. A couple from England whom we had never met once sent us a large cheque which helped us when again we were in great need. I remember sitting down just to make sure the amount was as I first read it to be. We were filled with great joy both at their care and at God's goodness to us. I must say those occasions have never been forgotten nor the care of these dear believers toward us.

We have a framed statement that hangs on the wall of our home to which we have turned on many occasions, just bowing the head and thanking God, knowing He will provide. It says,

> "Say not my soul, from whence shall God relieve thy care?
> Remember that Omnipotence hath servants everywhere:
> His method is sublime, His thoughts supremely kind;
> God never is before His time, and never is behind."

4:11-13—The Experience of Paul

4:11—His Destitution knowing Poverty

> *Not that I speak in respect of want: for I have learned, in whatsoever state I am, [therewith] to be content.*

Though the language is veiled, it is evident that he was in great straits when this fellowship arrived. He sets out the pattern of all who look to God alone; he does not complain, nor does he make his needs known to others, for he looks to God and will leave all to God.

When he speaks of "want" he uses a word that refers to destitution. It is used of the widow who *"cast in all that she had"* into the treasury when she was in *"want."* How beautiful these two mites appeared in heaven's courts! Did she see the two trumpets that took her coins into the temple coffer chests, knowing one was for the temple service and the other for the poor, and say to herself, "Do I love the Lord my God with all my heart? I do." So she cast one mite into that trumpet. Then looking at the trumpet that took the gift for the poor would think, "Do I love my neighbour as myself? I do." So she cast in the other. She like Paul had *"learned in whatsoever state I am, therewith to be content."*

It was not an easy path and it must have been a very difficult school to be in. The lessons were hard but the exams had been passed, and in this, Paul was content. All believers are called to this in 1 Timothy 6:8, *"having food and raiment let us be therewith content."* As our God provides the basic necessities of life, that is enough. If we are blessed with abundance, let us use it for the glory of God.

4:12—His Deliberations Regarding his Daily Portion

I know both how to be abased, and I know how to abound: every where and in all things I am instructed both to be full and to be hungry, both to abound and to suffer need.

The experiences of life had caused Paul to perceive by intuitive knowledge (*oida*, know) the downs and the ups of life. If the Lord Jesus in chapter 2:8 knew how to humble Himself, for Paul it was something that he had to perceive, *"how to be abased."* Human nature would shrink from it, but God takes His servants through difficult paths that they might know what it means to be like Christ, for God cannot use a proud man. Paul's experiences in his service for God had often brought him low, but now he is contented with his circumstances, having been humbled by his experiences in service.

If there are the downs, thankfully God does not continually take us there, for there are also the ups of life, *"I know how to abound."* The word used *perisseuo* is found twice in this verse and five times through the epistle. In chapter 1:9, it is that *"your love may abound,"* and this touches the **heart**. Again, in 1:26 the thought is *"that your rejoicing may be more abundant* *in Christ Jesus."* Paul looks for abounding **happiness**. In our present verse, where it is against the background of daily needs being met, Paul has in mind what would be good for his **health**. When we come to verse 18 it is his **holiness** that is paramount, for it is against the background of the gift being a sacrifice to God.

4:12b—His Discipline in the Pathway

Paul uses a word that is only found here in the New Testament, when he says *"I am instructed."* The word is "initiated" in the Received Text, and W. E. Vine says the meaning is "to initiate into the mysteries." We are told the source of this initiation, *"every where and in all things."* The places and events that he knew as he served the Lord were God's school to instruct His servant. The experiences he passed through were the tools in the Lord's hand to make Paul a dependent man, to cast him upon God that he might know the secret of His keeping power. Perhaps this is one of the reasons that the Lord takes many of His servants through difficult experiences in a financial way as they serve Him. Though these are often very unpleasant at the time, nevertheless it does seem that they are needful to the spiritual well being of the Lord's servants.

Paul not only knew how to abound but also *"to suffer need."* This is a word that would indicate that he had known what it is to be destitute. He was following in the footsteps of those worthies recorded in Hebrews 11:37, who among their many trials are said to have been *"destitute, afflicted, tormented."* He has been like the prodigal of Luke 15:14 when *"he began to be in want."* The word carries the thought of wanting, lack or failure. Such was the school of the Apostle under the hand of God. What lessons he learned! Yet it is good to see that though there was a Marah (Ex. 15:22-25) for Paul, there was no murmuring under the circumstances. Rather he knew something of the branch cast in (4:13), to make those bitter waters sweet.

THE SAME MIND

4:13—HIS DEPENDENCY ON DIVINE POWER

I can do all things through Christ which strengtheneth me.

This servant of God could endure the experiences he was called to pass through only because he had learned in this school to depend on Christ. Is not this where the Lord wants to bring those who serve Him? They are not looking to men or for material gain from their service, but are wholly dependent upon the Lord.

A number of years ago, there was a young man who had just left his employment to serve God on the ground of faith alone, with no known visible support from any source. An older servant of God asked how he was finding the way. The young man said, "Well you have been this way before me and you will know what it is like." The older man replied, "Brother, at this stage God has got to try you to see if you are made of the material he can use." Demas failed the test (2 Tim. 4:10), "[he] *loved this present world.*" Another venerable servant said, "The jangling of the chain got on his nerves" (J. Douglas).

Three things are in the verse as Paul thinks of the Muscle, the Might and the Minister:

He says, "I can." This is no vain boast in human effort. He acknowledges that he is strong (*ischuo*) and that ability is his to enable him to endure the trials of life that he knows as he serves the Lord. This ability has its source in the power that is put into him, for the word "strengtheneth" (*endunamoo*) has been translated "poured strength into." *Bullinger's Critical Concordance* says "to strengthen in, i.e. to render strong, impart strength to."

In Acts 9:22, Paul *"increased in strength"* in his preaching. He thanks Christ Jesus the Lord for *"enabling"* him to minister when put into the ministry (1 Tim. 1:12) and now he values the strength imparted to suffer adversity in that service. He was also thankful for this strength in the hour of his trial before Nero, when all forsook him, but *"the Lord stood with me, and strengthened me" (2 Tim. 4:17).* So, from the beginning to the end of his service, in all circumstances, Paul knew what it was to be strengthened.

The minister of all this was the Lord Jesus; all is *"through Christ."* The Lord will not call any to His service without pouring His strength into them in all that they pass through.

4:14-17—The Example of the Philippians

In the earlier verses that we looked at, relating to the gift sent by the Philippian believers, we saw that giving must be (by):

4:10	Exercise, "flourished again"
4:10	Thoughtful, "your care" (you were thinking)
4:10	Opportunity, "ye lacked opportunity"

In the verses we are now looking into, we see:

4:14	It is a beautiful thing, "ye have well done" (*kalos*)
4:14	It is fellowship
4:15-16	They were consistent
4:17	It is beneficial, "fruit"
4:18	It is worship
4:19	It is reciprocal

These latter points deserve expansion, as they are a great source of encouragement to those who desire to give to those who serve the Lord.

4:14—Paul's Appreciation of Their Giving

Notwithstanding ye have well done, that ye did communicate with my affliction.

Such was the gift at this time of trial that Paul was passing through that it came to him as a beautiful thing, *"ye have well done."* The word "well" (*kalos*) means "good, beautiful, pleasant, noble, splendid" (Gordon D. Fee, *Philippians*, page 438). How his heart must have rejoiced to receive this from the hand of Epaphroditus as he was feeling the pressure of the way through which he was passing. It would draw out his heart

THE SAME MIND

to them and cause there to be thanksgiving to God (4:18). He cannot help but express his appreciation in such a way that the assembly would know his heartfelt thanksgiving for this timely gift.

THEIR ASSOCIATION IN HIS TRIAL

Such was the appreciation of Paul that he saw this gift as a link with him in the trial he was passing through. He uses a word that only occurs three times, *sugkoinoneo*. It is found in Ephesians 5:11 and in Revelation 18:4. The word means, to be a partner with; we should not be a partner with the world's *sin* (Eph. 5:11), nor with the civil system of Babylon when we see that God has **sentenced** it to judgement. But what a blessed thing to become a partner in the servant's **suffering**, as their godly care had brought these saints into partnership with Paul. We saw in chapter 1 how their giving was to the gospel (1:5), and with his ministry (1:7); here Paul teaches how it also makes them partners in his tribulations.

The Lord Jesus foretold of the tribulations that the church would pass through when He said, *"In the world ye shall have tribulation"* (John 16:33). Affliction was not only for the Apostles, for the Thessalonians knew what it was to follow in the same pathway. And ye *"became followers of us, and of the Lord, having received the word in much affliction, with joy of the Holy Ghost"* (1 Thess. 1:6). These tribulations were a proof of true conversion, for in the parable of the sower it is said that *"when tribulation or persecution ariseth because of the word, by and by he is offended"* (Matt. 13:21). There was no such offence by the Thessalonians for they were encouraged by the fact that Timothy was sent to comfort them, *"That no man should be moved by these afflictions: for yourselves know that we are appointed thereunto"* (1 Thess. 3:3). Paul could make a boast about them *"in the churches of God for your patience and faith in all your Persecution and tribulations that ye endure"* (2 Thess. 1:4). Paul calls his trials but *"light affliction which is but for a moment."* He sees them as working for him *"a far more exceeding and eternal weight of glory"* (2 Cor. 4:17). It is little wonder he can write *"we glory in tribulations also"* (Rom. 5:3), knowing it is God's path for His saints that will bring great profit to the saints. In all this, we see that the Philippians, by their giving, are made partners in it.

What is a profit for the believer's eternal benefit will one day be the punishment of a Godless world. For the same word is used of the tribulation that will come upon them when the wrath of God is poured out in what we call Tribulation Days. The believer will know tribulation from the world, but the world will know tribulation from God (Matt. 24:21; 24:29; 2 Thess. 1:6).

4:15—ALONE IN THEIR GIVING

> *Now ye Philippians know also, that in the beginning of the gospel, when I departed from Macedonia, no church communicated with me as concerning giving and receiving, but ye only.*

The Apostle continues his theme of the fellowship that they had with him and the partnership they had in the work of God. They were fully aware that they alone had supported him as he continued his service in other regions beyond Macedonia. Their giving is a lesson book to other churches who fail miserably in the responsibility of supporting the gospel.

Even at this late stage in the church's history with the divine record in their hands, many are misers instead of ministers of that which God has blessed them with. Many are like the Corinthians, who failed to support Paul as he served God among them, reminding them that *"I robbed other churches, taking wages of them, to do you service. And when I was present with you, and wanted, I was chargeable to no man: for that which was lacking to me the brethren which came from Macedonia supplied"* (2 Cor. 11:8-9).

What an indictment it is of the carelessness of many when he writes, *"No church communicated with me as concerning giving and receiving but ye only."* How often have we heard of assemblies with many thousands in the bank that has been entrusted to them for the work of God, that seem to be leaving it for the Man of Sin to use when the believers are raptured to heaven.

THE SAME MIND

One was very thankful to learn of one company of God's children that was doing this a number of years ago and, realizing the error of their ways, decided to do as the Word would teach and distribute all of it into the work of God. Thereafter they saw all their own needs met, and have continued the practice of putting all their offerings into divine service. They have become like the Philippians in their giving and not like the Corinthians.

The word "giving" occurs only in James 1:17 apart from here, but what a lovely example the Philippians were following, for *"every good gift and every perfect gift is from above, and cometh down from the Father of lights, with whom is no variableness, neither shadow of turning."* The word "gift" (*dosis*) is the word for giving. It is in the heart of God to give, and if He will give the gift of His Son (John 3:16; 2 Cor. 9:15) *"how shall he not with him also freely give us all things?" (Rom. 8:32).*

There is not only the giving but also the receiving on the part of the servant, for there is a grace in receiving the support of your fellow saints. It is not for God's servants to look for collections from the unbeliever, for we are taught about those who *"went forth, taking nothing of the Gentiles"* (3 Jn. 7). They went for His name's sake, and looked to the Lord alone to meet their needs. Many, like Lightfoot, make these expressions a commercial term, "Credit and debit, a general expression for pecuniary transactions. The phrase refers solely to the passing of money between two" (*Philippians*, page 163). Commercial transactions are carried out for mutual benefit and, though unwittingly, these believers were going to receive much as a result, as we shall see in verse 19.

4:16—THE ABUNDANCE OF GIVING

> *For even in Thessalonica ye sent once and again unto my necessity.*

Having remembered their giving when he left Macedonia he now relates to it whilst he was still in that province. After he was constrained to leave following the prison experiences there, they travelled some 95 miles to Thessalonica. It would seem from the historic record of Acts 17 that Paul did not remain too long in that city. Verse 2 would indicate that he reasoned with the Jews in the synagogue for three sabbath days, when unbelieving Jews caused an uproar. The brethren sent Paul and Silas away by night to Berea. Though some would reckon that Paul must have had a longer stay, what the divine record given by the Spirit of God indicates causes me to find it difficult to see how he could have been there much longer than the three weekends that are specified for our learning. Nevertheless, such was the heart of the Philippians for Paul that the assembly sent gifts to him on at least two occasions, *"once and again,"* for it certainly means more than once. Again, when we think of the distance they would have to travel along the Ignation Way, it entailed much labour on their part to bring their offering. We can see how Paul would count them as partners in his ministry. The journey to Corinth was not too much for some of their company to take to bring a gift to him there, and even now as he writes, Epaphroditus is by his side, having suffered much to secure this present exercise of the assembly to Paul. Not many are as diligent as the church at Philippi. They are a silent witness to all of what we should be, but they are also a finger of condemnation to others who fail in their support of the work and of the servants of God.

4:17—THE ADVANTAGE OF GIVING

Not because I desire a gift: but I desire fruit that may abound to your account.

How blessed to know that the Lord is no man's debtor, and that *"whatsoever a man soweth, that shall he also reap" (Gal. 6:7).* This verse is written against the background of supporting those who teach the Word of God (Gal. 6:6). The Corinthians were encouraged by the obvious principle that Paul sets out in 2 Corinthians 9:6, *"He which soweth sparingly shall reap also sparingly; and he which soweth bountifully shall reap also bountifully."* This truth is now brought before the Philippian saints as he writes, *"Not because I desire a gift: but I desire fruit that may abound to your account."*

There was no covetous spirit in Paul. He can say to the Ephesian elders, with whom he had laboured for the space of three years, *"I have coveted no man's silver, or gold, or apparel" (Acts 20:33)*. There was no Achan of Joshua 7:21 in Paul, nor was there any spirit of Gehazi, who followed after Naaman to make a gain from a spiritual work that had been accomplished by God (2 Kgs. 5:20-24). Though in need when the gift came and thankful to God for the care of the church, nevertheless he can say, *"Not because I desire a gift."* The word *epizeteo* is the intensive form of the word *zeteo* that is used of Herod *"seeking the young child to destroy him" (Matt. 2:13)*; also of the Scribes and Pharisees who *"sought how they might destroy him" (Mark 11:18)*. It is as if they would leave no stone unturned in their efforts to slay the Lord Jesus. There was no self-seeking spirit in Paul to use his service for God to make financial profit for himself; his interest was the future blessing of the saints.

As A. T. Robertson writes, "It is not the gift so much as the giving that brought joy to Paul's heart" (*Paul's Joy in Christ*, page 145). His primary interest was the blessing that it would ultimately bring to them, and he was seeking this. The word "desire" here is that found in the former part of the verse. Unlike the spirit that marked them, which he exposed in chapter 2:21 when *"all seek their own,"* Paul is now seeking their eternal benefit as he sees that they have made "an investment which would repay rich dividends in the service of the Kingdom, as accumulated interest" (R. P. Martin, *Philippians*, page 181). He was looking for interest being added to their bank account. Some may have fat purses here but scant profit there; they are not *"Laying up in store for themselves a good foundation against the time to come" (1 Tim. 6:19)*. Like those rich people whom Paul warns in that passage who are:

> In **Danger** of being high-minded,
> **Dependent** on the wealth they possess, and do not
> **Distribute**, nor are they rich in good works. Their
> **Destiny** is bleak as they fail to put into heaven's bank.

These principles are all seen in 1 Timothy 6:17-19. As W. Secker has pithily written, "Many think it must go well with them hereafter because it is well with them here: as if silver and gold which came from the bowels of the earth, would carry them to the bosom of God in heaven" (*The Nonesuch Professor*, page 52). Or, as he has written in page 42, "It is a reproach to many rich men, that God has given them so much, and that they should give the poor so little. Some observe that the most barren grounds are nearest to the richest mines." Let us seek to lay up treasure in heaven by our unstinted giving to the work of God.

4:18—THE AROMA OF GIVING

But I have all, and abound: I am full, having received of Epaphroditus the things [which were sent] from you, an odour of a sweet smell, a sacrifice acceptable, wellpleasing to God.

The full appreciation that is felt by the Apostle is seen in this verse. As he writes, he thinks of the **abundance** that he enjoys through this gift that was brought by Epaphroditus. He also sees it as a sweet smelling **aroma** as far as God is concerned. Then in verse 19 he will give an **assurance** to them that there is nothing lost in giving, for God will richly repay all that is given to Him.

He confirms to the Philippians that this gift has met every need, *"I have all."* But it not only met present need, there was enough to guarantee his future needs. This is evident when he uses the word *"abound."* This word is used of all that was left over after the feeding of the multitude when it is recorded, *"and there was taken up of the fragments that **remained** to them twelve baskets."* Paul is here thinking of his full baskets. How generous were these believers to Paul, and how rich in their giving toward God! The word that is used to express the fulness of what was sent to him is found five times in the epistle where we see that it should be the benchmark of:

    1:11   A Righteous life

2:2   A Rejoicing heart
4:12 His Resources in service (twice)
4:18 Relieving a need.

This fellowship had filled all Paul's needs and he can express with pleasure that he is full.

If the support of the saints toward him met his need, he now reveals how such giving brings pleasure to God. Using the language of the Levitical offerings, he recognises that the gift is nothing less than a peace offering that has been brought to God. The peace offering of Leviticus chapter 3 was in reality a fellowship offering. It was given to God out of deep appreciation for all that God had done for them. The offerer not only wants God to benefit from it, but knows that the priests will also have a share in it, whilst he himself also partakes of the offering. The peace offering is always referred to as a *"sacrifice."* Hence Paul speaks of this fellowship as a "sacrifice" to God. He, as the officiating priest, had his portion, and he had all and abounded. To have all would give him the wave breast, and to abound would supply the heave shoulder (see Lev. 7:28-34).

God also received that which gave Him pleasure. As the internal organs and the internal fat of the animal was caused to ascend as it was burnt on the altar, so the internal affections of these believers that moved them to such liberality meant much to God and was to Him an odour of a sweet smell.

In the peace offering, there was not only the priest's portion and God's portion, but the offerer also fed from this offering. In verse 19, Paul reveals the part that they have as God supplies all their needs.

Let us reflect upon what we give to God. We can be like the Philippians and give liberally, thus bringing pleasure to God, or like those of Corinth who were beggarly and miserly, and when Paul recalls the giving from such as them he calls it *"your carnal things"* (1 Cor. 9:11).

Returning to the *"odour of a sweet smell,"* it is interesting to find that this occurs with:

The Devotion of Mary—John 12:3

Such was the pouring of the ointment as she displayed her love for Christ, that all received the benefit of her delightful action. Some, like Judas, will always complain when they see such love in action, though he did not complain about the supper with which he filled his own stomach, only at that which was for the Lord's honour.

The Declaration of the Gospel —2 Corinthians 2:14

The figure that Paul uses is that of a Roman triumph. When a general returned from a mighty victory, he would be given a triumphal welcome home and the streets would be filled with perfume as they burned incense in appreciation of him. Our Lord has accomplished the greatest victory that was ever wrought and Paul sees His triumph and the gospel preached is the incense offered making *"manifest the savour of his knowledge by us in every place."*

The Destiny of Humanity —2 Corinthians 2:16 (twice)

Paul continues the theme of the triumph, recalling that, during his welcome, the general would have in his train those he had conquered, and would now be bringing them to face the lions or the stake for crucifixion. They smelled the odour but to them it was a savour of death unto death; they were soon to die.

Also in the retinue would be those who had been delivered by his victory and, as they smelled the same perfume, it was to them *"the savour of life unto life."*

The scene is not of a Roman triumph alone; for the same idea is found in the song of Deborah, after the defeat of the Canaanites as recorded in Judges 5, see particularly verse 12.

A Dedicated Walk—Ephesians 5:2

Such is the true walk of a believer when he walks in love; it is a *"sweet-smelling savour."*

The Distribution of the Gift—Philippians 4:18

Enough has been written to recognise now what unstinted giving is to God.

If in Philippians we have the sacrifice of our **purse**, in Romans 12:1 it is the sacrifice of our **person**. In Philippians 2:17, Paul speaks of a sacrifice through **preaching** and Hebrews 13:15 bids us *"offer the sacrifice of praise to God continually, that is, the fruit of our lips giving thanks to his name."*

4:19—Assurance for the Assembly

But my God shall supply all your need according to his riches in glory by Christ Jesus.

The believers are to learn that they will not be impoverished by giving to God, for Paul knows his God and can speak of *"my God."* In the school of experience, he has learned much of God in a personal way, and this knowledge he now imparts to the saints by way of encouragement.

Many take this verse as a *carte blanche* statement for all to appropriate in any circumstances, but we must remember that it is written against the background of the fact that these Macedonian saints may well have impoverished themselves in their desire to meet Paul's needs. The words that are used are akin to those that Paul uses to describe his own condition. When he says *"my God shall supply,"* he uses the word for describing his state when he received their gift, *"I am full."* They had left Paul full, and the *supply* of God would leave them full as it replenished the empty coffers that they knew by their fellowship with Paul. Again, when he uses the word *"need"* it reflects upon his own condition before the gift arrived. It is the word for *"wants"* (2:25) and *"necessity"* (4:16). The Philippians had given in such a way that it was out of *"their deep poverty"* (2 Cor. 8:2). Now the servant of God assures them that, as his wants and necessities had been met by God, so the same Lord would also meet their needs. He leaves no doubt in the matter as he says *"my God **shall** supply all your need."* We must not lay hold on the truth taught here lightly, as if we can do as we will with our finances, like sowing to the flesh, and expect God to sustain us in our folly. No, if we sow sparingly, we shall also reap sparingly (2 Cor. 9:6). These Philippians had given abundantly, and God would not leave them impoverished when they had given to Him.

The divine provision to supply the needs of faithful saints does not impoverish God, for it is *"according to his riches in glory."* We have been well taught that it is not "out of his riches in glory." The Lord is no less rich by giving, but we do see the inexhaustible supply from which He draws to sustain His own here in the world.

The riches of God are boundless. It is the *"riches of his goodness"* that bring us the gospel (Rom. 2:4). How sad when men despise it! It is the *"riches of his grace"* that bring us forgiveness (Eph. 1:7), and the *"exceeding riches of his grace"* will be manifested when the saints are displayed with Christ (Eph. 2:7). We find the *"riches of his glory"* will bring in an inheritance in the saints (Eph. 1:18). The same *"riches of his glory"* are those by which He strengthens us in our inner man (Eph. 3:16). I take this to be the new man of Ephesians 4:24. The same *"riches of the glory"* now revealed in the *"mystery among the Gentiles; which is Christ in you, the hope of glory"* (Col. 1:27), cause us to wonder at such movements of God toward us. Here we are told that these same *"riches in glory by Christ Jesus"* will supply every need of those who give to God to further His work in the gospel.

GREETINGS TO THE SAINTS
4:20-23

Now unto God and our Father be glory for ever and ever. Amen.

Salute every saint in Christ Jesus.

The brethren which are with me greet you. All the saints salute you, chiefly they that are of Caesar's household.

The grace of our Lord Jesus Christ be with you all. Amen.

4:20—GLORY GODWARD

As the care of the church toward him is contemplated, how that he now abounds and is full, and knows that the Lord will recompense them for their faithfulness, Paul is filled with awe and wonder. He must raise a paean of praise heavenward. He does so by this doxology, which, like others in the New Testament, uses the plural of unto the ages, *"for ever and ever."* The literal translation is *"to the ages of the ages."* Eternal glory will be manifested for all God's goodness to us.

This expression *"unto the ages of the ages"* occurs seven times in the epistles and thirteen times in the book of Revelation, of which, nine are Godward and four manward. Of the four manward references, three relate to the sufferings caused by the Judgement of God (Rev. 14:11; 19:3; 20:10), and one to the eternal reign of the saints with Christ (22:5). Again, it is interesting to note that, whenever a four is introduced in the Word of God, it always divides into a three and a one.

The seven references in the epistles all spring out of appreciation for God's goodness to us in Christ:
- The Salvation of Sinners—Galatians 1:5
- The Sustaining of the Servant—Philippians 4:20
- The Sovereignty of God—1 Timothy 1:17
- On Strengthening His Servant—2 Timothy 4:18
- Through Sanctification of the Saints—Hebrews 13:21
- Through Service in the Assembly—1 Peter 4:11
- By Sustaining Saints in Suffering—1 Peter 5:11

If Paul speaks of *"my God"* in verse 19, he writes of Him as *"our Father"* in this verse, indicating that all the saints should join in the adoration and praise of such a one as this, who sustains us at all times.

4:21-22—GREETINGS MANWARD

Salute every saint in Christ Jesus. The brethren which are with me greet you. All the saints salute you, chiefly they that are of Caesar's household.

In keeping with his desire, manifest throughout the epistle, to promote unity, there are no names mentioned, for this might have endangered the spirit he sought to create. There is just the simple desire to "salute every saint in Christ Jesus." All are embraced; none are excluded. Again, he links all the brethren who are with him in the salutation, as sending their greetings. A distinction seems to be made between the brethren that are with him (are these his co-workers?), and those in verse 22, who could be believers from Rome. It is good to know that Paul had links with Caesar's household, possibly those who were saved as a result of his preaching as seen in 1:13.

He speaks of some as saints, this is what we are Godward, and others as brethren, this is what we are manward.

4:23—GRACE INWARD

> *The grace of our Lord Jesus Christ [be] with you all. Amen. [[[To [the] Philippians written from Rome, by Epaphroditus.]]]*

Paul brings his letter to a close by desiring that they know something of the grace that has brought them into all the blessings of God. He also ends as he begins, by embracing "all."

May God bless this epistle to our hearts.

Bibliography

I have endeavoured to credit all referenced material, however should any have been omitted I apologize and will seek to rectify this in any future publication.

Author	Title of Book	Publisher
Alford, Henry, D. D.	Philippians, The Greek Testament	Moody Press
Article from the	Imperial Bible Dictionary	Blackie and Sons Limited
Baxter, J. Sidlow	Explore the Book	Zondervan
Biggs, C. R. D.	Epistle of Paul to the Philippians	Methuen and Co.
Bloomfield, S. T., D. D.	Bloomfield's Greek Testament, Vol. 2	Longman. Orme, Brown, Green and Longmans
Brown, & Jamieson Fausset	Commentary on the whole Bible	Zondervan
Bruce, F. F.	The Book of the Acts	Marshal, Morgan and Scott
Bullinger, W. E.	Critical Lexicon and Concordance	Regency Reference Library
Caffin, B. C.	Philippians, The Pulpit Commentary	Macdonald Publishing Co.

PHILIPPIANS: THE MIND OF CHRIST

Author	Title of Book	Publisher
Caldwell, J. R.	The Charter of the Church 1 Cor.	Pickering and Inglis
Conybeare and Howson	Life and Epistles of St. Paul	Longman. Green, Longman and Roberts
Darby, J. N.	Synopsis of the books of the Bible	Bible Truth Publishers
Darby, J. N.	The New Translation	Bible Truth Publishers
Fee, Gordon D.	Paul's Letter to the Philippians	William B. Eerdmans
Fritz, Rienecker	Linguistic Key to the Greek New Testament	Zondervan
Gaebelin, Arno C.	Philippians, The Annotated Bible	Loizeaux Brothers
Gordon, Sam	Joy Philippians	Ambassador
Grant, F. W.	Philippians, The Numerical Bible	Loizeaux Brothers
Gwynn, J.	Philippiansm, The Bishops Bible	John Murray
Henry, Airay	Philippians	Tentmaker Publications
Ironside, H. A., Litt. D	Philippians	Loizeaux Brothers
Kelly, William	1 Corinthians	Morrish
Kelly, William	Philippians and Colossians	Ralph E. Welch Foundation
Kittel, Gerhard	Theological Dictionary of the New Testament	Wm. B. Eerdmans
Lauren, Roy L.	Where life Advances Philippians	Kregal Publications

THE SAME MIND

Author	Title of Book	Publisher
Lightfoot, J. B.	Epistle to the Philippians	Macmillen and Co.
Lincoln, William	Philippians	Gospel Tract Publications
MacArthur, John, Jn.	Philippians	Moody Press
Martin, R. P.	Epistle to the Philippians. Tyndale	William B. Eerdmans
Maxwell, Sydney	Philippians, What the Bible Teaches	John Ritchie Ltd.
Metcalfe, John	Philippians	The Publishing Trust
Meyer, F. B.	Devotional commentary on Philippians	Kregal Publications
Meyer, Heinrich A. W.	Philippians and Colossians	T and T Clark
Motyer, Alec	Message of Philippians	IVP
Moule, H. C. G., D.D.	Philippian Studies	Hodder and Stoughton
Pentecost, J. Dwight	The Joy of Living Philippians	Zondervan
Rainy, Robert, D. D.	Epistle to the Philippians Expositor's Bible	Hodder and Stoughton
Rainy, Robert, D. D.	Paul's Joy in Christ	Broadman Press
Ramsay, Prof. W. M.	St. Paul the Traveller and Roman Citizen	Hodder and Stoughton
Robertson, A. T.	Philippians, Word Pictures in the New Testament	Broadman Press
Secker, William	The Nonsuch Professor	Zoar Publications
Strauss, Lehman	Philippians	Loizeaux brothers

PHILIPPIANS: THE MIND OF CHRIST

Author	Title of Book	Publisher
Strong, James	Exhaustive Concordance	Welch Publishing Co.
Vaughan, C. J., D. D.	Epistle to the Philippians	Macmillan and Co.
Vincent, Marvin R., D. D.	Philippians, Word Studies in the New Testament	Wm. B. Eerrdman
Vines, W. E.	Dictionary of New testament Words	Oliphants
Vine, W. E.	Epistles to the Philippians and Colossians	Oliphants Ltd.
Walvoord, John F.	Philippians Triumph in Christ	Everyman's Bible Com. Moody Press
Wiersbe, Warren	Be Joyful	Victor Books
Wigram, George V. & Ralph D. Winter	The Word Study Concordance	Tyndale House Publishers, Inc.
Willis, G. Christopher	Sacrifices of Joy	Christian Book Room Kowloon, Hong Kong

OTHER COMMENTARIES BY
🗲 GOSPEL FOLIO PRESS

The Gospel of Mark
Harold St. John

A helpful & detailed outline, brief and thought-provoking comments are given on the 100 paragraphs of the Gospel narrative. Difficult points are discussed and the reader is encouraged to form their own conclusions.

Binding: Paper | Page Count: 200 | ISBN: 1882701968

In the School of Christ
David Gooding

This book is a study of John chapters 13-17, focusing on Christ's teaching on holiness. It contains many lessons taught by Jesus concerning the heart of the Christian faith.

Binding: Paper | Page Count: 272 | ISBN: 1882701194

Seeds of Destiny
Warren Henderson

This is a devotional book which explores Genesis in relation to the rest of Scripture. It contains over 100 devotions, and is suitable as either a daily devotional or as a reference source for deeper study.

Binding: Hard Cover | Page Count: 390 | ISBN: 1897117019

To Order Call: 1-800-952-2382 • orders@gospelfolio.com

OTHER COMMENTARIES BY
GOSPEL FOLIO PRESS

True to the Faith
David Gooding

In a vivid and original study of the book of Acts, David Gooding brings to life the world of the early church and leaves the reader with the clear vision of what it really means to be true to the faith.

Binding: Paper | Page Count: 415 | ISBN: 1882701208

An Unshakeable Kingdom
David Gooding

Hebrews is often considered one of the most difficult books to understand. This book is a primer on Hebrews and is written especially for those attempting to come to grips with the epistle's major themes.

Binding: Paper | Page Count: 256 | ISBN: 1882701798

Windows on Paradise
David Gooding

One of the most beautiful features of the Gospel of Luke is the way it depicts Christ. This commentary examines in detail some of the case-histories of people who were reclaimed and restored by Christ.

Binding: Paper | Page Count: 192 | ISBN: 188270147X

Webstore: www.gospelfolio.com